Realizing Freedom: Hegel, Sartre, and
the Alienation of Human Being

Realizing Freedom: Hegel, Sartre, and the Alienation of Human Being

Gavin Rae
American University in Cairo, Egypt

palgrave
macmillan

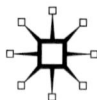

First published 2011 by
PALGRAVE MACMILLAN

Palgrave Macmillan in the UK is an imprint of Macmillan Publishers Limited,
registered in England, company number 785998, of Houndmills, Basingstoke,
Hampshire RG21 6XS.

Palgrave Macmillan in the US is a division of St Martin's Press LLC,
175 Fifth Avenue, New York, NY 10010.

Palgrave Macmillan is the global academic imprint of the above companies
and has companies and representatives throughout the world.

Palgrave® and Macmillan® are registered trademarks in the United States,
the United Kingdom, Europe and other countries.

ISBN: 978–0–230–31435–1

This book is printed on paper suitable for recycling and made from fully
managed and sustained forest sources. Logging, pulping and manufacturing
processes are expected to conform to the environmental regulations of the
country of origin.

A catalogue record for this book is available from the British Library.

A catalog record for this book is available from the Library of Congress.

10 9 8 7 6 5 4 3 2 1
20 19 18 17 16 15 14 13 12 11

Printed and bound in Great Britain by
CPI Antony Rowe, Chippenham and Eastbourne

Contents

Abbreviations of Works Cited

The following is a list of abbreviations for the various texts written by Hegel and Sartre used throughout the text. Other works cited can be found by comparing the in-text citation with the bibliography at the end of the book.

Hegel

PN   Hegel, G.W.F. (2007), *Philosophy of Nature*, (trans. Miller, A.V.), Oxford University Press: Oxford. [The number refers to the paragraph, R to 'Remarks,' and A to 'Additions'.]

PH   Hegel, G.W.F. (2004), *Philosophy of History*, (trans. Sibree, J.), Dover: New York.

LA   Hegel, G.W.F. (2004), *Introductory Lectures on Aesthetics*, (trans. Bosanquet, B; ed. Inwood, M.), Penguin: London.

HP   Hegel, G.W.F. (2003), *Introduction to the Lectures on the History of Philosophy*, (trans. Knox, T., & Miller, A.V.), Oxford University Press: Oxford.

PR   Hegel, G.W.F. (1991), *Philosophy of Right*, (trans. Nisbet, H.B.), Cambridge University Press: Cambridge. [The number refers to the paragraph, R to 'Remarks,' and A to 'Additions'.]

EL   Hegel, G.W.F. (1991), *The Encyclopaedia Logic*, (trans. Gereats, T.F., Suchting, W.A., & Harris, H.S.), Hackett: Cambridge. [The number refers to the paragraph, R to 'Remarks,' and A to 'Additions'.]

PM   Hegel, G.W.F. (1988), *Philosophy of Mind*, (trans. Miller, A.V.), Clarendon Press: Oxford. [The number refers to the paragraph, R to 'Remarks,' and A to 'Additions'.]

PS   Hegel, G.W.F. (1977), *Phenomenology of Spirit*, (trans. Miller, A.V.), Oxford University Press: Oxford.

Sartre

BEM   Sartre, J.P. (2008), *Between Existentialism and Marxism*, (trans. Matthews, J.), Verso: London.

WL   Sartre, J.P. (2007), *What Is Literature?* (trans. Frechtman, B.), Routledge: London.

CDR 1   Sartre, J.P. (2006), *Critique of Dialectical Reason*, vol.1, (trans.
         Hoare, Q; ed. Elkaim-Sartre, A.), Verso: London.
CDR 2   Sartre, J.P. (2006), *Critique of Dialectical Reason*, vol. 2, (trans.
         Hoare, Q; ed. Elkaim-Sartre, A.), Verso: London.
TOTE   Sartre, J.P. (2004), *The Transcendence of the Ego*, (trans. Brown,
         A.), Routledge: London.
BN   Sartre, J.P. (2003), *Being and Nothingness: A Study in
         Phenomenological Ontology*, (trans. Barnes, H.), Routledge:
         London.
WD   Sartre, J.P. (1999), *War Diaries: Notebooks from a Phoney War
         1939–1940*, (trans. Hoare, Q.), Verso: London.
NE   Sartre, J.P. (1992), *Notebooks for an Ethics*, (trans. Pellauer, D.),
         University of Chicago Press: London.
TE   Sartre, J.P. (1992), *Truth and Existence*, (trans. van den Hoven,
         A.; ed. Aronson, R.), University of Chicago Press: London.
ASJ   Sartre, J.P. (1976), *Anti-Semite and Jew: An Exploration of the
         Etiology of Hate*, (trans. Becker, G.J.), Schocken Books: New
         York.
EH   Sartre, J.P. (1973), *Existentialism and Humanism*, (trans.
         Mairet, P.), Methuen: London.
I   Sartre, J.P. (1970), 'Intentionality: A Fundamental Idea of
         Husserl's Phenomenology,' (trans. Fell, J.P.), *Journal of the
         British Society for Phenomenology*, vol.1, n.2, May, (pp. 4–5).
SM   Sartre, J.P. (1968), *Search for a Method*, (trans. Barnes, H.),
         Vintage: London.
SG   Sartre, J.P. (1963), *Saint Genet: Actor and Martyr*, (trans.
         Frechtman, B.), Pantheon: New York.

Preface and Acknowledgements

This book examines the important, if often overlooked, role that alienation plays in Hegel's and Sartre's work and, in doing so, offers one of
the first sustained, comparative analyses of their thinking available in
the English speaking world. As such, it fills two gaps in the existing
literature. But alienation's intimate relationship to authenticity, ethics,
ontology, freedom, and social relations means that this book offers far
more than a comparison of these two thinkers on this one concept.
It offers a holistic analysis of their respective philosophies of human
being. The aim is to show that, while Sartre was influenced by Hegel, it
is Hegel's analysis that is more developed, consistent, and subtle.

While the difficulty of Hegel's and Sartre's thinking and writing styles
has long been acknowledged, the aim is to present their thinking in a
holistic, clear, and concise manner that identifies the salient differences
between the two. As such, newcomers will find that it engages with all
of their key texts to offer a useful and clear introduction to the philosophies of two of the giants of philosophical history. Readers famil-
iar with Hegel's and Sartre's work will find a detailed, well-researched
exposition of their ideas that exposes the subtle, yet fundamental, differences between the two on a range of issues, including the nature of
consciousness and the human being, ontology, metaphysics, phenomenology, ethics, anthropology, psychology, and politics.

The latter is particularly relevant given the history of this project.
This book was started in England, mostly written in Scotland, and
finally completed amidst a social uprising in Cairo, Egypt. It was, in
many respects, fitting that a book on alienation should be completed
in Cairo just as the social uprising that swept away the Mubarak regime
was being played out. After all, here was a living example of what can
happen when individuals, long alienated by repressive government policies, finally decide that they have had enough. Whatever the outcome
of this social uprising, the fact that it happened for the reasons it did
re-enforces the book's central point: alienation is an issue of crucial
importance to human being.

But given that its gestation spans three countries and two conti-
nents, there are numerous people I want to thank. My doctoral thesis
supervisor, Stephen Houlgate, played an invaluable role in shaping the
structure and content of the thesis from which this book emanates.

His comments were always appreciated and I am in no doubt that the final work would be far inferior without his very patient and careful reading of the various drafts produced. Similarly, my second supervisor, Peter Poellner, was a supportive, willing, and critical reader, whose comments greatly improved the early Sartre chapters. Bruce Baugh and David Detmer provided insightful comments on an earlier, shorter version of Chapter 3 which appeared in *Sartre Studies International* (vol.15 (2), pp. 52–75) under the title 'Sartre and the Other: Conversion, Conflict, Language and the We'. David Jones and Michael Schwartz provided encouragement and comments on an earlier version of Chapter 4, entitled 'Sartre, Group Formations, and Practical Freedom: The Other in the *Critique of Dialectical Reason*', which is forthcoming in *Comparative and Continental Philosophy*. Caleb Heldt and Tanya Chhabra were kind enough to read and suggest certain content, stylistic, and grammatical changes to an earlier, full draft, while my editor at Palgrave Macmillan, Priyanka Gibbons, was not only kind enough to support publication of the work, but, along with her assistant Melanie Blair, was available to offer timely responses to my questions. Lastly, but by no means least, I want to thank my family, and in particular my Mother to whom this book is dedicated, for supporting me throughout my long and costly academic apprenticeship. Without their continuing support, I wouldn't have been able to start let alone complete this difficult project.

Introduction

What is it to be human? What place do we have in the world? How should we live? Why should we act in this manner? What can we be and what prevents us from realizing this? Far from being dry, abstract, and academic, these questions are existentially important and have, therefore, long captured human attention. But while important in-themselves, they concern us here because they are intimately related to the issue that forms the basis of this book: alienation.

In popular parlance, 'alienation' is typically associated with feelings of isolation, hopelessness, powerlessness, loss, anxiety, frustration, despair, and/or loneliness. These sensations arise because the individual explicitly perceives and experiences some sort of disconnection between his perception of what/who he is and what/who he thinks he should be. In other words, he explicitly experiences a discrepancy between how he actually lives and how he perceives he should live. For example, he may feel disconnected from his society because it does not conform to how he thinks it should look and/or allow him to act; or he may feel frustrated because his job does not allow him to creatively express himself. This discrepancy may lead to a sense of loss, a general malaise, a feeling of uneasiness, or the more powerful negative sensations listed above.

However, as this book will argue, alienation does not simply describe a psychological state in which an individual negatively experiences some sort of self/self and/or self/society separation. Alienation is primordially an ontological and ethical concept that describes the complex relationship between the actual living individual, his ontological structure, and historically sensitive ethical norms that delineate what he should be and how he should act. The psychological sense of the term is rooted in this primordial onto-ethical ground, but limits itself to describing the experience that arises when an individual explicitly

1

2 Realizing Freedom: Hegel, Sartre, and the Alienation of Human Being

experiences a disconnection between his self-identity and the ethical norms that delineate how he/his social world should be.

However, as Hegel and Sartre show, this purely empirical, psychological approach fails to appreciate that there may be a discrepancy between an individual's sense of self and what he truly is. By limiting itself to the relationship between an individual's sense of self and specific ethical norms, the psychological approach fails to bring the individual to question whether his sense of self affirms or accords with what he truly is. The consequence could be that he *feels* perfectly at home in his being despite that way of being alienating him from what he truly is and should be.

Rather than being grounded in an individual's subjective sense of self, alienation is grounded in, and gains meaning in contrast to, an alternative state of being that describes what the individual truly is and, importantly, should strive to be. In other words, being alienated requires that the individual be alienated from something; this non-alienated state will be called 'authenticity'.

In general terms, therefore, alienation describes a situation or state of being in which an individual is separated from, at least, one of the aspects deemed necessary to live in accordance with a normative conception of the preferable, or authentic, self. Each notion of the authentic self acts as a standard against which a way of being can be compared to determine whether that way of being is authentic. If the actual self's way of being conforms to the notion of the authentic self that underpins the discussion, it is authentic; if not, it is alienated. Implicit to any discussion of authenticity and alienation, therefore, is a description of what the actual self should strive to look like. This ensures that authenticity and alienation are descriptive concepts that explain how an actual self lives and prescriptive concepts that delineate the ethical validity of an individual's way of being and identify how he should be (Rae, 2010).

Importantly, however, because each specific conception of alienation is grounded in a normative conception of an authentic, or preferable, self, each will have a different understanding of what alienation entails. Alessandro Ferrara shows this by distinguishing between 'antagonistic' and 'integrative' conceptions of the authentic self. Antagonistic conceptions of the authentic self view 'authenticity as primarily linked with breaking free from the constraints of an entrenched social order' (1997: 82). If the authentic self is characterised in an antagonistic way to society, as Ferrara insists the early works of Sartre, Heidegger, and Nietzsche characterise it, then the actual self will be alienated if it integrates itself into the norms and values of its society.

However, Ferrara names Hegel and Taylor as two thinkers who have challenged this view of the authentic self. Rather than being authentic by setting oneself in opposition to society, Ferrara argues that these thinkers maintain that authenticity requires that the actual self be integrated into a specific form of society. Contrary to the antagonistic perspective, therefore, integrationists argue that existing in a relation of pure opposition to society is exactly what causes the actual self to be alienated. This disagreement arises because the two perspectives start from fundamentally different foundational premises regarding the constitution of the authentic self. This leads each to insist that the other perspective misunderstands what authenticity entails and requires.

What we see, therefore, is that different conceptions of the authentic self lead to different analyses and understandings of alienation. Thus, when discussing a particular thinker's conception of alienation we first have to identify and understand the conception of the authentic self that underpins the discussion. Given that this book aims to undertake an analysis of the different ways in which Georg Wilhelm Friedrich Hegel (1770–1831) and Jean-Paul Sartre (1905–1980) understand that the human being can be alienated, it will first have to identify how each thinker conceptualizes the authentic self. Only then can the different ways in which they understand that the actual self can be alienated be discussed.

But we cannot simply turn to a passage to identify what Hegel and Sartre mean by the authentic self; we will have to tease out its meaning by looking at their analyses of human being. Thus, while an important topic in-itself, the central role it plays in Hegel's and Sartre's thinking and its intimate relationship to the many important philosophical themes they discuss, such as freedom, ethics, ontology, metaphysics, individual identity, social relations, and politics, means that 'alienation' is the perfect door through which to gain access to Hegel's and Sartre's wider philosophical projects.

The importance of alienation for Hegel and Sartre

There is still the issue of whether alienation does, in fact, play the crucial role in Hegel's and Sartre's thinking that I maintain it does. Happily, commentators have long agreed that alienation plays a crucial role in their respective philosophies. For example, while Jean Hyppolite insists that alienation is 'the key concept of the *Phenomenology of Spirit*' (1997: 178), Hans-Georg Gadamer goes further by recognizing that Hegel's entire philosophy 'assigns a central role to the problem of the alienation of the self and the overcoming of it' (1976: 106). In agreement, Georg Lukács notes that alienation occupies 'a central position in the Hegelian system' (1975: 538), while David Cooper goes so far as to maintain that 'for Hegel, alienation is not so much the central issue of philosophy as the *only* one' (1999: 26).

But Hegel's position is also justified by the central place he occupies in historical studies of the phenomenon of alienation. For example, Richard Schacht (1970: 3) notes that, historically, it was Hegel who elevated the phenomenon of alienation to a position of philosophical importance and in so doing established the guidelines for subsequent discussion of it. Indeed, for this reason, Hegel has been called 'the god-father of alienation' (Williamson & Cullingford, 1997: 264). Engaging with Hegel's analysis of this concept will, therefore, allow us to better understand the phenomenon.

Commentators have also noted the central role alienation plays in Sartre's thought. For example, Douglas Kirsner insists that Sartre's *oeuvre* 'focuses on our radical alienation from ourselves and our world' (1985: 206), Ronald Aronson (1980: 2) undertakes a genealogy of Sartre's work that shows he 'sought to grasp the individual as the source of the society and its alienations, then the society as the source of individuals and their alienations' (1980: 2), while John Glenn Jr (1984: 525) simply maintains that Sartre's is a philosophy of alienation.

But while one of the rationales for this study emanates from the crucial role that alienation plays in Hegel's and Sartre's thinking, there is another reason: Hegel's influence on Sartre. While it does not appear that Sartre sat in on Alexander Kojève's famous lectures on Hegel's *Phenomenology of Spirit*, there is no doubt that Sartre was influenced by the Hegelian renaissance that was taking place in 1930s France. As Bernard Levy notes, 'Sartre, like all his contemporaries, inevitably had to do with Hegel. The real dialogue, the really decisive and ultimately acrimonious head-to-head was the one he engaged in with Hegel' (2003: 412).[1]

But we do not need to refer to commentators to determine the extent of Hegel's influence on Sartre; not only does Sartre insist that 'Hegel represents a high point in philosophy' (NE: 60), but extended discussions of Hegel can be found throughout his works. For example, in *Being and Nothingness*, Sartre provides an explicit and critical discussion of Hegel in his account of intersubjective relations (BN: 260–268) that shows that, despite Joseph Catalano's insistence that 'in *Being and Nothingness*, [...] there is no real use of dialectic, truncated or otherwise, nor is there a meaningful confrontation with Hegel or Marx' (1986: 22), a crucial aspect of Sartre's philosophical thought emanates from a direct confrontation with Hegel. Furthermore, throughout the *Notebooks for an Ethics*, Sartre discusses various aspects of Hegel's thought; in *Search for a Method*, he insists that existentialism is grounded in Hegel's notion of becoming (SM: xxxiv); while, in the *Critique of Dialectical Reason*, Sartre provides an extended critique of, what he insists is, Hegel's metaphysical dialectic (CDR 1: 18–27). It is safe to say, therefore, that Sartre was influenced by Hegel. What is not clear is the extent of this influence. One of the sub-arguments this book makes is that while Sartre was influenced by Hegel, his reading of Hegel's thinking was, in many respects, fundamentally flawed. This ensured that Sartre developed his thinking in opposition to a flawed interpretation of Hegel that resulted in him claiming uniqueness for a concept of authenticity that is remarkably similar to Hegel's actual view.

However, while Sartre comes close to Hegel in terms of the types of activities required for the individual to become free, there are a number of fundamental differences in their respective analyses of the human being's ontological structure that, I argue, show that it is Hegel's analysis of alienation and its various related issues that is more subtle, consistent, and developed than Sartre's.

But there is a further issue that impacts on the Hegel/Sartre relationship: the 'spectre' of Marx (Derrida, 2006: 1). Marx's reaction to Hegel, and Sartre's apparent reconciliation with Marx would appear to indicate that any discussion of the Hegel/Sartre relationship must pass through Marx. It might be expected, therefore, that I will spend significant time discussing Marx. For a number of reasons, however, this will not be the case.

First, there are a number of books that deal with Marx's views on alienation and his relationship to Hegel and Sartre to which the interested reader can turn. Secondly, introducing Marx into the equation would complicate the structure and argument of the book to such a degree that the final outcome would be a book that tried to do and say too much. For example, it would require not only the chapters on Hegel and Sartre already present, but additional chapters on Marx's reading of Hegel, the development of Marx's own thought, Sartre's reading of Marx, and the way in which it impacts on Sartre's reading of Hegel. But the main reason why Marx does not play a fundamental role in this analysis is the comparative focus of this book.

If this book simply aimed to undertake a chronological analysis of the Hegel/Sartre relationship that showed the ways in which Hegel influenced Sartre's thinking, then an intensive engagement with Marx would be warranted and necessary. However, not only are there a number of excellent books that take this approach (Baugh, 2003; Butler, 1987), but this book aims to do more than chart the ways in which Hegel influenced Sartre; it defends a particular philosophical position. Thus, while it will note Hegel's influence on Sartre, it will focus on showing that, while 'alienation' is a key concept for both thinkers, and despite Sartre coming after Hegel historically, it is Hegel's conceptualization of the ontology of human being that provides the more subtle, multi-dimensional, and logically consistent accounts of alienation and authenticity. The argument to be developed, the range of issues to be discussed, and the availability of books that do focus on Marx's relationship to both thinkers mean that this book focuses on the Hegel/Sartre relationship un-mediated by third parties. This direct comparison is crucial if a comparative analysis of Hegel's and Sartre's philosophical arguments is to be undertaken, and especially if the argument to be defended is to be outlined in as clear and systematic fashion as possible.

But given the long-recognized relationship between Hegel and Sartre, we would be forgiven for thinking that there would already be a plethora of commentaries comparing their respective thought. Surprisingly, however, this is not the case. While there are discussions of Hegel's analyses of the human being and alienation, these tend to offer only partial analyses of his thought. For example, Michael Hardimon (1994) provides an excellent discussion of Hegel's account of the ways in which the individual is alienated from his social world, but, because he limits the discussion to Hegel's *Philosophy of Right* and *Philosophy of History*, does not take into consideration Hegel's analysis of the different ways in which consciousness is alienated as this is outlined in the *Phenomenology of Spirit*.

Similarly, while there are commentaries that discuss Sartre's analyses of the human being and alienation, these misrepresent Sartre's thought and/or fail to discuss the multi-faceted role that alienation plays in his thinking. For example, while Jonathon Webber (2009) and David Detmer (2008) discuss Sartre's theory of authenticity, they both focus on other aspects of Sartre's thinking and so do not place alienation at the centre of their respective endeavours. In contrast, by focusing on the role that alienation plays in their thinking, I am not only able to do full justice to the complex role this concept plays in Hegel's and Sartre's thought, but am also able (and indeed required) to engage with the issues that Webber and Detmer discuss.

Furthermore, when similarities and differences between Hegel's and Sartre's accounts of alienation have been noted, these remarks tend to be made in passing and so do not provide an adequate or extended discussion of the similarities/differences in their views and/or simply do not relate to their theories of alienation. For example, Klaus Hartmann (1966) provides a comparative study of both thinkers by examining Hegel's influence on the logic of Sartre's *Being and Nothingness*. However, not only does he not explicitly discuss alienation in either thinker, but, by limiting his discussion to Sartre's *Being and Nothingness*, he is unable to take into consideration subsequent developments in Sartre's thought. Similarly, while Christopher Fry (1988) provides a comparative analysis of the underlying logic of Hegel's and Sartre's thought, and admittedly does touch on Sartre's views on the alienation of consciousness, he does not discuss these in detail, analyse Hegel's theory of alienation, or produce a comparative discussion of the thoughts of both thinkers on this issue.

Due to the central role that alienation plays in Hegel's and Sartre's philosophy and human existence in general, and the lack of an extensive and extended commentary that compares their respective accounts of alienation, there is the need for an extended, comparative discussion of the ways in which Hegel and Sartre understand that the human being can be alienated. This book attempts to fill this surprising gap.

Structure and method of the work

The general argument developed shows that while Hegel and Sartre agree that alienation is a constitutive aspect of the human being's existence and are, therefore, allies in the battle against it, Sartre's analysis of alienation is not as consistent as Hegel's, nor is it able to provide the same depth as Hegel's. Put differently, it is Hegel who provides an analysis of alienation that is more nuanced, subtle, complex, and multidimensional. Hegel achieves this because not only does his conception of consciousness's ontological structure recognize the logic that underpins Sartre's analysis of consciousness's ontological structure, but he goes beyond it by recognizing its failings and, importantly, conceptualizing consciousness in such a way that it is *possible* that consciousness can overcome the failings and shortcomings he identifies in the logic that underpins Sartre's position.

Furthermore, I maintain that while Sartre's account of practical freedom draws close to Hegel's in recognizing that being practically free requires the individual to develop certain intersubjective relations with others, his account of the type of action required to secure the individual's practical freedom is not always consistent and does not sit well with his analysis of the conditions required to secure consciousness's ontological freedom. The conclusion drawn is that it is Hegel's analysis of the issues involved that is the more subtle, consistent, and multidimensional of the two.

But while I maintain that Hegel's analysis is superior to Sartre's, I am not uncritical of Hegel's position. In particular, I argue that his analysis of the position of women in relation to the wider community causes problems for his analysis of freedom and his attempt to describe a universally free community. Similarly, by maintaining that children are the ethical component of marriage, Hegel appears to exclude same-sex couples from fulfilling the conditions (i.e. being married and having children) that he insists are necessary to secure the universal freedom that is a condition of individual freedom.

But while we may not agree with Hegel regarding the type of actions and objective structures necessary for individuals to escape from alienation, I suggest that the general framework he employs to think about issues such as human being, individual fulfilment, ethics, and social relations provides us with significant insights into what it is to be human and the type of action required for us to be at home in our world. Thus, while the resolution of these issues remains open, it is Hegel and not Sartre who provides us with the best understanding of them.

There are, however, two main ways in which this argument could be outlined. I could discuss several themes that link their respective analyses and compare Hegel's and Sartre's thinking on these issues as and when a similarity and/or difference arises or I could present each thinker's thought independently from the thought of the other and then discuss the similarities/differences between them.

The benefit of the former approach is that it would offer a dialectical analysis of the two thinkers that shows the similarities and differences between the two on specific issues. The great problem with this approach, however, is that it risks presenting each thinker's thought in a disjointed manner that does not allow the reader to truly understand each thinker's world-view. This links into one of the arguments I will propose regarding the coherence of Hegel's and Sartre's thinking.

That Hegel's philosophical project forms a coherent system is well-known and fairly uncontroversial. The interconnectedness of the various aspects of Hegel's thought ensures that any attempt to discuss an aspect of his thinking in isolation from the other aspects: a) risks offering a one-dimensional analysis that fails to capture the complexity of Hegel's thinking; or b) would simply fail to allow the reader to properly understand the interconnectedness of his thought. For these reasons, it is necessary to present Hegel's thinking en bloc.

However, while the coherence of Hegel's thinking is well-established in the secondary literature, the coherence of Sartre's thinking is disputed. For example, Thomas Anderson (1993: 1) insists that Sartre's philosophical development is constituted by a radical rupture between his early so-called existentialist writings and his later Marxist-inspired analyses. In contrast, and for reasons to be outlined, I will argue that Sartre's later writings, and in particular his analysis of the ways in which the individual's practical freedom is extended in certain group formations, complement and extend the analyses undertaken in his earlier works. Showing this requires that I present Sartre's philosophy en bloc. As such, this book is split into two parts: the first deals with Sartre's thinking; the second outlines Hegel's thought and compares it to Sartre's.

In relation to the structure of Sartre's works, there is a more or less neat division between the issues that he addresses in different periods of his writings. Because Sartre recognizes that consciousness plays a key role in human being, his early philosophy, exemplified by *Being and Nothingness* and *Notebooks for an Ethics,* outlines the ontological structure of consciousness and the different ways consciousness can live its ontological structure. This is complemented by his later works, in particular the *Critique of Dialectical Reason*, which focuses on the various ways in which the *concrete individual's* social existence alienates him from his practical freedom. Following this structure, I first outline Sartre's analysis of the ways in which consciousness can be alienated before discussing his analysis of the ways in which the concrete individual's practical freedom is constrained or enhanced by his social world. Chapter 1 examines Sartre's existential ontology as described in *Being and Nothingness* and the *Notebooks for an Ethics*. It outlines the way Sartre conceptualizes consciousness and demonstrates the general implications of this for his theory of alienation. In particular, it demonstrates that Sartre holds that, ultimately, whether consciousness is alienated depends on the pre-reflective fundamental project it chooses to adopt. Chapter 2 develops this by examining Sartre's theory of bad faith to show the ways in which consciousness's chosen pre-reflective fundamental project can alienate it. Chapter 3 deepens Sartre's analysis by showing that the alienation of consciousness does not simply emanate from its own subjective actions; consciousness's relations with others can also alienate it. Chapter 4 turns to Sartre's *Critique of Dialectical Reason* to examine how he understands that group membership and the actions of others can constrain or enhance the individual's practical freedom.

Having examined Sartre's analysis of consciousness's ontological structure and his theory of alienation, I turn to Hegel. In Chapter 5, I discuss the purpose and method of Hegel's *Phenomenology of Spirit*, while Chapter 6 complements this by discussing the complex role alienation plays in this famous text. Chapters 7 and 8 turn to Hegel's *Philosophy of Right* to outline his analysis of freedom and provide a critical analysis of the objective structures and cultural ethic he maintains are necessary to allow the individual to be free. These chapters also compare and contrast Hegel's and Sartre's thinking to show that it is Hegel's thought that is the more subtle, consistent, and multi-dimensional of the two.

1
Sartre's Existential Ontology

While not always consistent, Sartre's analysis of human being is remarkably complex and multi-dimensional. Sartre reaches the conclusions he does, however, because he employs a particular method. Understanding this method requires that we recognize that its primary purpose is to challenge and ultimately overcome the appearance/essence dualism upon which he insists philosophical thought has long been based.

This dualism is underpinned by the following two arguments: first, that the phenomenal being requires a hidden essence to explain its being; and secondly, that a hidden essence is required to explain how consciousness can be mistaken about its phenomenal object. In other words, consciousness is mistaken about what the object is because it does not go beyond the object's appearance to its hidden essence.

Sartre rejects these arguments. He insists that consciousness must not 'point over its shoulder to a true being which would be, for it, absolute. What [the object] is, it is absolutely, for it reveals itself *as it is*. The phenomenon can be studied and described as such, for it is *absolutely indicative of itself*' (BN: 2). Rather than maintain the essence/appearance dualism, Sartre collapses the distinction and maintains that the appearance of the being discloses what it truly is.

But he also argues that, contrary to the reasoning that underpins the appearance/essence dualism, the correlate of misinterpreting an object is not the positing of a true, hidden essence that needs to be uncovered; it is to look at the object from a different perspective or to take a harder, more patient look at the object. Because consciousness can relate to its object in an infinite number of ways, it can adopt a new perspective on its object until it discovers the perspective that actually allows it to know what its object truly is.

With this, Sartre insists that discovering what a being truly is requires an examination and description of the *phenomenon*, or appearance, of that being. Sartre understands this descriptive method to be 'phenomenology.' The focus on ontology, or what being truly is, the rejection of a transcendent realm, and the subsequent emphasis on the phenomenon as the means to attain true knowledge of being allows Sartre to maintain that not only is his philosophy a 'phenomenological ontology,' but it is only phenomenological ontology that discloses what being truly is.

But, for Sartre, phenomenology does not simply disclose what being truly is. Sartre's ontological categories provide part of the standard against which he compares consciousness's actual *mode of being*. While the discussion of bad faith will disclose that there is more to it than this, in the first instance, authenticity requires that consciousness reflectively understand its ontological structure; if it does not, its mode of being is inauthentic. Because he holds that the phenomenological method discloses what a being truly is and whether consciousness reflectively exists in accordance with what it is ontologically, Sartre insists that the phenomenological method is the true method of philosophy.

The purpose and status of *Being and Nothingness*

From this, we can say that Sartre's phenomenological ontology 'operates' on two different, but related, levels: I will call these two levels the *ontological* level and the *experiential* level (Aronson, 1980: 75–76; Due, 2000; Williams, 1997: 374). This distinction ensures that the purpose of *Being and Nothingness* is two-fold: first, it systematically outlines the ontological categories that will inform Sartre's analysis of being; this is what I will call the *ontological* level of his analysis. Secondly, the *experiential* level of his analysis outlines *a* particular way consciousness lives its ontological structure. More specifically, the concrete descriptions of different modes of being outlined in *Being and Nothingness* describe the modes of being consciousness adopts when its reflection is *impure*. For reasons that will be subsequently discussed, impure reflection is the form of reflection that alienates consciousness from what it truly is ontologically. So we may say that *Being and Nothingness*'s descriptions of concrete modes of being describe the alienating consequences that occur when consciousness does not properly reflectively understand its ontological structure.

Crucially, however, while impure reflection describes one possible form of self-reflection, it is not the only form of self-reflection possible. While consciousness's reflection can be *impure*, it can also be *pure*.

While these terms will be discussed in detail, at this stage, it is sufficient to note that because pure reflection allows consciousness to reflectively understand its ontological structure, it is not alienating. Consciousness *can*, but does not necessarily have to, reflectively understand itself in a way that does not alienate it. *Conversion* is the name Sartre gives to the movement from alienating, impure reflection to authentic, pure reflection.

While the meaning and content of the conversion will be explained, highlighting the conversion at this stage is important because it sheds light on both the *status* of *Being and Nothingness* within Sartre's *oeuvre* and how we are to understand its content. Because it describes consciousness's mode of being 'before conversion' (NE: 6), *Being and Nothingness* describes the alienation that arises when consciousness fails to reflectively understand what it is ontologically. On my understanding, therefore, *Being and Nothingness* is a *critical* work. It is in his *Notebooks for an Ethics* that Sartre seeks to describe the way consciousness exists when its reflective self-understanding is *pure* or non-alienating. While *Being and Nothingness'* descriptions of alienated modes of being point towards authentic modes of being, the *Notebooks for an Ethics* seek to make the content of these post-conversion, authentic modes of being *explicit*. In other words, *Being and Nothingness* and the *Notebooks for an Ethics* complement one another: the former describes modes of being grounded in *inauthentic*, impure self-reflection; the latter describes modes of being grounded in *authentic*, pure self-reflection.

But how does this complementary relation relate to Sartre's Marxist-inspired *Critique of Dialectical Reason*? While some commentators (Warnock, 1970: 113–130; Anderson, 1993: 87–110) argue that the *Critique of Dialectical Reason* constitutes a fundamental break with the content, structure, and logic of Sartre's early work, there is, in fact, no radical break between *Being and Nothingness/ Notebooks for an Ethics* and the *Critique of Dialectical Reason*. The two periods of writing address the same problems in two different, but intimately related, ways. Whereas *Being and Nothingness* and the *Notebooks for an Ethics* outline Sartre's *ontological* categories *and* describe the various ways *consciousness* can reflectively understand and live its ontological structure, the *Critique of Dialectical Reason* complements these works by taking the *facticity* of consciousness as its starting point and providing a dialectical analysis of the way the *concrete individual* chooses to live his concrete socio-historical situation and the way the concrete individual's concrete socio-historical situation impacts on his *practical freedom*. While I will return to this issue in Chapter 4, at this point, it is sufficient to note that the content of the *Notebooks for an Ethics* and the *Critique of Dialectical Reason* complement and extend the arguments of *Being and Nothingness*.

The ontological characteristics of being-for-itself

The ontological level of Sartre's analysis discloses two types of being: being-in-itself and being-for-itself. The existent beings of each ontological category share the same fundamental *ontological characteristics*. I will start with the ontological characteristics that define the being of being-for-itself. While at times he writes otherwise, Sartre more often than not conflates being-for-itself with consciousness. While he insists that consciousness is unified, its unity is composed of two aspects: a pre-reflective aspect and a reflective aspect.

Pre-reflective consciousness describes the fundamental aspect of consciousness; it is the 'very being of consciousness' (BN: 100). The defining ontological characteristics of pre-reflective consciousness are that it is non-positional, insofar as it does not define itself in relation to objects, 'non-substantial' (BN: 12), object-less, content-less, and empty; it is essentially nothing. By this, Sartre does not mean that consciousness does not exist; he simply means that the defining ontological characteristic of consciousness is to be no-thing. Consciousness is not an inert thing; it is constant activity.

Sartre goes to great lengths to point out that its ontological nothingness means that the pre-reflective consciousness is ego-less. The I does not exist *within* consciousness, nor does the I accompany all forms of consciousness; the I only appears if consciousness reflectively objectifies itself. Thus, the self-objectification of 'the *I* only appears on the occasion of a [certain] reflective act' (TOTE: 16). But this does not mean that the ego is unimportant; it simply means that consciousness cannot be equated with the ego.

Because it is ontologically nothing, the pre-reflective consciousness cannot be described in objective form, nor does it think of its world in objective form; it is best thought of as a non-conceptual, non-objectified, and non-objectifying *self-awareness*. Perhaps Dan Zahavi captures it best when he calls the experience of pre-reflectivity 'an immediate, implicit, irrelational [...] and non-propositional self-acquaintance' (1999: 33).

As the foundation of consciousness, pre-reflective self-awareness accompanies all forms of reflection. But Sartre goes further than this and insists that 'it is the non-reflective consciousness which renders [...] reflection possible' (BN: 9). There are two separate, but related, reasons why Sartre comes to this conclusion: one emanates from the complexities of consciousness's acts; the other from the logic of Sartre's analysis of consciousness's ontological structure.

The complexity of its activities means that consciousness simply cannot be reflectively aware of both itself and everything its act requires. If consciousness is to successfully complete an activity, it must simply be able to *do* the activity without reflectively understanding everything it is doing or everything the activity entails. Peter Poellner makes this point through the example of skiing. He notes that 'skiing down a slope requires a fine-tuned ongoing proprioceptive awareness of limb position and tactile sensitivity to ground resistance, e.g. when responding "automatically" to unseen humps in the ground by bending one's knees' (2003: 50) Its complexity means that, if we are to ski at all, a large portion of the activity must be done without reflectively understanding what exactly is being done. Poellner's point is that large aspects of consciousness's daily activity are undertaken without it reflectively understanding what it is doing. This is necessarily so because if consciousness were reflectively aware of everything its various acts entailed, it 'would [...] find [itself] mentally exhausted simply by having walked a short distance down the street' (2003: 50).

But, while large portions of consciousness's activity are undertaken without reflective knowledge of the activity, this does not mean that consciousness's non-reflective activity emanates from an unconscious. According to Sartre, there is no *unconscious*; all consciousness is *self-conscious*. To explain how consciousness can engage in an act without reflectively understanding everything that act entails, or using the unconscious to explain its actions, Sartre distinguishes between consciousness's *pre-reflective* self-awareness and its *reflective* self-understanding. Because consciousness is always pre-reflectively self-aware, it can engage in activities without necessarily reflectively understand exactly what it is doing. Sartre insists on the primacy of pre-reflectivity because it allows him to explain, without appealing to the notion of the unconscious, how consciousness is able to act despite not always being reflectively aware of what it is doing.

But while consciousness is ontologically nothing, it does not simply exist in a unified nothingness. There is a fissure in its ontological nothingness that means consciousness is never identical with itself. Put differently, consciousness always exists at a distance from itself (BN: 97–103). This self-distance is important for two reasons: first, it means that consciousness always presents itself to itself, which means it is always aware of itself. This justifies Sartre's claim that consciousness is always conscious of itself. Secondly, it is because consciousness exists at a distance from itself that it can determine for itself what it will be. Without this distance, consciousness would simply exist in passive nothingness; with this fissure, it is able to determine for itself how it will act while always existing at a distance from this act. This distance enables consciousness to withdraw from its mode of being and actively become other than it is.

But it may be thought that the notion that consciousness's nothingness is fissured contradicts Sartre's insistence that consciousness is unified. Sartre recognizes this objection and rejects it (BN: 101–102). He does so because he thinks that only the introduction of *something* into consciousness would disrupt the unified nothingness of consciousness. Because the division Sartre describes is simply a division of nothingness, which he thinks does not actually divide anything, and because its fissure does not 'add' anything to consciousness's essential nothingness, Sartre insists that consciousness's nothingness can be fissured while still remaining unified.

But to fully understand the essential nothingness of being-for-itself and why this being is different to being-in-itself, we have to engage with the relationship between negation, nothingness, and nihilation.

Briefly, Sartre understands the term 'negation' to mean a *negative judgement* (BN: 30). It describes the possibility that each question may be answered in the negative. The possibility of negation, however, depends on *nothingness*. The discussion is not particularly clear or extended, but Sartre appears to insist that nothingness grounds negation because, while negation turns something into nothing, nothingness 'envelops the *not* within itself as its essential structure' (BN: 42). A condition of each act of negation is that it exists 'within' and emanates from nothingness; it is only because there is nothingness that acts of negation are possible. As Sartre notes, 'nothingness stands at the origin of the negative judgement because it is itself negation. It founds the negation as *an act* because it is the negation as *being*' (BN: 42).

But nothingness cannot, by definition, exist. Nothingness is a possible *modification* of being that 'lies coiled in the heart of being – like a worm' (BN: 41). Because this modification needs to be brought into the world, 'there must exist a being (this can not be the In-itself) of which the property is to nihilate Nothingness, to support it in its being, to sustain it perpetually in its very existence, a *being by which nothingness comes to things*' (BN: 46).

For nothingness to come to existence requires a being that is capable of turning something into nothing. It requires a being whose existence is defined by the act of *nihilation*. This act of nihilation can take the form of *altering* an object or, more radically, simply *annihilating* the object so that whereas it once existed, it no longer does. But Sartre warns that defining a being in terms of the act of nihilation does not mean that the being exists *prior* to the act of nihilation; it means that the being and the act of nihilation are entwined: the being only comes into existence through the act of nihilation and the act of nihilation only comes to existence through this being. Sartre calls the being that is ontologically defined by the act of nihilation: being-for-itself.

The act of nihilation is crucial to Sartre's analysis because it not only explains how nothingness 'exists,' but also describes a being that is not simply *something* or *nothing*. Whereas being simply is what it is, and nothingness is simply no-thing, the act of nihilation allows being-for-itself to *withdraw* from being without fully annihilating its existence. Because this nihilating being has the possibility of deciding for itself whether to be something or nothing, it exists 'between being and non-being' (BN: 47). But it is important to note that the act of nihilation is not initially a reflective act; the act of nihilation is a condition of consciousness's existence, insofar as consciousness only exists if it *pre-reflectively* nihilates being-in-itself. As Dan Zahavi explains, 'consciousness is nothing apart from not being the transcendent object which it reveals. And it is precisely in this strong sense that consciousness needs intentionality, needs the confrontation with something different from itself in order to *be self-aware*; otherwise, it would lose every determination and dissipate as pure nothingness' (1999: 128).

While consciousness always *pre-reflectively* nihilates being-in-itself, consciousness can also *reflectively* nihilate itself and other objects. This enables it to reflectively determine what it will be. Consciousness is able to reflectively nihilate being because it is *'its own nothingness'* (BN: 47). But we should not think that this nothingness is the nothingness that is brought into existence by the act of nihilation. This would be circular: an act of nihilation would be dependent on nothingness which would be dependent on an act of nihilation. To escape this circularity, Sartre implicitly distinguishes between two senses of nothingness: while I previously noted that 'nothingness as non-being' describes a possible modification in being, there is another sense of nothingness: 'nothingness as an ontological characteristic.' However, the two senses do not have equal status; it is only because 'nothingness is an ontological characteristic' of consciousness that consciousness can bring 'nothingness as non-being' to the world.

But while consciousness is *always* pre-reflectively aware of its ontological nothingness, Reidar Due points out that its pre-reflective self-awareness 'is not [necessarily] experienced *as such* in all of [its] acts and in all of [its] being' (2005: 39). While consciousness is ontologically nothing, and is always *pre-reflectively* aware of this, it does not always *reflectively understand* this. This brings us to the reflective aspect of consciousness. Whereas pre-reflective consciousness is an immediate, undifferentiated, non-conceptual, non-objectified self-awareness, reflective consciousness is positional, insofar as it defines itself in terms of its position to other objects, has an explicit self-understanding, is mediated, insofar as it determines itself by explicitly differentiating itself from objects, and is judgemental.

Reflective consciousness's experience of itself and its world is, therefore, different to the experience of pre-reflective consciousness. While this may make it appear that reflection describes or creates a new form of consciousness, it is, in actuality, simply a specific *modification* of consciousness's pre-reflective, non-conceptual awareness. Dan Zahavi explains what this modification entails: 'when we reflect, we thematise a till then pre-reflectively self-aware experience, say, a perception of a chair. During this thematisation, the perception continues being conscious of its object, the chair, but it undergoes a certain modification. It is turned into a psychical (quasi) object, and is experienced as being owned or had by an ego' (1999: 141). While Sartre does recognize that 'it is difficult to explain the upsurge *ex nihilo* of the reflective consciousness' (BN: 173), he is clear that the modification that brings consciousness to reflectivity does not emanate from, nor is it caused by, something external to consciousness; reflection arises from 'an intrastructural modification which the for-itself realises in itself' (BN: 175). In other words, reflection emanates from consciousness's own activity.

By distinguishing between *pure* and *impure* reflection, Sartre demonstrates that not all forms of reflection are the same. Reflection is *pure* if consciousness reflectively understands itself as it is *ontologically*; that is, pure reflection describes the consciousness that reflectively understands that it is ontologically nothing and reflectively understands what this means for its being.

The consciousness of pure reflection nihilates all attempts to objectify it by either rejecting the objective description given to it or continuously reflectively altering its identity so that no single identity becomes synonymous with it. By continually reflectively altering its identity, consciousness is able to occupy the middle ground between being and non-being. This enables consciousness to constantly become without actually becoming anything.

The consciousness of pure reflection also explicitly understands that its judgements are not necessarily valid beyond their current application. In other words, when the consciousness of pure reflection expresses an opinion, it explicitly understands that this opinion is only valid for its immediate activity; it does not establish a timeless, ahistoric truth (NE: 507). Because the consciousness of pure reflection has a clear, lucid, and accurate, reflective understanding of its ontological nothingness, Sartre holds that pure reflection is the 'ideal form' (BN: 177) of reflection.

In contrast, and while impure reflection has all the understanding of pure reflection, it surpasses pure reflection's self-understanding by insisting that consciousness is more than it actually is. Impure reflection fails to recognize and affirm the essential nothingness of consciousness. As Sartre notes, 'reflection is impure when it gives itself as an "intuition of the for-itself in in-itself"' (BN: 184). In other words, the consciousness of impure reflection reflectively understands itself to be defined by a fixed, objective, ontological essence, characteristic, or talent.

But Sartre does recognize that consciousness can escape from impure reflection's self-objectification and come to the pure form of reflective self-understanding in which it reflectively understands that it is ontologically nothing. This self-recovery entails 'a modification which it effects on itself and which [takes] the form of a catharsis' (BN: 182). 'Conversion' is the name Sartre gives to this catharsis. Importantly, escaping from impure reflection does not 'add' anything to consciousness (NE: 497). Through conversion, consciousness chooses to reflectively understand what it is pre-reflectively aware of; namely, that it is ontologically nothing.

This has implications for Sartre's account of authenticity. If consciousness is ontologically nothing, and if it is *authentic* when it reflectively understands that it is ontologically nothing, then the process of becoming authentic does not require consciousness to develop its self-understanding; authenticity simply requires that consciousness reflectively recognize what it is ontologically. Consciousness's journey to authenticity entails a process of *self-revelatory recognition*. As Sartre notes, '[authentic pure] reflection is recognition rather than knowledge. It implies as the original motivator of the recovery a pre-reflective comprehension of [consciousness's essential nothingness that] it wishes to recover' (BN: 178).

But while consciousness can escape from impure reflection, it can never completely overcome the temptation of impure reflection. Indeed, while Sartre holds that consciousness must constantly battle against the self-objectification of impure reflection, he seems to think that the 'chips are stacked against' *pure* reflection (NE: 11). While consciousness must choose whether to reflectively understand itself *authentically* by reflectively understanding itself to be ontologically nothing *or* reflectively understand itself *inauthentically* by reflectively understanding itself to be ontologically something, consciousness's pre-reflective ontological desire to be something means the identity thinking of inauthentic, impure reflection is 'stronger' or more 'natural' than authentic, pure reflection. This is why Sartre calls the identity thinking of impure reflection, consciousness's 'natural attitude' (NE: 6).

Thus, Sartre thinks it likely that consciousness will naturally slip into inauthentic, impure reflection with the journey to authentic, pure reflection requiring significant effort. This does not mean that consciousness cannot spend significant amounts of time 'in' pure reflection; it means that: 1) alienating, impure reflection is always a possibility consciousness can reflectively choose; and 2) authentic, pure reflection takes a lot of effort to achieve. On this point, Sartre writes that 'the authenticity of your previous momentum doesn't prevent you [from] falling next instant into the inauthentic. The most one can say is that it's less difficult to preserve authenticity than to acquire it' (WD: 219). While the authentic, pure form of self-reflection is difficult to achieve and must be continually re-enacted to prevent consciousness from falling back into the inauthentic, impure form of self-reflection, Sartre does offer consciousness the slight comfort that, having chosen to undertake the difficult conversion to the authentic, pure form of self-reflection, it is a little easier to maintain the authentic, pure form of self-reflection than it was to convert from the inauthentic, impure form of self-reflection to the authentic, pure form of self-reflection in the first place. I will return to this issue later in this chapter.

Because it is ontologically nothing, Sartre maintains that the content of consciousness does not emanate from within itself. He also rejects the notion that while the world exists outside consciousness, it is subsequently incorporated into consciousness. The later view he dismissively calls the view of 'digestive philosophy' (I: 4). Instead, Sartre maintains that consciousness is always intentional; consciousness is always *consciousness-of-something*. When consciousness thinks, it always thinks of something; when it imagines, it always imagines something; when it is aware, it is always aware of something.

For Sartre, consciousness's intentionality ensures that its *content* emanates from the outside world rather than from within itself. For Sartre, this means that 'we are [...] delivered from the "internal life:" in vain would we seek the caresses and fondlings of our intimate selves, like

Amiel or like a child who kisses his own shoulders, since everything is finally outside, everything, even ourselves. Outside, in the world, among others. It is not in some hiding-place that we will discover ourselves; it is on the road, in the town, in the midst of the crowd, a thing among things, a man among men' (I: 5).

However, while consciousness gains its content from its intentional relation to the objects of its world, the two never synthesize. The object never enters into consciousness, nor does consciousness 'add' anything to being-in-itself; consciousness's content simply emanates from the object before it. There is always an ontological difference between the being of consciousness and the being of the object. Although I am not sure it is, Mark Meyers (2008: 87) maintains that this is the 'central paradox' of Sartre's argument: while consciousness is dependent on being-in-itself for its existence, the ontological difference between the two types of being ensures they remain ontologically distinct.

We can perhaps better understand this 'paradox' by further examining the relation between being-in-itself and being-for-itself. On the one hand, because the content of being-for-itself is determined by its relation to being-in-itself, Sartre maintains that being-in-itself has 'ontological primacy' (BN: 639) in the relation. However, at other times, he also appears to argue that they are mutually entwined: '[being-in-itself] has no priority over consciousness, and consciousness has no priority over it. They *form a dyad.* Of course this being could not exist without the for-itself, but neither could the for-itself exist without it' (BN: 115).

Timothy Sprigge finds Sartre's description of the entwined relation between consciousness and being-in-itself somewhat unsatisfactory. For Sprigge, 'there is a certain clash between the Sartrean view that things within the in-itself have definite natures which settle deterministically what they will do in any circumstances, and the view that, until played on by the light provided by the for-itself, the in-itself is a plenitude of being with no definite character or articulation into distinct things' (1984: 135). In other words, Sprigge argues that Sartre holds that the *ontological* structure of being-in-itself is both differentiated and undifferentiated.

This leads to another apparent ambiguity in Sartre's account relating to his insistence that being-in-itself is an undifferentiated mass of being that only becomes differentiated when consciousness differentiates it *and* his insistence that the *content* of consciousness emanates from its relation to being-in-itself. If, as Sprigge insists it is, being-in-itself is a unified, undifferentiated mass of being, consciousness's intentional relation to being-in-itself would ensure that consciousness's content was also undifferentiated and Sartre would have to hold that the experience of different objects is a purely subjective experience. Put differently, different objects such as cats, dogs, tables and so on would not exist in-themselves; they would only exist if consciousness chose to differentiate the unitary, undifferentiated mass of being-in-itself in the way necessary to create these objects. If, however, consciousness gains its content from its intentional relation to being-in-itself, and if Sartre is to be able to account for the *experience* of different objects, being-in-itself must be ontologically differentiated. It appears to Sprigge, therefore, that there is a tension in Sartre's account between his theory of intentionality and his description of the ontological structure of being-in-itself. I disagree, but to make my case I first have to examine the being of being-in-itself.

The ontological characteristics of being-in-itself

Gregory McCulloch (1994: 3) notes that there are two senses to Sartre's description of 'being-in-itself:' first, being-in-itself describes the ontological characteristics of a particular *entity*. More specifically, being-in-itself describes an entity that is '*solid*' (BN: 22), consists of 'full positivity' (BN: 22), is non-temporal, and undifferentiated. 'The in-itself is full of itself, and no more plenitude can be imagined, no more perfect equivalence of content to container. There is not the slightest emptiness in being, not the tiniest crack through which nothingness might slip in' (BN: 98). Because the ontological structure of existents defined by the ontological characteristics of 'being-in-itself' is undifferentiated, not much more can be said about them. As Sartre summarizes it: 'Being is. Being is in-itself. Being is what it is' (BN: 22).

But it may be objected, as Nik Farrell-Fox does, that 'homogenising all the various features of the natural world into a single inorganic and passive externality, fails to distinguish between the more active elements of that world, such as plants and animals, and the more passive, inorganic ones, such as rocks and sand – nor does he make any such distinction between naturally occurring forms (animals, rivers etc.) and synthetic human constructions (chairs, machines, dams, buildings etc.)' (2003: 45–46). In other words, Sartre's ontological description of being-in-itself is too simplistic.

While there is textual evidence to support Farrell-Fox's interpretation, insofar as Sartre talks of 'the undifferentiation of the in-itself' (BN: 21), that 'at the start *everything* is given to me in undifferentiated form' (TOTE: 19), and 'the in-itself' (BN: 22), which makes it appear that being-in-itself is simply a unitary, undifferentiated, solid mass of being, I think Farrell-Fox's objection and the interpretation of being-in-itself it is grounded in are ultimately unsatisfactory.

Farrell-Fox's criticism emanates from the same interpretation of being-in-itself that underpins Sprigge's criticism: the ontological category being-in-itself describes a *unitary, undifferentiated mass of being*. Because being-in-itself is interpreted as an ontologically *un*differentiated mass of being, Farrell-Fox is able to claim that, for Sartre, particular objects, such as tables, chairs, rocks and sorts, do not actually exist *in-themselves*. All that exists in-itself is an undifferentiated mass of being that consciousness subjectively differentiates and divides into various objects. Particular objects only come to exist once consciousness differentiates the ontologically undifferentiated mass of being-in-itself. On Farrell-Fox's interpretation, the particular objects of the world do not *actually* exist; they simply and wholeheartedly exist *for consciousness*. Similarly, because he interprets being-in-itself to be 'a plenitude of being with no definite character' (Sprigge, 1984: 135) prior to the differentiation consciousness creates through its nihilating act, Sprigge argues that Sartre is unable to explain how consciousness can have differentiated knowledge of its world. In other words, Sprigge questions how Sartre can hold that consciousness can have differentiated knowledge of its world when consciousness only gains knowledge from its intentional relation to being-in-itself and when the ontological structure of being-in-itself is undifferentiated. This interpretation of being-in-itself insists that the undifferentiated ontological structure of being-in-itself conflicts with Sartre's theory of consciousness's intentionality.

The interpretation is, however, ultimately based on a misinterpretation of Sartre's thought. Being-in-itself does not describe a unitary, undifferentiated mass of being; it is the term Sartre uses to describe certain forms of being that exist with common *ontological characteristics*. In other words, being-for-itself and being-in-itself are both aspects of 'being,' insofar as both exist; importantly, however, they are different forms of being, insofar as *a* being is characterized as being-for-itself if it 'has' the ontological characteristic of nothingness, while *a* being is characterized as being-in-itself if it has the ontological characteristic of something-ness. The fundamental difference between the two types of being is that, because it is ontologically nothing, consciousness is able to *nihilate* itself, whereas a being with the ontological characteristics of being-in-itself can only be what it is. This is not to say that being-in-itself does not change, nor is it to say that being-in-itself can not be dynamic. It is to say that being-in-itself *cannot nihilate itself* to determine its own mode of existence; only being-for-itself can nihilate itself and determine its own being. Thus, the ontological category 'being-in-itself' does not describe a unitary, undifferentiated mass of being; it describes the ontological characteristics *a* particular being has: namely, that particular being is ontologically solid, undifferentiated, passive, and lacks the capacity for self-nihilation.

Understanding that being-in-itself describes ontological characteristics common to different objects overcomes the obstacles that arise if being-in-itself is understood to designate a single, undifferentiated ontological mass of being. It means that Sartre's descriptions of consciousness' relations to an alarm clock, tools, or stones (BN: 61; NE: 354, 383) are not descriptions of objects consciousness has created and that only exist in consciousness's subjective imagination; they are descriptions of consciousness's relation to *actual* alarms, tools, and stones that *actually* exist in ontological opposition to consciousness.

Sartre is most clear on this in *Truth and Existence* when he adopts the first-person perspective to explain that 'when I touch velvet, what I make exist is neither a velvet that is absolute and in itself nor a velvet relative to some sort of structure superimposed [*structure de survol*] by a transmundane consciousness. I make *velvet* exist *for flesh*' (TE: 8). Put differently, there are actual, particular objects that confront consciousness although these take on the particular properties and meaning consciousness gives them. Thus, while consciousness intentionally relates to an ontologically undifferentiated object (in this case, a piece of cloth), what this ontologically undifferentiated, particular object means for consciousness in terms of its colour, consistency, and feel depends on consciousness's subjective interpretation of the ontologically undifferentiated, particular object it intentionally relates to.

Consciousness does not simply create its object out of an undifferentiated mass of being-in-itself; consciousness *unveils* the particular object before it in a particular way by subjectively *interpreting* the ontologically undifferentiated, particular object before it. Understanding that being-in-itself describes particular beings that share the same fundamental ontological characteristics overcomes the tension that Farrell-Fox and Sprigge argue exists between Sartre's analysis of the ontological structure of being-in-itself and his analysis of the intentionality of consciousness. It means that the differentiated content of consciousness emanates from its intentional relation to the different objects of its world, each of which is defined by common ontological characteristics.

The second sense of being-in-itself McCulloch identifies is that it describes 'a *way* or *mode* or *manner* of being' (1994: 3) consciousness can pre-reflectively adopt. If consciousness adopts a pre-reflective fundamental project that leads it to reflectively understand that it has an essential identity, Sartre maintains it will adopt a mode of being with fixed predetermined actions and/or a fixed conception of itself. In other words, when consciousness pre-reflectively understands itself to have a fixed identity or ontological characteristic, such as being intelligent or lazy, rather than reflectively understanding that it is, in actuality, ontologically nothing, Sartre maintains that it has adopted the mode of being-in-itself. We will see that this is crucially important for Sartre's account of alienation. Because the consciousness that reflectively understands itself to have a fixed ontological identity fails to reflectively understand that it is ontologically nothing, Sartre insists it is alienated from what it truly is ontologically.

The fundamental ontological difference between being-in-itself and being-for-itself creates an *ontological* duality in Sartre's account of being. Because being-for-itself is ontologically nothing, it cannot ever become the full, ontological positivity of being-in-itself. Even when being-for-itself reflectively understands itself to have a fixed essence and so adopts the mode of being-in-itself, it never *actually* becomes the *entity* 'being-in-itself.' In contrast, because being-in-itself cannot nihilate itself, it can only be what it is; it can never have the possibilities inherent to the being of the for-itself. There is not and cannot be any synthesis between being-for-itself and being-in-itself. The irreducible ontological difference between both beings ensures that, for Sartre, each is, and can only ever be, *ontologically* distinct.

Facticity

Because Sartre insists the defining ontological characteristic of consciousness is nothingness, he notes that consciousness can never be constrained or adopt a mode of being-in-itself without pre-reflectively deciding for itself to be constrained or adopt the mode of being-in-itself. Consciousness's ontological nothingness means it is always free to decide for itself what it will be and what it will do. Writing in the first-person, Sartre famously states that 'I am condemned to be free. This means that no limits to my freedom can be found except freedom itself or, if you prefer, that we are not free to cease being free' (BN: 462). Sartre even goes so far as to say that the tortured individual remains free because 'whatever the sufferings which have been endured, it is the victim who decides, as a last resort, what the moment is when they are unbearable and when he must talk' (WL: 167). There is no determination that constrains consciousness's freedom. At each and every moment of consciousness's existence, it pre-reflectively affects the nihilating withdrawal from being-in-itself through which it becomes and remains absolutely free. But consciousness does not simply have the potential to free itself from its given reality. Sartre goes further and says that consciousness *is* freedom: 'Man does not exist *first* in order to be free *subsequently*; there is no difference between the being of man and his *being-free*' (BN: 49).

However, while nothingness discloses the fundamental ontological characteristic of consciousness, Sartre recognizes that consciousness is always embodied in a particular situation. He calls this, consciousness's *facticity*: 'it is […] facticity which permits us to say that the for-itself *is*, that it *exists*, although we can never *realise* the facticity and although we always apprehend it through the for-itself' (BN: 107). Consciousness's facticity comprises a multiplicity of concrete social phenomena, including its birth at a particular place and historical time which determines certain economic facts regarding luxury and the way objects can appear to consciousness, its body, race, social class, nationality, character, and past (BN: 352). These aspects combine to embed each being-for-itself in the world. Not only do they make it a concrete being, but they also shape the concrete possibilities available to it.

However, on my understanding, Sartre holds that consciousness's facticity is not an aspect of its ontological structure. Consciousness's facticity is the *area of happening* that embeds consciousness in the actual world and allows consciousness's ontological freedom to be exercised in the actual world. Because consciousness is intimately related to its facticity without its facticity being a constitutive aspect of its ontological structure, consciousness's relationship to its facticity is complex and nuanced (BN: 535). On the one hand, consciousness is always embedded in the world by its facticity; but, on the other hand, because of the transcendence that results from its pre-reflective nihilation of being-in-itself, consciousness is ontologically other than its facticity. The result is that, rather than being constituted by the world, Sartre maintains that 'consciousness is *in contact* with the world' (WD: 181). Similarly, and in relation to its body, Sartre holds that while consciousness is pre-reflectively aware of its body, consciousness is not synonymous with its body. 'Non-positional [pre-reflective] consciousness is consciousness (of the) body as being that which it surmounts and nihilates by making itself consciousness – i.e., as being something which consciousness is without having to be it and *which it passes over* in order to be what it has to be' (BN: 353–354).

While Sartre recognizes that consciousness is always embodied, he maintains that consciousness always pre-reflectively nihilates its body. This pre-reflective act secures consciousness's ontological nothingness. But Sartre warns that this does not mean that consciousness exists 'within' its body. As Sartre explains, 'I am neither *in my body* nor behind it, nor *am* I my body, but neither am I *other* than it – I exist it' (NE: 316). As I understand, this means that while consciousness is always embodied, it is not synonymous with its body, nor is consciousness constituted by its body. By insisting on a distinction, albeit a subtle and nuanced one, between consciousness and its body, Sartre is able to hold that, no matter how constrained its body may be, consciousness always remains free to determine itself and its situation.

The important aspect of my interpretation is that while consciousness is embedded in its objective facticity, it is *not* a living synthesis of subjective freedom and objective facticity. If it were, objectivity would be an aspect of consciousness's ontological structure. This, however, contradicts Sartre's insistence that consciousness's ontological structure is defined by its ontological opposition to objectivity. Consciousness's objective facticity is the *area of happening* on, in, and through which consciousness struggles to assert its subjective freedom in-line with the ends of its pre-reflective fundamental project (BN: 503–511).

For Hegel, however, consciousness and its body are *ontologically* entwined. Hegel explains that 'in so far as I am alive, my soul (the concept and, on a higher level, the free entity) and my body are not separated; my body is the existence [*Dasein*] of freedom, and I feel through it' (PR: 48R). While Hegel talks of a distinction between 'soul' and its body, it is clear that this means consciousness and its body. Thus, for Hegel, consciousness does not choose how it will live its body; it *is* its body. On Hegel's understanding, Sartre's ontological distinction between consciousness and its body fails to understand that the two are *ontologically* entwined. This failure leads Sartre to insist that consciousness is ontologically different to its body, despite being dependent on its body to embed it in the world and allow it to practically express itself. Sartre's consciousness is, if you like, *ontologically disembodied*, but *experientially embodied*; it is ontologically distinct from its body, yet experientially dependent on its body. For Hegel, however, it is not possible to be experientially embodied and not be ontologically embodied.

But this does not mean that Hegel thinks that consciousness and its body are *synonymous*; it means that there is a dialectical interplay between consciousness and its body that shapes consciousness's *ontological structure*. By insisting that thought discloses being, Hegel is able to insist that an alteration in consciousness's self-understanding alters its being and an alteration in its being alters its self-understanding. Put differently, consciousness's self-understanding is shaped by its bodily interactions and its bodily interactions are shaped by consciousness's self-understanding. Thus, whereas Sartre appears to maintain that consciousness is detached from the torture imposed on its body to the extent that it is able to determine the meaning of its beating, Hegel maintains that consciousness is intimately tied to the experience of torture; its body's beating impacts on and shapes consciousness's reaction to its body's beating. Hegel's consciousness does not remain unaffected by its bodily interaction in the way that Sartre appears to think it can and does.

Understanding the way Sartre conceptualizes consciousness's relation to facticity is crucial to understanding the role objectivity plays in Sartre's thought. However, Sartre's analysis of consciousness's relation to objectivity is complex. While he holds that consciousness's ontological structure is defined by its ontological opposition to all forms of objectivity, Sartre notes that consciousness's *actual existence* is shaped by its objective facticity. This ensures that to understand a particular consciousness's *actual* mode of being, it is necessary to understand its facticity and how consciousness reflectively lives it. It is only by identifying and understanding consciousness's facticity that we can identify how consciousness's facticity shapes its experiences. This allows us to identify the empirical possibilities open to that particular consciousness in its particular objective situation. In turn, this allows us to identify whether that particular consciousness lives its freedom *authentically*, by reflectively affirming its ontological nothingness in its particular situation, or whether it lives its particular situation *inauthentically*, by reflectively understanding that its situation defines it ontologically.

Thus, while Sartre insists that *consciousness's ontological structure* can be understood without identifying and understanding its facticity (consciousness is always *ontologically* nothing), he holds that understanding how a particular consciousness *actually exists* requires that consciousness's facticity and the way consciousness reflectively lives its facticity be identified.

Freedom

But Sartre's insistence that consciousness is *always* free is one that is highly striking. How is Sartre able to claim that the tortured are free?

How is he able to claim that nothing impinges on consciousness's freedom? To understand his thought requires that we engage further with his understanding of freedom.

To start with, it must be noted that Sartre's understanding of freedom is not undifferentiated. David Detmer (1988: 60) correctly notes that, throughout Sartre's argument, the concept 'freedom' refers to two different, but related, *general* senses of the term. I will follow Detmer's characterization and call them 'ontological freedom' and 'practical freedom.'

Ontological freedom describes the freedom that emanates from consciousness's pre-reflective nihilation of being-in-itself. Consciousness's existence is, in the first instance, defined by the negative because its existence is dependent on a pre-reflective act that nihilates being-in-itself. But consciousness also has the capacity to reflectively nihilate being-in-itself. This reflective act of nihilation allows consciousness to effect an *idealistic* nihilation of its given reality which, in turn, allows it to choose its existence. There is no determination that constrains consciousness's freedom. This is because consciousness's ontological nothingness always allows it to do, at least, one of two things.

First, Sartre's conception of ontological freedom ensures that being-for-itself is always capable of effecting a reflective idealistic *nihilation* of its *given reality*. Sartre argues that the ever-present possibility that consciousness can affect a reflective nihilating withdrawal from the given reality ensures that 'there exists [...] for the questioner the permanent objective possibility of a negative reply' (BN: 29). To any question, statement, or argument there is always the possibility of answering 'No!' It is because consciousness can always refuse the given reality by simply saying 'No!' that Sartre maintains that consciousness always remains free from it.

Secondly, consciousness's ontological freedom ensures that it is free to determine the *meaning* of its given reality. While Sartre does not reject the notion of an objective world, indeed the intentionality of consciousness requires there to be one, what he does reject is that the *meaning* of this world is synonymous with its being. The meaning of the world emanates from and is grounded in being-for-itself. Sartre explains that 'we choose the world, not in its contexture as in-itself but in its meaning, by choosing ourselves' (BN: 485). It is consciousness that gives the world its meaning by choosing what the meaning of the objective event will be for it. While the objective event impacts on consciousness, consciousness is able to determine the extent to which the objective event will impact on its existence by determining the meaning that the objective event will have for its life. Because consciousness is free to choose the meaning of each objective event, it is not constrained by these objective events. By affecting the nihilating withdrawal from its objective event, consciousness is able to either simply reject this event or alter the meaning of the event for it. Either of these tactics allows it to remain free from its world and choose what it will be and do.

While ontological freedom refers to the fundamental aspect of consciousness's ontological structure, practical freedom delineates consciousness's capacity to actually express itself in the concrete world. There are two related senses to this form of freedom, the second of which is dependent on the first. Practical freedom delineates: 1) the freedom consciousness has from any constraints or impediments to its actual, concrete activity; and 2) the process whereby consciousness creatively expresses itself in the actual world. It is only if consciousness's world does not constrain it that consciousness can freely choose how it will creatively express itself. Thus, for Sartre, being practically free requires that consciousness first nihilates its world. Only this initial act of nihilation allows consciousness to create a space for itself from which to choose how it will practically express itself.

But, importantly, in the *Critique of Dialectical Reason*, Sartre explains that consciousness's practical act of creative self-expression will necessarily create objects/objective structures that subsequently impinge on its capacity to be practically free. This is because Sartre implicitly distinguishes between the *act of objectification* that he deems to be the expression of consciousness's practical freedom and the *being of objectivity* which he insists alienates consciousness from its capacity to practically express itself. For Sartre, while the *act of objectification* allows consciousness to express its individuality in objective form, the object created as a result of consciousness's act of creative self-expression will become a static entity that stands before consciousness as something to be overcome before it can practically express itself in the future (CDR I: 177–178). Consciousness is never 'at one' with the object it creates; nor does it appear that consciousness can see itself in the object it creates. The object consciousness creates always subsequently appears to it as an other that impinges on its capacity to be practically free. Importantly, however, the practical activities of other consciousnesses also create objects that impinge on consciousness's capacity to practically express itself. For this reason, Sartre holds that to secure its practical freedom, consciousness must 'enter into conflict with the situation in which [it] finds [it]self' (CDR I: 253). It is by battling with, and overcoming the resistance from, its external world that consciousness becomes and remains practically free.

The important point is that, while consciousness's act of creative self-expression allows it to express its subjective freedom, the object created as a result of its self-objectification necessarily appears to it as an other that must first be nihilated before consciousness can practically express itself. Consciousness's practical freedom is, therefore, a double-edge sword: on the one hand, it allows consciousness to freely and practically express itself; on the other hand, the objects created by consciousness's act of practical self-expression will fold back on consciousness to constrain its future practical freedom.

According to Sartre, therefore, while the process of self-objectification always allows consciousness to authentically express its subjective freedom in the actual world, the object created as a result of its act of creative self-expression always subsequently appears to consciousness as a constraint that must first be overcome before it can choose how to express itself practically. For Sartre, consciousness can only become practically free if it overcomes a resisting world.

Sartre slips between the two senses and three usages of the notion 'freedom' to show that no matter how determined consciousness's situation appears to be, consciousness's ontological structure is never shaped, constrained, or determined by its situation and its experiences do not need to be determined by its situation either. Even when consciousness cannot effect an objective change in the actual world, it can always alter what the world means for it. In choosing its values, consciousness chooses and so controls the meaning of its world. This allows Sartre to insist that freedom *is* synonymous with human reality.

But it is not entirely clear how Sartre can consistently claim that consciousness, which, it will be remembered, is defined by the act of nihilation, can also creatively express itself in the world. It appears that Sartre's account of consciousness's activities is not wholly consistent with his analysis of consciousness's ontological structure. Put differently, on the one hand, Sartre's analysis of consciousness's ontological structure insists that the activity of consciousness is defined by the pure nihilation of the given. On the other hand, however, he insists that consciousness is not simply defined by the act of pure nihilation; it also creatively and positively expresses itself in the actual world. There appears to be a tension in Sartre's account between what his analysis of consciousness's ontological structure allows it to do (nihilate the given reality) and what Sartre wants consciousness to be able to do in the actual world (creatively and positively express itself in the actual world).

Hegel would certainly think that Sartre is inconsistent on this point. If consciousness's ontological structure is defined in terms of the act of nihilation, Hegel maintains it is not able to construct anything; 'its actualisation can only be the fury of destruction' (PR: 5R). According to Hegel, therefore, the pure nihilation constitutive of Sartre's analysis of consciousness's ontological structure prevents it from being able to construct anything; its activity can only be purely negative. To account for consciousness's creative capacity, Hegel holds that the will of consciousness is not simply negative; it also has a positive, creative aspect. This overcomes the tension identified in Sartre's analysis because it allows Hegel to explicitly recognize that consciousness can express itself both negatively and positively/creatively in the actual world (PR: 7).

But while Sartre describes two *general* senses, and *three* specific usages, of the concept 'freedom,' he also argues that the two general senses of the concept are related. More specifically, Sartre maintains that being-for-itself's *practical* freedom is dependent on its *ontological* freedom. It is because being-for-itself is *ontologically* free that it can always affect the idealistic nihilating withdrawal from determinate reality, which can then allow it to freely choose how it will act in the actual world. The *fundamental* sense of Sartre's conception of freedom is, therefore, consciousness's *ontological freedom*.

But while consciousness is always pre-reflectively aware of its ontological freedom, it does not always reflectively understand this. An aspect of Sartre's account of authenticity is that consciousness comes to *reflectively understand* that it is ontologically nothing. Thomas Anderson objects to this. He argues that making authenticity dependent on consciousness's reflective self-understanding does not distinguish between the *content* of consciousness's various acts; it only distinguishes between the forms of reflective understanding that consciousness adopts when it acts. As such, 'it would seem to allow an individual to do or accept absolutely anything so long as she were clearly conscious of it and accepted personal responsibility for it' (1993: 55).

Indeed, Sartre himself seems to notice this aspect of his account. He recognizes that defining authenticity in terms of consciousness's reflective self-understanding may 'lead to conflicting political decisions. The Jew can choose to be authentic by asserting his place as Jew in the French community, with all that goes with it [in terms] of rights and martyrdom [...] But he may also be led by his choice of authenticity to seek the creation of a Jewish nation possessing its own soil and autonomy' (ASJ: 139). Why does this trouble Anderson and not Sartre? I think there are two reasons.

First, Anderson appears to forget that consciousness's reflective self-understanding also determines its actual mode of being. Because Sartre insists that authenticity requires a specific form of reflective self-understanding, namely one where consciousness reflectively understands that it is ontologically nothing, he also appears to think that when consciousness reflectively understands this, it will simultaneously adopt a mode of being that conforms to its ontological nothingness. In other words, when consciousness reflectively understands that it is ontologically nothing, its mode of being will affirm this nothingness by purposefully not adopting a fixed identity. Instead, consciousness will affirm its freedom. This allows Sartre to distinguish between *inauthentic* modes of being where consciousness freely and reflectively chooses a mode of being which *does not* subsequently affirm its ontological freedom, and *authentic* modes of being where consciousness freely and reflectively chooses a mode of being that *does* subsequently affirm its ontological freedom. This distinction brings a critical aspect to Sartre's analysis of consciousness's modes of being.

Secondly, Anderson criticizes Sartre because he reduces Sartre's account of authenticity to whether consciousness reflectively understands that it is ontologically nothing. This prevents Anderson from recognizing that, while this is an aspect of Sartrean authenticity, there are other aspects to his account that outline the concrete content of authentic acts. While Sartre insists that an aspect of authenticity requires that consciousness reflectively understand that it is ontologically nothing, we will see that he complements this by adding other conditions to authentic being: in particular, consciousness must also be practically free in the actual world and must ensure that the other is practically free. By making consciousness's authenticity dependent on the realization of its own, and other's, practical freedom, Sartre insists that, while ontological freedom is the primordial form of freedom, it is practical freedom that consciousness should focus on achieving.

But to reiterate, the realization of consciousness's practical freedom does not occur at the expense of consciousness's ontological freedom; the two senses of freedom do not exist in an either/or relation. Affirming its *practical freedom* requires that consciousness live in a manner that reflectively affirms its *ontological freedom*. For Sartre, consciousness is only practically free if it: 1) is able to freely act in the actual world; and 2) does this without adopting a fixed identity and/ or unreflectively acting in accordance with predetermined rules and actions.

The universal value and the fundamental project

Sartre deepens his conception of freedom by showing how it relates to consciousness's values. This allows him to again demonstrate consciousness's freedom. For Sartre, there are no a priori, *ethical* judgments that consciousness must follow. Because meaning comes to the world from the actions and choices of consciousness, each consciousness must determine for itself the values it holds. As Sartre explains in *Existentialism and Humanism*, 'you are free, therefore choose – that is to say, invent. No rule of general morality can show you what you ought to do: no signs are vouchsafed in this world' (EH: 38). Each consciousness must choose for itself what it considers to be good/bad, right/wrong. Nothing is given to it in terms of absolute, moral values or meaning; consciousness must perpetually make its own moral world. Consciousness may not understand this or may understand it and flee from its freedom, but, for Sartre, this is still consciousness's choice (EH: 48).

Failure to reflectively choose its values means that consciousness exists in the 'spirit of seriousness' (BN: 646). The consciousness of the spirit of seriousness 'considers values as transcendent givens independent of human subjectivity, and it transfers the quality of "desirable" from the ontological structure of things to their simple material constitution' (BN: 646). In other words, the consciousness of the spirit of seriousness reifies abstract notions of good/bad, right/wrong by taking them to be independent of consciousness. This ensures that consciousness lives its life according to the dictates of another; it does not choose its own values. By pre-reflectively choosing to live in accordance with a priori, transcendent values, consciousness voluntarily alienates itself from its freedom. As Sartre explains: 'The spirit of seriousness is voluntary alienation, that is, submission to an abstraction that justifies one: the thought that man is the inessential and the abstract the essential' (NE: 60).

The spirit of seriousness also describes a consciousness that approaches existence with a specific subjective attitude: it takes itself and its world excessively seriously. It lives with a heavy weight on its metaphorical shoulders and is unable to see the lighter side of life. Existence becomes a burden to it; one that impinges on its subjective freedom. It repudiates all attempts to *enjoy* its world; it simply seeks to fulfil its existential needs. Thus, '*bread* is desirable because it is *necessary* to live (a value written in an intelligible heaven) and because bread is nourishing' (BN: 646); it is not desired because it tastes good or brings pleasure to consciousness.

Rather than live with a spirit of seriousness, Sartre exhorts consciousness to live with a *spirit of play* (WD: 327). Consciousness must realize that its existence is akin to that of an artist; it must continuously reflectively create itself. Consciousness must be willing to experiment with its being and try out alternative ways of being (NE: 508, 514–515).

However, for Sartre, consciousness's freedom to choose its mode of being comes at a terrible cost: it is wholly responsible for its being. 'Man being condemned to be free carries the whole weight of the world on his shoulders; he is responsible for the world and for himself as a way of being' (BN: 574). Consciousness must choose what it does and how it lives. There are no objective, ethical laws that can guide its actions. At each moment, consciousness must choose its existence from a myriad of existential possibilities.

The responsibility that accompanies consciousness's absolute freedom ensures that if consciousness's reflection is *pure*, it will not reflectively experience its absolute freedom happily. The perpetual choice that accompanies its absolute freedom and the absence of a priori, ethical standards means that consciousness exists in the unenviable situation of having to choose what to do and be without being able to discern what it is to do or be. This paradox causes consciousness anguish: 'Anguish, abandonment, responsibility, whether muted or full strength, constitute the *quality* of our consciousness in so far as this is pure and simple freedom' (BN: 486). The paradox of Sartre's conception of consciousness is that while consciousness is free, its pure reflective experience of this freedom is not a joyous or happy experience. Consciousness's reflective experience of its absolute freedom pains it. This is the reason why consciousness may flee its freedom by reflectively adopting the mode of being-in-itself. Bad faith is the attempt to flee from the anguish and misery that emanates from consciousness's reflective experience of its absolute freedom.

But the exercise of consciousness's absolute freedom is not arbitrary. Each consciousness has its own *fundamental project*, its own fundamental, existential choice as to the goal its life will be directed towards and the ethical values it will adhere to. Its pre-reflective fundamental project encases consciousness within a matrix of pre-reflective goals and values that shape its reflective experience.

It is crucial to understand consciousness's fundamental project because this choice will shape how consciousness sees the world, relates to it, and comports itself. But Sartre warns that there are no guidelines as to which fundamental project consciousness must choose; some may choose to be writers, others doctors, teachers, nurses, soldiers, or even madmen. The choice is purely individual, although it is shaped by consciousness's interaction with others. It is also possible for consciousness to alter its fundamental project if it so desires, although, because this requires that consciousness alter its entire world-view, this will result in significant existential upheaval.

However, consciousness's fundamental project is itself grounded in, and shaped by, a pre-reflective *universal value*. This pre-reflective universal value is the desire to synthesize with being-in-itself to become a being-in-itself-for-itself; or, as Sartre provocatively calls it: God. Thus, 'the best way to conceive of the fundamental project of human reality is to say that man is the being whose project is to be God' (BN: 587).

Consciousness pre-reflectively desires to be God because while it is ontologically nothing, it is not satisfied with simply being nothing. It pre-reflectively desires to 'fill' its ontological nothingness by becoming something; 'the supreme value toward which consciousness at every instant surpasses itself by its very being is the absolute being of the self with its characteristics of identity, of purity, of permanence, etc., and as its own foundation' (BN: 117–118).

But consciousness does not simply want to replace its ontological nothingness with the something-ness of being-in-itself; consciousness 'does not want to lose itself in the in-itself of identity at the limit of its surpassing. It is for the for-itself as such that the for-itself lays claim to being-in-itself' (BN: 114). Consciousness wants to become something determinate and fixed, while at the same time remaining absolutely free. Only by *synthesizing* with being-in-itself will consciousness be absolutely free to choose its existence, while at the same time escaping the contingency and nothingness that this absolute freedom entails. Only then will consciousness be able to freely and absolutely choose its existence, while at the same time being secure in its being (Levy, 2002: 94).

But consciousness's ontological desire to be God does not determine or constrain its freedom. The ontological desire to be God is a *pre-reflective* desire towards which consciousness's existence can be, but does not necessarily have to be, orientated.

However, Sartre explains that if consciousness chooses to adopt a pre-reflective fundamental project that seeks to fulfil its pre-reflective ontological desire to be God, it will necessarily fail because: 1) becoming something would annihilate the nothingness that defines its ontological structure; and 2) there is no element that can mediate the oppositional, ontological relation between being-for-itself and being-in-itself: 'Negativity cannot be overcome and it is not a question [...] of dreaming about assimilating this Not-me as in Hegel or Fichte. No digestion' (NE: 498).

The tragedy of Sartre's consciousness is that its pre-reflective ontological desire to be God ensures that if it were to become the thing it desires to be, it would lose the nothingness that defines its ontological structure. Its inevitable failure ensures that the consciousness that tries to become God suffers its existence. 'The being of human reality is suffering because it rises in being as perpetually haunted by a totality which it is without being able to be, precisely because it could not attain the in-itself without losing itself as for-itself. Human reality therefore is by nature an unhappy consciousness with no possibility of surpassing its unhappy state' (BN: 114).

Conversion and the desire to be God

But while *Being and Nothingness* describes the alienating consequences that arise when consciousness adopts the pre-reflective fundamental project of being God and reflectively understands itself to be ontologically something, at the very end of *Being and Nothingness*, Sartre points out that consciousness's ontological freedom means it does not have to reflectively understand itself in this way, nor does it have to adopt a pre-reflective fundamental project that has the desire to be God as its end. Sartre returns to this point in the discussion of the 'conversion' in his *Notebooks for an Ethics* (NE: 471).

There are two related aspects to the conversion: first, conversion involves a specific alteration in consciousness's pre-reflective fundamental project; 'there is a conversion from the [pre-reflective fundamental] project to-be-for-itself-in-itself and appropriation or identification to a [pre-reflective fundamental] project of unveiling and creation' (NE: 482). Whereas the pre-converted consciousness understands that it *must* seek to become God, its perpetual failure to fulfil this desire may lead consciousness to re-evaluate whether it should continue to attempt to fulfil this desire. Through this re-evaluation, consciousness comes to understand that it does not simply have to seek to become God; consciousness comes to understand that its freedom is at the source of this futile imperative. Sartre thinks this recognition will lead consciousness to abandon its previous desire to be God and place freedom as the end towards which its existence is directed (EH: 38, 51–52).

By adopting a pre-reflective fundamental project that has freedom as its end, the converted consciousness reflectively recognizes that it is free to choose itself. The result is that consciousness undergoes a process of continuous, reflective self-creation. Perpetually reflectively recreating itself allows consciousness to reflectively express its freedom without actually reflectively understanding itself to be anything or, in fact, actually becoming anything. For Sartre, consciousness's reflective refusal of the pursuit of being and its continuous acts of reflective self-creation are at the foundation of authentic being (NE: 475, 514–515).

Secondly, accompanying this alteration in its pre-reflective fundamental project is a radically new form of reflective self-understanding (NE: 472). Conversion describes the movement from the *impure* form of reflective self-understanding to the *pure* form of reflective self-understanding. Whereas the consciousness of impure reflection thematizes its ontological nothingness, thereby reflectively understanding itself to be an ego or something, conversion is the process whereby consciousness, having been in the natural attitude of impure reflection, comes to reflectively understand that it is ontologically nothing. By reflectively understanding its ontological nothingness, the converted consciousness has 'a thematic grasping of freedom' (NE: 474). It no longer reflectively understands itself to be something, nor does it reflectively understand itself to have to follow a priori, transcendent, ethical imperatives; the converted consciousness achieves 'a new, *"authentic,"* way of being [it] self' (NE: 474), which reflectively understands and affirms its ontological freedom.

There are, however, two separate, but related, issues with the conversion. First, Sartre never explains at what point its experience would, or should, lead consciousness to undertake this self-conversion. Indeed, by stating that 'there are no *reasons* within this world for changing one's point of view' (NE: 357), it appears that there is a degree of randomness as to which form of reflection consciousness will choose at any moment. Secondly, while the pre-converted consciousness of impure reflection experiences the perpetual failure of its attempt to be something, the fate of the converted consciousness of pure reflection is even worse. Not only does it share impure reflection's experience of perpetual failure, it also explicitly experiences the anxiety that accompanies pure reflection of the absolute freedom that emanates from its ontological nothingness. For Sartre, consciousness faces two miserable options: it can either exist *inauthentically* by choosing the impure form of self-reflection that will lead it to experience constant failure or exist *authentically* by choosing the pure form of self-reflection that will lead it to experience perpetual failure and anxiety.

Faced with these options, it is not clear why consciousness would choose to adopt the authentic, pure form of reflection over the inauthentic, impure form of reflection. As Alfred Stern argues, 'a life in authenticity, as preached by Sartre, gives us only *one* reward for the sufferings it imposes upon us: the moral satisfaction of living no longer in bad faith, of being sincere, of being no longer bad *salauds*. But only an irrationalist approach to existence can consider this moral satisfaction an adequate reward for the sufferings of anxiety' (1968: 235). Perhaps it is more rational for consciousness to seek to escape from the anxiety that results from its adoption of the authentic, pure form of self-reflection by reflectively understanding itself in terms of the inauthentic, impure form of self-reflection? When consciousness does this, it may not be authentic in the Sartrean sense of the term, but at least it experiences only failure rather than failure *and* anxiety.

But while conversion allows consciousness to overcome its pre-reflective ontological desire to be God, a one-off conversion does not allow consciousness to overcome its pre-reflective ontological desire to be God *forever*.

Because the desire to be God is a pre-reflective ontological condition of consciousness, it can never be overcome once and for all. Consciousness is continually faced with the choice of whether to pre-reflectively affirm or negate its pre-reflective ontological desire to be God. For this reason, Sartre explains that 'the authentic man cannot suppress the pursuit of being through conversion' (NE: 37). Conversion simply brings consciousness to reflectively understand: 1) that it is ontologically nothing; and 2) the futility of its pre-reflective ontological desire to be God. With this recognition, Sartre thinks consciousness will no longer pursue its pre-reflective ontological desire to be God. Instead, consciousness will adopt a pre-reflective fundamental project that leads it to reflectively understand that it is ontologically nothing and reflectively affirm its practical freedom. For Sartre, this is the foundation of authentic being.

But, because consciousness must constantly choose itself, and because the desire to be something is a pre-reflective condition of consciousness, no sooner has the converted consciousness overcome its pre-reflective ontological desire to be something than it again faces the decision as to whether to adopt a pre-reflective fundamental project that affirms its ontological nothingness or whether to adopt a pre-reflective fundamental project that affirms its pre-reflective desire to be God. For Sartre, consciousness is caught in an eternal return of the same: no matter what it reflectively chooses, it is always returned to this same choice (WD: 219).

For this reason, consciousness's existence is a constant failure: if it adopts a pre-reflective fundamental project that affirms the impure form of self-reflection, it fails to reflectively live in accordance with its ontological nothingness; if, however, it chooses a pre-reflective fundamental project that affirms the 'reflective nothingness' (BN: 177) of pure reflection, it is immediately thrown back into the choice of whether to choose a pre-reflective fundamental project that affirms the pure or impure form of self-reflection.

But we must resist the temptation to characterize consciousness's inevitable failure as wholly negative. Stephen Wang points out that 'existential failure is what saves [consciousness] from the immobility and stagnation associated with success [...] The perpetual failure to fix our identity is the very thing that reassures us of our freedom' (2006: 8). The inevitable failure that results from its ontological structure means that consciousness is always free to alter its mode of being.

While Sartre holds that consciousness ultimately fails in whatever it does, the way it lives with this failure plays a large role in Sartre's account of authenticity: consciousness can be authentic by facing this failure, incorporating it into its existence, and affirming its freedom, despite reflectively understanding that it will ultimately fail. Alternatively, it can flee from this failure and live in the inauthenticity of the spirit of seriousness. While there are differences between the two thinkers, there is, as Christine Daigle (2004) notes, something Nietzschean about Sartre's conception of authenticity: the authentic, 'strong' consciousness will reflectively affirm its freedom despite the obstacles it faces; in Sartre's case, its inevitable failure and the anxiety it reflectively experiences when its reflection is pure. In contrast, the inauthentic, 'weak' consciousness flees from its freedom and seeks security and certainty in the form of a fixed identity.

Conclusion

But before examining the different ways in which consciousness can flee from its freedom, it may be helpful to point out some aspects of his account that have not so far been discussed. For Sartre, consciousness alienates itself when it adopts a pre-reflective fundamental project that leads it to live in accordance with its pre-reflective ontological desire to be something. If this happens, consciousness will either adopt a fixed identity or live in accordance with the dictates of another. This alienates consciousness:

> By alienation, we mean a certain type of relation that man has with himself, with others, and with the world, where he posits the

ontological priority of the other. The other is not some specific person but a category or, if you will, a dimension, an element. There is no object or privileged subject that has to be considered as other, but *anything* can be other and the other can be anything. It is just one way of being. In a conception of the world based exclusively on the other, the subject derives all his projects and everything about his existence from *what he is not* and from what does not exist as he does' (NE: 382).

However, as noted, while it requires a specific and difficult conversion, consciousness can adopt a pre-reflective fundamental project that leads it to reflectively understand that it is ontologically nothing. The foundation of authentic being is that consciousness's pre-reflective fundamental project leads it to reflectively live in accordance with its ontological nothingness. In other words, consciousness is authentic when it affirms its ontological nothingness by refusing the certainty of a fixed identity. Consciousness reflectively recognizes that it is ontologically nothing and continually reflectively affirms this by choosing a mode of being that leads it to reflectively recognize its ontological freedom and reflectively affirm its practical freedom.

We will see exactly what this entails in subsequent chapters, but Sartre warns that 'if you seek authenticity for authenticity's sake, you are no longer authentic' (NE: 4). Consciousness cannot place authenticity as its goal. To seek to be authentic fails to understand that because consciousness can not be *anything,* it can not be authentic in the sense that being-in-itself is an entity. For Sartre, 'authenticity reveals that the only meaningful project is that of *doing* (not that of being)' (NE: 475). Authenticity is not an identity to be attained; it describes a particular pre-reflective fundamental project and reflective form of self-understanding that consciousness must continuously choose to realize.

Sartre's insistence that authenticity requires consciousness to adopt a pre-reflective fundamental project that affirms its lack of ontological identity leads to a specific consequence: consciousness will explicitly experience the anguish that accompanies its reflective experience of its absolute ontological freedom. Sartre holds that being authentic is not a pleasurable or fulfilling experience for consciousness. Being authentic requires consciousness to choose to reflectively experience the anxiety that results from its absolute freedom.

But is there not something strangely disheartening about Sartre's conception of authenticity? Can the struggle for authenticity only ever end in anxiety and a sense of unease? Can we really say that the choice of an *alienated* mode of being allows us to escape our ontological anxiety? Is Sartre correct to insist that human life always fails? What legitimizes Sartre's privileging of consciousness's ontological structure over its experience when deciding on the value of consciousness's mode of being? Why *would* and why *should* consciousness choose to experience the anxiety of authenticity, rather than the anxiety-free state of alienation, when there appears to be no justification, imperative, or external reason for doing so? To better understand these issues we have to turn to those sections where Sartre explicitly discusses alienation. The following two chapters will discuss Sartre's theories of bad faith and social relations. It is to the former that I now turn.

2
Fleeing from Freedom: Sartre and Bad Faith

Sartre's account of bad faith is crucial to his philosophy because it discloses his theory of self-deception, consciousness's relationship to objectification and objectivity, and what it is to exist authentically and inauthentically. For these reasons, 'any comprehension of Sartre's view of consciousness must rest on a thorough grasp of the character and implications of bad faith' (Natanson, 1980: 97).

But understanding Sartre's account of bad faith requires that we engage with the following questions: what is bad faith? What are the characteristics of bad faith? What is the structure of bad faith? In what way, if any, does the self-deception of bad faith differ from modes of being such as lying and sincerity? What is the relationship between Sartre's theory of bad faith and his conceptions of alienation and authenticity? To begin to answer these questions, I will start by distinguishing the deception of bad faith from the deception of lying.

Lying and bad faith

Sartre acknowledges that bad faith is frequently identified with lying. However, while he acknowledges that lying and bad faith share certain characteristics, he maintains they differ in a number of important respects.

In the first instance, bad faith and lying differ in terms of their intentionality. Sartre explains that while lying is a negative attitude, and is, therefore, only a possibility of consciousness, the act of lying is not directed towards the same consciousness. Lying is an explicit act where one consciousness explicitly aims to deceive another consciousness.

But Sartre notes that consciousness can only deceive the other if it believes a proposition that contradicts that which it seeks to persuade the other to believe. In other words, it is only if consciousness is aware of the truth that it can explicitly conceal the truth by lying about it. This leads Sartre to define lying as the wilful and purposeful covering of the truth, where this covering-up is falsely passed off as the truth. It is the intentional concealment of a presumed truth that distinguishes the act of lying from other acts, such as acts of ignorance, duping or being mistaken, where the truth is not disclosed but where there is no purposeful concealment of the truth. This allows Sartre to maintain that 'the ideal description of the liar would be a cynical consciousness, affirming truth within himself, denying it in his words, and denying that negation as such' (BN: 71).

Lying's concealment of the truth creates a specific relation between consciousness and its act where the lying consciousness remains at a distance from its outer manifestation. When consciousness lies, it reflectively knows the truth, but reflectively conceals this truth by saying something else. Lying creates a split in the *reflective* consciousness between its deceptive outer manifestation and its inner truth. However, it is important to note that there is no moment of alienation here because consciousness does not lose itself in its lie; when lying, consciousness remains in control of its own intentionality.

But while purposeful concealment is a crucial aspect of lying, because lying involves consciousness purposefully concealing the truth from the other, so too is the existence of the other. While bad faith conceals the truth in a way similar to lying, it differs from lying in its intentionality. Bad faith does not seek to conceal the truth from the other; the consciousness of bad faith seeks to conceal its truth from *itself*. This leads Sartre to insist that 'we shall willingly grant that bad faith is a lie to oneself, on condition that we distinguish the lie to oneself from lying in general' (BN: 71). But the question arises: how can consciousness deceive itself about itself if, as the last chapter showed, it is always pre-reflectively aware of what it truly is ontologically?

The structure and choice of bad faith

The answer is grounded in Sartre's understanding of consciousness's ontological structure. Jonathon Webber (2002: 50–51) explains that the paradox of self-deception can be easily explained if the notion of the unconscious is utilized. Appealing to the unconscious explains self-deception because while consciousness's intentions and activities would form part of its unconscious, consciousness would not be conscious of these unconscious drives. Because the unconscious aspect of consciousness would, by definition, not be present to consciousness, the central problem of Sartre's account of the self-deception of bad faith would not arise: consciousness would not need to reconcile its ever-present self-knowledge with its self-deception of this self-knowledge. However, because Sartre rejects the notion of an unconscious, this option is closed to him. To account for the apparent paradox of self-deception, Sartre maintains that the consciousness that exists in bad faith is characterized by a distinction between the content of its *pre-reflective self-awareness* and the content of its *reflective self-understanding*.

Webber argues that because Sartre insists consciousness's self-understanding is not always conceptual, and because Sartre holds that this non-conceptual self-awareness is a sufficient condition of self-knowledge, he is able to maintain that consciousness's pre-reflective, non-conceptual self-awareness qualifies as *self*-knowledge. Thus, consciousness is always pre-reflectively *self*-aware of its ontological nothingness. However, in bad faith, consciousness does not reflectively understand what it is pre-reflectively aware of; namely, that it is ontologically nothing. By distinguishing between its pre-reflective, non-conceptual self-awareness and its reflective, conceptual self-understanding, and making non-conceptual self-awareness a sufficient condition of self-knowledge, Sartre is able to insist that consciousness can be pre-reflectively or non-conceptually aware of what it truly is ontologically while at the same time not reflectively or conceptually understanding this. In other words, the consciousness of bad faith is able to deceive itself because, while it is pre-reflectively aware of its ontological nothingness, it does not reflectively understand this.

But bad faith does not *happen* to consciousness; consciousness *chooses* to live in bad faith. Sartre explains that 'there must be an original intention and a project of bad faith; this project implies a comprehension of bad faith as such and a pre-reflective apprehension (of) consciousness as affecting itself with bad faith' (BN: 72). However, Sartre explains that it is not a 'question of a reflective, voluntary *decision,* but of a spontaneous determination of our being. One *puts oneself* in bad faith as one goes to sleep and one is in bad faith as one dreams' (BN: 91). Bad faith is a *pre-reflective* project that Sartre thinks consciousness naturally 'slips' (NE: 13) into. For this reason, he calls it, consciousness's 'natural attitude' (NE: 6).

By slipping into bad faith, the norms of bad faith become consciousness's pre-reflective norms. These pre-reflective norms shape the reflective activities of consciousness without consciousness necessarily reflecting on what it is doing. While Sartre recognizes that consciousness can choose to *reflectively* understand itself in the objective terms of bad faith, he thinks that if consciousness's pre-reflective fundamental project is in bad faith, it does not usually reflect on its self-understanding; consciousness tends to simply *un*-reflectively affirm the values constitutive of the mode of being of bad faith. In this way, the self-objectification of bad faith crystallizes over consciousness.

Disclosing bad faith through concrete examples

To further understand bad faith, Sartre examines specific, concrete examples of the phenomenon. The first is the famous example of the woman who is on a first date with an admiring man. Sartre maintains that the woman suspects full well the intentions of the man. She knows that sooner or later she will have to make a decision in regards to his proposal, but she does not want to make this decision; she does not want to affirm or deny his advances. By seeking to ignore aspects of the situation, the woman does not truly *live* the moment. She does not undertake the nihilating withdrawal that would place her between being and non-being and open her up to the possibilities inherent in the situation. Instead, she reduces her moments with him to their sheer objective status. She does not pay attention to the implicit meanings of his conduct, but concerns herself only with its explicit meaning: 'If he says to her, "I find you so attractive!" she disarms this phrase of its sexual background; she attaches to the conversation and to the behaviour of the speaker, the immediate meanings, which she imagines as objective qualities' (BN: 78).

Her entire interaction with the man tries to escape from the fluency and multi-dimensionality of the lived experience. She interprets his actions in the most literal, straight-forward manner. 'The qualities thus attached to the person she is listening to are in this way fixed in a permanence like that of things, which is no other than the projection of the strict present of the qualities into the temporal flux' (BN: 78). The woman does not want to make a decision as to the man. She does not want to give herself to him, but nor does she want to reject him. She aims to continue the relationship without giving herself to him in the way that the evidence before her reveals that he desires. To do this, she must disarm his conduct towards her.

She does this by maintaining the relationship with him in a specific way. She attracts the man's attention, but does not affirm the relationship by reflectively responding to his actions. 'She refuses to apprehend the desire for what it is; she does not even give it a name, she recognizes it only to the extent that it transcends itself toward admiration, esteem, respect and that it is wholly absorbed in the more refined forms which it produces, to the extent of no longer figuring anymore but as a sort of warmth and density' (BN: 78–79). She disarms his conduct towards her by fleeing from the sexual intent inherent to the man's actions. Rather than face up to the sexual intent of his actions, she purposefully chooses to avoid the evidence in front of her regarding the man's intentions. She does this because she does not desire to bring the relation to a conclusion. 'She intentionally rests content with the *ambiguity* of the evidence *in order* to be able to hold on to the desired interpretation and be permitted to continue the game' (Poellner, 2004: 58).

However, their relationship develops when he takes her hand. This alters the situation; the woman is no longer able to simply drift along in relation to the man. She must decide what to do. Here, her problems begin. 'To leave the hand there is to consent in herself to flirt, to engage herself. To withdraw it is to break the troubled and unstable harmony which gives the hour its charm. The aim is to postpone the moment of decision as long as possible' (BN: 79). The desire to drift in the moment, to not affirm her subjectivity by making a decision, ensures that 'the young woman leaves her hand there, but she *does not notice* that she is leaving it' (BN: 79). She does not affirm her subjectivity by making a conscious and explicit decision. Rather, she employs two 'strategies' to evade her free decision: first, she flees from her immersion in the sensual world and takes sanctuary in the safety and security of her subjective imagination. By fleeing from the content of the sensuous world, she is able to flee from the need to make a decision with regards to the man's action. Secondly, she purposefully objectifies a part of herself, thereby detaching herself from it. The two strategies support one another ensuring that 'during this time the divorce of the body from the soul is accomplished; the hand rests inert between the warm hands of her companion – neither consenting nor resisting – a thing' (BN: 79).

The combination of her passivity and self-objectification ensures that she not only objectifies herself, but also negates her freedom: 'While sensing profoundly the presence of her own body – to the degree of being disturbed perhaps – she realises herself as *not being* her own body, and she contemplates it as though from above as a passive object to which events can *happen* but which can neither provoke them nor avoid them because all its possibilities are outside of it' (BN: 79).

Sartre's example of the bad faith of the woman on the first date discloses that consciousness can: 1) deceive itself about the other's intentions if it purposefully avoids gaining, or facing, evidence that discloses the other's true intentions; and 2) deceive itself about itself if it fails to reflectively understand that it is a subjective consciousness that lives an objective body in an objective situation. In the above example, the woman objectifies her hand and so takes it to be something wholly other than herself. By taking itself to be wholly unencumbered from its body, her consciousness fails to realize that it is, in actuality, a subjective freedom that chooses how it will live a situated body.

But we have to remember that while Sartre maintains that consciousness chooses how it will live its objective body in an objective situation, neither its body nor its situation constrains its ontological freedom; consciousness's ontological nothingness ensures it is always free to make of its body and situation what it will. Sartre insists that when it is authentic, consciousness is able to co-ordinate its facticity and freedom so that neither is privileged. While the authentic consciousness is reflectively aware that its facticity creates an objective horizon that delineates its existential possibilities, it reflectively understands that its facticity does not determine or constrain its ontological freedom.

Thus, while consciousness always transcends its facticity through the *pre-reflective* nihilating act that distinguishes it from being-in-itself, consciousness only becomes authentic if it *reflectively* understands that it constantly pre-reflectively nihilates its facticity and subsequently reflectively affirms this nihilating act.

Reflectively nihilating its situation does not, however, mean that consciousness *annihilates* its situation. While consciousness can alter its situation, it can never *annihilate* its situation because consciousness is always situated in the world. If consciousness were to *annihilate* its world, it would simultaneously annihilate itself.

According to Sartre, therefore, the authentic form of self-reflection requires that consciousness reflectively understands that it is ontologically nothing; and that, while it exists in a specific situation, it is not constrained by this situation. For Sartre, consciousness's empirical situation is no obstacle to whether it reflectively understands its ontological structure authentically. For consciousness to authentically understand its ontological structure requires that it simply choose to alter its pre-reflective fundamental project to one that allows it to reflectively understand that it is ontologically nothing.

However, the picture is a little more complex than this. For Sartre, being authentic does not simply require that consciousness choose to reflectively understand that it is ontologically nothing; it also requires that consciousness accept responsibility for its actions and situation.

To understand why this is the case, it may be helpful to turn to Sartre's discussion of sincerity.

Sincerity

While sincerity's exhortation that 'a man be *for himself* only what he *is*' (BN: 81) may appear to be fundamentally different to the self-concealment of bad faith, Sartre maintains that sincerity is, in fact, an aspect of bad faith. Sartre highlights this through the example of the homosexual.

Sartre describes a man who engages in homosexual acts and recognizes that he has committed these homosexual acts. However, at the same time as he recognizes his homosexual feelings, he finds ways to purposefully disavow the acts that affirm his homosexuality. He maintains that his acts are somehow different to other homosexual acts or that they were nothing but a game that do not disclose anything of his being. Put simply, he does not take *responsibility* for his acts. He does so, not because he does not know that he has committed homosexual acts, but because 'he does not wish to let himself be considered as a thing' (BN: 87).

The homosexual is, therefore, not only reflectively aware of his ontological nothingness, but also reflectively understands that to be authentic requires that he flee from the temptation to seek sanctuary in an ontological identity. By not accepting responsibility for his homosexual acts, he evades the objectifying term 'homosexual' and so remains free from any ontological identity.

However, while this allows him to live in accordance with his ontological nothingness, Sartre insists it does not allow him to live *authentically*. Because consciousness is not simply a pure, subjective freedom, but is always embodied in an objective situation, Sartre holds that consciousness is not authentic when it simply affirms its ontological freedom. Authenticity requires that consciousness reflectively understand that it is ontologically nothing and also reflectively take responsibility for its objective body, situation, and past actions.

The reasoning behind this is never made explicit, but I think it goes something like this. As noted, Sartre holds that authenticity requires that consciousness reflectively understand that its ontological nothingness means it is always free. Because consciousness's ontological freedom means it could always have acted differently, Sartre holds that consciousness has always freely chosen its actions and is, therefore, always responsible for them. Because being authentic requires that consciousness reflectively understand and accept responsibility for its ontological freedom, and because its past actions emanate from its ontological freedom, Sartre holds that authenticity requires consciousness to reflectively accept responsibility for its past actions. By not reflectively taking responsibility for his freely instantiated past actions, the homosexual is in bad faith.

But Sartre warns that consciousness is not only in bad faith when it does not reflectively affirm its ontological freedom or reflectively take responsibility for its objective acts; it is also in bad faith when it attempts to construct itself in a way not supported by its actions. In other words, consciousness is in bad faith when, for example, it apprehends itself as being courageous when it does not, or has not, acted courageously (BN: 90). Thus, if consciousness does not reflectively take responsibility for its past objective acts, as in the case of Sartre's homosexual, or constructs an identity that is not supported by its objective acts, it exists inauthentically.

While the authentic consciousness recognizes that it is a subjective freedom that lives an objective body in an objective situation, the fundamental project of the consciousness in bad faith is so structured that it maintains that its freedom and facticity exist in strict opposition to one another.

This discloses the ambiguous role that objectivity plays in Sartre's analysis of consciousness. For Sartre, the pure ontological nothingness of consciousness ensures it can never be anything; objectivity has no role to play *in* consciousness's ontological structure. Or, as Sartre puts it, consciousness is 'the radical exclusion of all objectivity' (BN: 265). Consciousness *is* pure subjectivity *and* is authentic when it reflectively understands and affirms this. But at the same time as consciousness is *ontologically* opposed to all forms of objectivity, consciousness only exists by virtue of being situated in an objective world. *Experientially*, consciousness is intimately related to objectivity. While it may be thought that Sartre's analysis of consciousness's ontological structure would insist that consciousness becomes authentic when it reflectively recognizes that it is ontologically nothing, his discussion of bad faith insists that to privilege its pure ontological freedom over its objective situation is to be inauthentic. According to Sartre's discussion of bad faith, while an aspect of authenticity requires that consciousness reflectively understand that it is ontologically nothing; other aspects of authenticity require that consciousness reflectively: 1) understands and accepts that it is always embodied in an objective situation; and 2) takes responsibility for the objective acts it has committed.

Interestingly, it also appears that Sartre holds that undergoing the conversion that brings consciousness to authenticity alters its attitude towards objective rules. Whereas, in *Existentialism and Humanism* (EH: 38), Sartre rejects transcendent ethical values as an imposition on consciousness's self-determining freedom, and, in the *Critique of Dialectical Reason*, he appears to hold that consciousness's relation to objective structures and rules is a purely oppositional one, insofar as consciousness can only secure its practical freedom by first overcoming the constraints imposed on it by the objective structures and social norms of its social world (CDR I: 253), in *What is Literature?*, Sartre maintains that, if consciousness effects the conversion, it recognizes that objective rules do not necessarily constrain its self-determining freedom. Adopting the first-person perspective, Sartre explains that 'if we ourselves produce the rules of production, the measures, the criteria, and if our creative drive comes out from the very depths of our heart, then we never find anything but ourselves in our work. It is we who have invented the laws by which we judge' (WL: 29). Thus, whereas the pre-converted consciousness insists that all objective rules constrain its subjective freedom, the converted consciousness relates to objective rules differently. If the converted consciousness sees itself reflected back to itself through these objective rules, it can see them as an extension of its own freedom.

Sartre's discussion of consciousness's relation to objectivity takes on a different form depending on whether he is discussing consciousness's *ontological structure* or its *experience*. As noted in the previous chapter, Sartre's analysis discloses that the defining ontological characteristic of consciousness is nothingness, which Sartre holds means that consciousness is always ontologically free. This ontological freedom ensures that consciousness is always free to choose, and so is responsible for, its mode of being. Because consciousness is defined by its ontological freedom, its lived experience does not alter, shape, or determine its ontological structure; irrespective of its actual lived experience, consciousness is always ontologically free. Thus, if we simply want to understand consciousness's ontological structure we will, on Sartre's understanding, discover that consciousness is pure nothingness; consciousness is ontologically opposed to all forms of objectivity.

However, if we want to understand what it is for consciousness to exist *practically*, we have to understand that while consciousness is ontologically nothing, its concrete experience is determined by the way it chooses to live its objective world. This then brings us to the question of the different ways consciousness *can* choose to live its objective situation which, in turn, brings us to the issue of authenticity. If consciousness's mode of being is *inauthentic,* it will either seek to evade its objective situation and take itself to be a pure, subjective freedom or will identify wholeheartedly with its objective situation and so evade its freedom. To exist *authentically*, consciousness must reflectively 1) recognize that it is ontologically nothing; 2) recognize that its ontological nothingness means it is always free; 3) recognize that it is embodied in an objective situation; and 4) take responsibility for its objective situation. As Sartre notes in *Anti-Semite and Jew,* 'authenticity, it is almost needless to say, consists in having a true and lucid consciousness of the situation, in assuming the responsibilities and risks that it involves, in accepting it in pride or humiliation, sometimes in horror and hate' (ASJ: 90).

But consciousness only comes to reflectively understand and accept that it is a subjective freedom that chooses how it will live a socially embedded body after it undergoes the conversion (NE: 20). Because the pre-converted consciousness exists with the inauthentic, impure form of self-reflection, it either privileges its pure, subjective freedom over its objective facticity or privileges its objective facticity over its pure ontological freedom (Rose, 2003: 13). But, while Sartre recognizes that it can, logically, choose either of these options, I think Sartre's discussion of the impure self-reflection of bad faith demonstrates that he thinks that the pre-converted consciousness tends to privilege its objective facticity over its ontological freedom, rather than vice-versa. In other words, Sartre thinks that, rather than thinking it is absolutely free, consciousness tends to think it is absolutely determined by its situation.

Conversion brings consciousness to reflectively understand that it is not determined by its situation. The converted consciousness recognizes that it is ontologically nothing and that this means it is free. But this cannot go so far that consciousness reflectively understands itself to be absolutely unencumbered. To be authentic, consciousness must reflectively understand and accept that while objectivity is not an aspect of its *ontological structure*, it is a crucial and inescapable aspect of its practical *experience*. The conversion strikes a difficult balance: it must bring consciousness to reflectively understand that it is ontologically free, while, at the same time, getting it to reflectively understand and accept that, because it exists in an objective situation, it is only ever practically free within the empirical possibilities of its objective situation.

But Sartre's discussion of bad faith does not simply describe an important existential phenomenon by distinguishing between the different pre-reflective fundamental projects open to consciousness; it brings a critical dimension to his analysis of human being. If consciousness is to be authentic, it must choose a pre-reflective fundamental project that brings it to reflectively affirm its ontological nothingness and take responsibility for its past actions; otherwise, consciousness will adopt an inauthentic pre-reflective fundamental project.

The failure of bad faith

But while the consciousness of bad faith takes itself to be something, its ontological nothingness means it never becomes the thing it desires to be. This is because 'I am on a plane where no reproach can touch me since what I really am is my transcendence. I flee from myself, I escape myself, I leave tattered garment in the hands of the fault-finder. But the ambiguity necessary for bad faith comes from the fact that I affirm here that I *am* my transcendence in the mode of being a thing' (BN: 80). Although the consciousness in bad faith experiences itself as an object, its ontological nothingness means it never *actually* is the thing it takes itself to be.

Sartre demonstrates the failure of bad faith through the famous example of the waiter in the cafe. The waiter is the epitome of politeness, helpfulness, and eagerness to please. His entire being appears to conform to the ideal waiter. However, it is precisely because his being-a-waiter is too perfect that it becomes evident that something is wrong. His being is not at ease in its situation; he does not comport himself in an organic and fluid manner. Every action of his is forced; he is merely a man playing-at-being-a-waiter (BN: 82). But why does the man play-at-being-a-waiter?

Sartre answers that it is due to consciousness's pre-reflective ontological desire to be something and the insidious pressure society exerts on consciousness to act in conformity with its conception of a waiter. The same pressure is placed on all workers; each worker must assume and fulfil a particular role in accordance with the dictates of the general public:

> The public demands of them that they realise it as a ceremony; there is the dance of the grocer, of the tailor, of the auctioneer, by which they endeavour to persuade their clientele that they are nothing but a grocer, an auctioneer, a tailor. Society demands that he limit himself to his function as a grocer, just as the soldier at attention makes himself into a soldier-thing with a straight look which does not see at all, which is no longer meant to see, since it is the rule and not the interest of the moment which determines the point he must fix his eyes on (the sight 'fixed at ten paces') (BN: 83).

This is an interesting development in Sartre's account of bad faith. The adoption of a pre-reflective fundamental project of bad faith does not simply emanate from consciousness's own subjective choice; it also emanates from the social identity consciousness's society confers on it. When I discuss Sartre's theory of social relations in the next chapter, I will return to this theme, but, for now, it is sufficient to note that this provides a glimpse of what will be made explicit: for Sartre, others objectify and so alienate consciousness.

However, I disagree with Mathew Eshleman's claim that the 'prevalent forms of bad faith involve collusion with or resistance to socially enforced identities' (2008: 2). While conforming to social pressure is an aspect of bad faith, it is not the dominant reason why consciousness adopts a pre-reflective fundamental project in bad faith. Eshleman fails to remember that a condition of consciousness's existence is its pre-reflective *ontological* desire to be something. This ensures that, irrespective of the actions of others, consciousness's ontological structure 'naturally' motivates it to adopt a pre-reflective fundamental project that is in bad faith. Consciousness only conforms to the social pressure of others because, by doing so, it pre-reflectively thinks it will fulfil its pre-reflective ontological desire to be something. The *fundamental* reason consciousness adopts the pre-reflective fundamental project of bad faith is not because of social pressure, but because it tries to fulfil its pre-reflective ontological desire to be something (Santoni, 2008: 29–30).

But no matter the extent to which consciousness tries to become the waiter its society demands it becomes, its ontological nothingness prevents it from succeeding in its aim. Sartre notes that 'if I represent myself as him [the waiter], I am not he; I am separated from him as the object from the subject, separated *by nothing*, but this nothing isolates me from him. I can not be he, I can only play at *being* him; that is, imagine to myself that I am he' (BN: 83). The individual can assume the life of a waiter; he can sweep the floors, serve drinks, attend to customers, get up at a certain time, and structure his existence around being-a-waiter; but the ontological nothingness of consciousness means *he will never be a waiter* in the sense that being-in-itself is an entity. The best that consciousness can achieve is to *play-at-being-a-waiter* by trying to conform to the socially determined norms and activities that are socially understood to define the role 'waiter.'

However, it is important to note that the waiter's playing-at-being-a-waiter is not an expression of the spirit of play that Sartre maintains is indicative of authentic being. The waiter's playing-at-being-a-waiter occurs because of his passive conformity to the other's conception of what being a waiter entails; it is not because of *the waiter's* spontaneous and reflective self-determination of what being a waiter entails. Only the latter is indicative of authentic being. For this reason, Sartre holds that the waiter's playing-at-being-a-waiter is an inauthentic form of play.

Good faith and the faith of bad faith

Up to this point, Sartre's description of bad faith has allowed him to identify two aspects of bad faith: bad faith occurs when consciousness adopts a pre-reflective fundamental project that leads it to reflectively objectify itself, and/or fails to take responsibility for its past actions. There is, however, a third aspect to bad faith that relates to its epistemological ground.

Sartre maintains that what distinguishes bad faith from other forms of deception, such as lying, is its faith. Indeed, he maintains that this is 'the true problem of bad faith' (BN: 91). The faith of bad faith determines consciousness's relation to its intentional object. Rather than disclose its object as and when it reveals itself to consciousness, the consciousness in bad faith ignores the given reality of the object, constructs its own truth, and imposes this onto its empirical reality.

Because of its pre-reflectively constructed preconceived schema, the consciousness of bad faith does not *know* the object as it is given; it has a pre-conceived *belief* about the object and takes this belief to describe what the object truly is. As Sartre explains, 'bad faith does not hold [to] the norms and criteria of truth as they are accepted by the critical thought of good faith. What it decides first, in fact, is the nature of truth. With bad faith a truth appears, a method of thinking, a type of being which is like that of objects; the ontological characteristic of the world of bad faith is what it is not, and is not what it is' (BN: 91). Importantly, the adoption of its preconceived schema is not a reflective act; consciousness pre-reflectively decides to shape its world in accordance with its preconceived schema.

Its preconceived schema ensures that the consciousness of bad faith is not affected by empirical evidence or critical thought. Rather than being open to its empirical reality and finding the truth of its world as it appears to it, the consciousness of bad faith turns away from the objective truth of its world and interprets its world according to its preconceived schema. Put differently, the consciousness that exists in bad faith does not allow reality to disclose itself to consciousness as it actually is; it distorts the given reality by imposing its preconceived schema onto reality.

Sartre holds that a concrete example of the preconceptual schema constitutive of bad faith is provided by the anti-Semite. The anti-Semite is in bad faith because he has chosen to hate the Jew before interacting with him. While we can provide the anti-Semite with empirical evidence that contradicts his predetermined conception of the Jew, the anti-Semite closes himself off to this empirical evidence and simply reaffirms his predetermined schema (ASJ: 20).

But while consciousness can relate to its world in bad faith, there is also the possibility of existing in good faith. While Sartre clearly thinks it is better to exist in good faith rather than bad faith, good faith is an achievement that is dependent on consciousness successfully undergoing the difficult conversion to pure reflection. While Sartre does not discuss good faith in much detail, Ronald Santoni (1995: 85) explains that there are two aspects to it: 1) an epistemological aspect; and 2) an ontological aspect.

The epistemological aspect of good faith describes the way the consciousness in good faith relates to its world epistemologically. While the consciousness of good faith exists with a preconceived notion of the given reality, in contrast to the consciousness of bad faith, it remains open to its given reality and is willing to alter its understanding in line with empirical evidence. This allows consciousness to disclose its given reality as it truly is.

The ontological aspect of good faith describes the way consciousness reflectively recognizes and lives with its ontological freedom. While the consciousness of bad faith flees from its ontological freedom, the consciousness of good faith reflectively understands and affirms its ontological freedom. For this reason, good faith is synonymous with authenticity and is, therefore, only a possibility once consciousness has undergone the conversion.

Conversion and bad faith

While the mode of being of bad faith is 'a constant and particular style of life' (BN: 73), the set pattern of being in bad faith is not total. Consciousness can escape from bad faith. However, it can only do so if it somehow effects a cathartic conversion. As noted in the previous chapter, conversion brings consciousness: 1) to a pre-reflective fundamental project that has freedom as its end; and 2) from the inauthentic, impure form of self-reflection to the authentic, pure form of self-reflection. While the consciousness of impure self-reflection reflectively understands that it has a fixed identity, the consciousness of pure reflection reflectively understands that it is ontologically nothing and that this ontological nothingness means it is free.

Because consciousness's fundamental project pre-reflectively shapes its values, attitudes, and beliefs, the adoption of a fundamental project that affirms freedom brings consciousness to spontaneously and pre-reflectively adhere to the norms, values, and activities that realize and affirm this end. While the movement to the authentic, pure form of self-reflection emanates from a subjective decision, the way of being instantiated by the conversion does not have to be a *momentary* achievement. Rather than merely experience moments of authentic self-insight, conversion can bring consciousness to exist in a way that continually pre-reflectively affirms the authentic, pure form of self-reflection.

There are two reasons for this: first, as I outlined in the previous chapter, the adoption of a specific form of reflective self-understanding is constitutively related to a specific mode of being. As such, if consciousness reflectively understands itself to have an ontological identity, it will act in a way that reflectively affirms this identity. In contrast, if consciousness effects the conversion that brings it to the authentic, pure form of self-reflection, it will act in a way that affirms its ontological freedom. For example, if consciousness's social role requires it to be a waiter, and while consciousness will carry out the duties of a waiter, it will not think of itself as being the entity: 'waiter.' The converted consciousness reflectively understands that it is free to determine what being a waiter means for it in terms of how it will undertake its role as a waiter. Thus, if consciousness achieves the conversion that brings it to the authentic, pure form of self-reflection, it still acts in the world, but it does not reflectively understand itself to have an ontological identity.

Secondly, in the *Notebooks for an Ethics*, Sartre continuously links the conversion to the founding of a new mode of being. For example, he discusses the mode of being of authentic love (NE: 9), insists that pure self-reflection requires an alteration in consciousness's relation to its body, world and other (NE: 12), and, most specifically, states that conversion creates 'a new, *"authentic"* way of being' (NE: 474). These comments indicate that the conversion to the authentic, pure form of self-reflection is more than a one-off momentary event;

conversion instantiates a new pre-reflective fundamental project that leads consciousness to reflectively understand and affirm its ontological nothingness.

But, at this point, it may be helpful to return to one of the questions posed at the end of the last chapter: why would consciousness effect the conversion that allows it to live authentically when, as noted, to live authentically is to explicitly experience the anguish that accompanies the authentic, pure form of self-reflection but not the inauthentic, impure form of self-reflection? While Heidegger appeals to a 'call of conscience' (2003: 314) and Hegel to an ontological 'urge' (HP: 77) to explain why consciousness attempts to overcome its alienation, Sartre never *explicitly* explains why consciousness would or should choose to effect the difficult conversion that allows it to become authentic. He simply maintains that 'consciousness alone can self-motivate itself to effect the conversion' (WD: 112).

The easiest way to demonstrate why consciousness should or would attempt to be authentic is to appeal to a transcendent (ethical or ontological) imperative. However, Sartre's insistence that consciousness is ontologically nothing, his criticisms of the spirit of seriousness, and his statement that 'no rule of general morality can show you what you ought to do' (EH: 38) appear to explicitly reject this. However, despite Sartre explicitly rejecting this, his account only makes sense if he is writing with the imperative 'Be Authentic!' in mind (Caws, 1979: 97; Manser, 1966: 64).

This leads Sartre to *implicitly* maintain that existing inauthentically is a debased form of existence. Indeed, why undertake the difficult conversion if the mode of being it leads to is *ethically* no different to that which precedes it and especially if, as noted, the mode of being that emanates from the conversion is experienced with more anguish than the one preceding the conversion? It only makes sense if the authentic, pure form of self-reflection is, despite its existential hardship, *ethically* superior to the inauthentic, impure form of self-reflection from which the conversion allows consciousness to escape.

This interpretation is further supported when we recognize that terms such as 'authentic,' 'inauthentic,' and 'alienation' are inherently ethical terms (Taylor, 2003: 25). Despite Sartre's insistence that his use of 'the term "inauthentic" [implies] no moral blame' (ASJ: 93), the simple use of the term 'inauthentic' to describe a mode of being implies that it is a less desirable mode of being than one that is authentic.

But it could be objected that Sartre is using these terms in a technical sense. The problem with this argument, however, is that the general tone of his argument and certain descriptions he provides of certain modes of being, such as bad faith and certain forms of intersubjective relations, are not ethically neutral. For example, in *Existentialism and Humanism*, he explains that 'I define [consciousness's] self-deception as an error. Here one cannot avoid pronouncing a judgement of truth. [...] Self-deception is evidently a falsehood, because it is a dissimulation of [consciousness's] complete liberty of commitment' (EH: 51). The implication is that modes of being in which consciousness flees from its freedom are ethically inferior to those that affirm consciousness's freedom.

Thus, despite his proclamations to the contrary, Sartre is doing more than merely objectively and dispassionately describing different modes of being; he is: 1) developing his theory against a predetermined ethical imperative that defines, irrespective of consciousness's experience and ethical judgement, what constitutes good and bad modes of being; and 2) actively, if not always explicitly, using this ethical imperative to prescribe how consciousness should act.

There is, therefore, an ethical objectivism that underpins Sartre's philosophy that takes the form: it is ethically better to be authentic than inauthentic; or, put differently, it is better to be free than un-free (Webber, 2009: 132). But I would go further and insist that while Sartre never makes this explicit, his argument necessarily implies that consciousness has a pre-reflective ontological desire to be authentic. Only if the ethical imperative 'Be Authentic' or 'Be Free,' which fundamentally means the same thing for Sartre, is a pre-reflective *condition* of consciousness would consciousness countenance, let alone actually choose to effect, the difficult and painful conversion to the anxiety-ridden, authentic mode of being. But why should consciousness desire to be authentically free? What justifies Sartre's argument?

Sartre offers two different, but related, arguments to justify his conclusion that freedom is the highest end to which the converted consciousness should strive. First, while Sartre recognizes that it is a personal choice whether to live authentically or not, he immediately contradicts this by stating that 'I declare [...] that the attitude of strict consistency alone is that of good faith' (EH: 51). The introduction of an absolute ethical imperative that makes authenticity dependent on the reflective affirmation of its ontological nothingness allows Sartre to hold that authenticity requires that consciousness be true to itself and affirm its freedom (EH: 51).

Secondly, Sartre simply 'pronounce[s] a moral judgement' (EH: 51) and states that 'I declare that freedom, in respect of concrete circumstances, can have no other end and aim but itself' (EH: 51). Sartre holds this position because having explained that all ethical values emanate from consciousness's freedom, it stands that 'freedom [is] the foundation of all values' (EH: 51). Thus, in choosing a value, which consciousness cannot not do, it is rational to choose to value that which allows consciousness to choose its values: freedom. The combination of these two arguments leads Sartre to hold that 'the actions of men of good faith have, as their ultimate significance, the quest of freedom itself as such' (EH: 51).

There are, however, at least two problems with Sartre's attempt to justify his conclusion that freedom is the highest end towards which consciousness should focus its attention. First, Sartre's criticism of the spirit of seriousness, his rejection of transcendent ethical values, and his insistence that consciousness's ontological freedom ensures it determines and is wholly responsible for its ethical values prevent him from justifying his ethic of authenticity by appealing to any foundational principle such as God, reason, intelligibility, consistency, justice, or the Delphic imperative 'Know thyself.' Sartre's insistence that authenticity requires that consciousness be consistent with what it truly is contradicts his rejection of universal, transcendent, ethical imperatives.

Secondly, Sartre's claim that consciousness should value freedom as the highest ethical end because freedom is the source of all ethical values, is dependent on his insistence that consciousness's freedom is the foundation of all moral values. This, however, raises the question: is consciousness's freedom the ground of all moral values? Rather than simply appeal to a prior argument, Sartre must defend and legitimize this argument.

However, unlike Hegel, for whom, as we will see, the issue of how to justify philosophy is of central importance to any philosophical undertaking, Sartre does not appear to have been overly concerned with how to justify his thought. It appears he simply writes what he believes to be true and, despite its inconsistencies, asks us to believe it based on the strength of his insight and conclusions (SG: 584). While we will see that Hegel's *Phenomenology of Spirit* aims to justify his philosophical thought by demonstrating the logical movement consciousness must make to reach the shape of itself whereby its experience discloses that it fully understands itself and its object, David Detmer notes that, rather than demonstrating why his way of thinking about the issue under discussion is correct, Sartre legitimizes his argument by appealing to the power of 'direct apprehension [...] of [the] point or principle' (1998: 187). In other words, Sartre justifies his ethic of authenticity by implicitly claiming that contemplation of the concept 'authenticity' brings him to *see* or *feel* that authenticity requires that consciousness act in the manner he describes.

However, the problem with simply insisting that authenticity requires that consciousness act in a certain way is, as Hegel notes, that '*one* bare assurance is worth just as much as another' (PS: 49). Because Sartre simply insists on specific conditions of authenticity, there appears to be no reason why other conditions are not equally justified. Sartre simply leaves us with a philosophical choice: either we accept his argument or we do not. In contrast, subsequent chapters will show that, rather than simply offering us this philosophical choice, Hegel attempts to demonstrate why his philosophical argument is correct without appealing to subjective intuition or an arbitrary foundation.

But my contention that a pre-reflective condition of Sartre's consciousness is that it pre-reflectively desires to be authentic means that consciousness has, at least, two fundamental pre-reflective desires: the pre-reflective desire to be something *and* the pre-reflective desire to be authentic by reflecting understanding itself to be ontologically nothing. Neither of these *determines* consciousness; consciousness has to choose which one it will seek to fulfil. Sartre appears to think that consciousness tends to *initially* fulfil its pre-reflective desire to be *something*. It is only if consciousness reflectively experiences the perpetual failure that accompanies the attempt to fulfil its pre-reflective ontological desire to be something that it will choose to undergo the difficult conversion process that allows it to come to the authentic, pure form of self-reflection.

But while consciousness can, with significant effort and existential upheaval, effect the conversion that brings it to the authentic, pure form of self-reflection, it should not be thought that adopting this authentic form of self-reflection is simply a one-off event. For Sartre, being authentic requires that consciousness continuously choose to affirm the pre-reflective fundamental project that instantiates the authentic, pure form of self-reflection. Because consciousness is free to determine its pre-reflective fundamental project, and because the understanding of freedom gained from the conversion is accompanied by a profound sense of anxiety, Sartre recognizes that there is always the possibility that consciousness may once again choose to exist in bad faith (BN: 94).

As a fundamental project, therefore, bad faith crystallizes over consciousness and impacts on every aspect of its existence. In the next chapter we are going to build on this insight by examining the ways in which bad faith impacts on consciousness's social relations. This will disclose that one of the crucial ways in which consciousness becomes alienated is through its relations with others.

3
Sartre, Alienation, and the Other

We have seen that while Sartre holds that consciousness is always pre-reflectively aware of its ontological nothingness, it alienates itself if it chooses to adopt the fundamental project of bad faith. It may appear, therefore, that the alienation of consciousness only ever emanates from, and is grounded in, consciousness's own activity.

However, Sartre explains that 'whatever our acts may be [...], we must accomplish them in a world where there are already others and where I am *de trop* in relation to others' (BN: 431). Because consciousness always exists in a world inhabited by other consciousnesses, understanding consciousness requires that we engage with its relationships to others. This will disclose that consciousness's relationship with others can also alienate it.

Sartre's analysis of social relations is not, however, one-dimensional. In the first instance, it seeks to disclose consciousness's ontological relation to the other. This level of his analysis discloses that the other is not an aspect of consciousness's ontological structure; the other is an aspect of the objective situation that consciousness exists. Because the other is not an aspect of consciousness's ontological structure, the other's disclosure only arises when it is encountered by consciousness. This leads Sartre to show that the primordial manner in which the other relates to consciousness is through what he calls 'the look.' In turn, this leads to a discussion of the various ways in which consciousness's pre-reflective fundamental project shapes its social relations.

But to outline his account of social relations, Sartre first engages with the way he thinks Husserl, Hegel, and Heidegger understand social relations. His aim in doing so is to clarify his own position and demonstrate how he differs from his predecessors. Sartre's reading of Husserl and Heidegger does not directly concern us here and so I will not engage with it in this volume; I will, however, engage with his critique of Hegel.

Sartre on Hegel's theory of intersubjectivity

To discuss Hegel's views on intersubjectivity, Sartre reduces Hegel's theory of intersubjectivity to the master/slave dialectic. Hegel's master/slave dialectic describes a particular way consciousness understands itself in the long developmental journey it must make to fully understand its ontological structure. This shape of consciousness arises when consciousness realizes that it cannot fully understand itself by simply negating an inanimate object to affirm its independence. With this realization, consciousness understands that its self-understanding is dependent on the establishment of a specific relationship with a *living* other in which both consciousnesses recognize each other's freedom.

In the first instance, Sartre recognizes and praises Hegel for establishing an important constitutive bond between consciousness's being and the being of the other. But while Sartre recognizes that 'Hegel's brilliant intuition is to make me depend on the other *in my being*' (BN: 261), he criticizes Hegel for being both epistemologically and ontologically optimistic.

According to Sartre, Hegel is *epistemologically* optimistic because he maintains that consciousness can know the pure subjectivity of the other. Sartre's strict subject/object *ontological* dualism rejects this; consciousnesses are *ontologically* opposed: 'Between the other-as-object and Me-as-subject there is no common measure, no more than between self-consciousness and consciousness of the other. I can not know myself *in* the other if the other is first an object for me; neither can I apprehend the other in his true being – that is, his subjectivity' (BN: 267). The ontological chasm between two consciousnesses means that it is not possible for one to know the ontological subjectivity of the other.

However, while Sartre insists that consciousness can never know the *ontological* subjectivity of the other, he does recognize that consciousness can *experience* the subjectivity of the other. This occurs through language and certain forms of social relation. But while consciousness can experience the subjectivity of the other, this experience does not disclose the nothingness that defines consciousness's ontological structure. This is because, for Sartre, to know the other is to objectify it, which nihilates the nothingness that defines its ontological structure. We cannot understand the other by experiencing it. Understanding the other requires that we actually become the other; an endeavour made impossible by the ontological chasm between us (BN: 264–267).

Hegel, however, does not divide consciousness's ontological structure from its experience; as we will see, he insists that consciousness's ontological structure develops through its experience. By collapsing the distinction Sartre makes between consciousness's ontological structure and experience, and making its experience the means through which consciousness learns about and develops its ontological structure, Hegel is able to insist that the experience of the other's subjectivity does disclose what the other is ontologically.

The dispute arises because Sartre does not undertake an internal critique of Hegel on this point; he simply takes his account of consciousness's ontological structure to be true and shows that, based on his premises, Hegel's account is wrong (Williams, 1992a: 296 & 1992b, 11). As this issue is based on the subtle, but fundamental, differences between their respective analyses of consciousness's ontological structure, its resolution will depend on the strength of their respective conceptions of consciousness.

But while Sartre charges Hegel with *epistemological* optimism, he also maintains a second, more fundamental charge against Hegel: *ontological* optimism. Sartre maintains that Hegel 'places himself at the vantage point of truth – *i.e.*, of the Whole – to consider the problem of the other' (BN: 267). For Sartre, Hegel creates a transcendent whole (what Hegel calls 'spirit') that encompasses, but is independent from, the two interacting individuals and exists independently from this interaction. Because Sartre insists that Hegel's transcendent whole incorporates and grounds social interactions, he holds it annihilates the ontological distance between the two interacting consciousnesses. While Hegel thinks he is talking of *two* consciousnesses, Sartre insists his mediating, transcendent whole means he is actually only talking about *one*. Put differently, Sartre maintains that there is no mediating aspect that allows consciousness to know what the other is *ontologically*, because, if there were, the common bond of this mediating aspect would annihilate the plurality of consciousnesses and negate the question of the other (BN: 267–268).

However, Sartre's criticisms fail to hit the mark because he fundamentally misunderstands what Hegel means by spirit and the relation spirit has to consciousness. There are two related aspects to Sartre's misunderstanding: first, Sartre assumes that the universal whole, what Hegel calls 'spirit,' is a transcendent other that exists prior to consciousness. Secondly, Sartre maintains that, for Hegel, spirit negates consciousness by *subsuming* consciousness within it.

As subsequent chapters will show, however, Hegel's conception of spirit is not a transcendent entity that exists independently of the consciousnesses it grounds; nor does it direct the activities of consciousness. Sartre completely fails to understand that, for Hegel, spirit is the non-determining substance of consciousness that is, initially, manifested as an implicit ontological potential that needs to be developed to be fully realized and is only developed by the actions of consciousness. Sartre's failure to appreciate Hegel's understanding of spirit means that his criticism simply fails to hit the mark. He portrays Hegel as setting up a straight metaphysical dualism between this world and a transcendent world of spirit and so fails to appreciate Hegel's stringent critique of metaphysical dualisms and the subtlety of his actual position. Despite this, however, Sartre's misreading does enable him to develop an original account of intersubjective relations. It is to this that I now turn.

The other and the ontological structure of consciousness

As Chapter 1 showed, Sartre's thought 'operates' on two levels: the ontological level that discusses the ontological structure of consciousness and reveals it is defined by nothingness; and the experiential level that describes the ways consciousness can live its ontological nothingness. Sartre's discussion of social relations conforms to this complementary division in that it first outlines the *ontological* relation between consciousness and the other, before discussing what this means for the content of social relations.

Sartre maintains that consciousness's *ontological* structure is thoroughly individualistic. Consciousness is 'a synthetic, individual totality, completely isolated from other totalities of the same kind' (TOTE: 7). Each consciousness exists in a unique independent space cut off from all other entities (BN: 255). It is this unique space that ensures that 'human bodies are made in such a way that they have to *oppose* one another' (NE: 288). The atomism of consciousness's ontological structure means *the other* does not enter into consciousness nor is it an aspect of consciousness's ontological structure. There is an 'ontological separation' (BN: 267) between consciousnesses that defines and preserves their ontological individualism. Slipping into the first-person perspective, Sartre explains that 'the other is the one who is not me and the one who I am not. This *not* indicates a nothingness as a *given* element of separation between the other and myself' (BN: 254). 'The fact is that being-for-others is not an ontological structure of the For-itself.' (BN: 306). Indeed, Sartre maintains that it is only because consciousness is ontologically detached from the other that there is an other. If the other was an aspect of consciousness's ontological structure, the difference between them would be usurped and the two consciousnesses would collapse into one (BN: 307).

There are two consequences to this: first, it means the other 'cannot be deduced from the ontological structure of the for-itself' (BN: 533). The other's existence is only disclosed to consciousness when consciousness encounters the other in the world (BN: 295, 306). Secondly, Thomas Anderson points out that it means 'the other's awareness of myself cannot help me attain greater awareness of myself as I am for myself' (1993: 29). Understanding consciousness's ontological structure does not require an understanding of consciousness's relationship to others; irrespective of its social interaction, consciousness is always ontologically nothing.

But it may be objected that, on numerous occasions, Sartre maintains that it is the other that makes consciousness what it is. Thus, he writes that it is the other's objectifying look that discloses to consciousness that it is 'somebody' (BN: 287), and, even more explicitly, that 'I need the mediation of the other in order to be what I am' (BN: 312). These statements make it appear that the other *constitutes* consciousness and so is a necessary aspect of consciousness's ontological structure.

This is not so, however; the other is not an aspect of consciousness's ontological structure, nor does it determine or constitute consciousness. While the other is ontologically distinct from consciousness, thereby ensuring that the other is not a constitutive aspect of consciousness's ontological structure (BN: 274), consciousness does need to interact with others to discover what it truly is. It is for this reason that Sartre writes that 'I need the other to realise fully all the structures of my being' (BN: 246).

Dan Zahavi (2008: 157–158) explains that while the Sartrean consciousness has a pre-reflective understanding of its body, *it* initially holds that its body is synonymous with the pure, subjective freedom it pre-reflectively understands itself to be (BN: 353; SG: 32). It is only once the other looks at it that consciousness comes to see its body as something objective. It is for this reason that 'through the other I am enriched in a new dimension of being: through the other I come to exist in the dimension of being, through the other I become an object' (NE: 499).

The other does not create consciousness, it *unveils* the objective facticity that is a necessary condition of consciousness's freedom, but which consciousness's pre-reflective self-understanding does not initially recognize (NE: 507). It is in this sense that the other holds the key to consciousness's being (BN: 246). The experience of the objectification that emanates from the other's look is necessary for consciousness to understand that it is not a pure, subjective freedom, but is a subjective freedom that chooses how to live an objective body in an objective situation.

But while the other's look discloses this to consciousness, it is not simply a passive form of objectification; the look of the other is imbued with an objective interpretation of consciousness. Thus, it is only through the other that consciousness becomes a coward, witty, intelligent, or evil (NE: 507). It is in this sense that consciousness becomes somebody through the other. It is because the other *discloses* consciousness's objective facticity to it, and recognizes consciousness in an objective way, that 'the other is indispensable to my existence, and equally so to any knowledge I can have of myself' (EH: 45).

But while the other tries to impose its objective description of consciousness onto consciousness, consciousness's ontological nothingness means it never actually is synonymous with the other's objective description of it, nor does it become the objective thing the other thinks it is (BN: 298–299). Consciousness's ontological nothingness means it is free to choose whether to accept or reject the other's objective description of it (SG: 49). Thus, while the other reveals consciousness's objective facticity to it, and tries to impose its objective description of consciousness onto consciousness, consciousness must choose how it expresses its subjective freedom within its objective facticity and whether to accept or reject the other's objective description of it.

For Sartre, the way consciousness reacts to the other's disclosure of its objective facticity is dependent on its pre-reflective fundamental project. Because consciousness tends to adopt a fundamental project in bad faith, an aspect of which leads it to perceive itself to be a free subject, Sartre maintains that consciousness's experience of the other's objectifying look causes it to feel ashamed.

But while consciousness tends to feel initially ashamed before the other's gaze, altering its pre-reflective fundamental project leads to an alternative reaction to the other. If consciousness chooses to undergo the conversion, it can come to reflectively understand that: 1) it is not a pure, subjective freedom that exists in strict opposition to objectivity, but is a subjective freedom that chooses how to live an objective body in an objective situation; and 2) the other has a necessary role to play in the disclosure of its facticity. With this realization, the converted consciousness alters its comportment towards the other. It no longer tries to objectify the other to maintain its subjective freedom. As we will see, the converted consciousness reflectively recognizes, respects, cares for, and affirms the other's freedom.

But, as William McBride explains, the converted consciousness also refuses 'to accept as mere givens the labels and values that the rest of society is constantly endeavouring to impose [on it]' (1991: 81). While the converted consciousness reflectively understands that it is embodied in an objective situation and that the other's objectification of it is crucial to this disclosure, conversion brings consciousness to reflectively recognize that it is ontologically free and is able to accept or reject the other's objective description of it. Thus, while the other discloses the objective aspect of consciousness's existence to consciousness, this disclosure is purely formal, insofar as it discloses that consciousness lives an objective body in an objective situation. It is up to consciousness to choose the content of its objective facticity by 'using' its ontological freedom to choose what its objective facticity will mean for it.

The ontological distinctness of each consciousness means that, rather than constituting consciousness, the other is an aspect of the objective facticity in, on, and through which consciousness chooses how it will express its subjective freedom. It is for this reason that Sartre places his discussion of consciousness's relation to its neighbour in his analysis of the relation between freedom and facticity (BN: 531–532).

Crucially, however, the other does not simply exist as a passive entity within consciousness's objective world. The other's expression of its subjective freedom *shapes* the objective world in which consciousness exists and expresses itself (BN: 547–548).

This interpretation of consciousness's ontological relation to the other is, therefore, fundamentally opposed to T-Storm Heter's insistence that Sartre's consciousness is *ontologically* social, insofar as the other is a necessary and constitutive aspect of consciousness's ontological structure (2008: 23).

While interesting, Heter's reading is contentious in that it is not simply a work of pure exegesis, but is a work that combines 'historical scholarship and original philosophy' (2008: Preface). By combining Sartre's insights with his own arguments, Heter is able to maintain that while certain aspects of Sartre's thought, namely the thought of *Being and Nothingness*, are unsatisfactory, if we reconstruct Sartre's arguments in-line with Hegel's, Sartre's position becomes not only more logically consistent, but also, so Heter argues, more philosophically palpable.

While Heter's argument would appear to support my own, insofar as it re-enforces my claim that Hegel's analysis of consciousness's ontological structure is more logically consistent, subtle, and multi-dimensional than Sartre's, there are certain problems with Heter's endeavour. In the first instance, Heter simply rejects aspects of Sartre's thought that do not accord with his argument that an ethics grounded in mutual recognition 'ought to be the cornerstone of Sartre's ethics' (2008: 36). Because Heter maintains that *Being and Nothingness*'s description of the ontological separation between consciousnesses prevents each consciousness from reflectively recognizing and affirming the other's freedom, and because he holds that the *Notebooks for an Ethics* describes a fundamentally different analysis of consciousness's ontological structure that recognizes that the other is a constitutive aspect of consciousness's ontological structure, Heter privileges the *Notebooks for an Ethics* over *Being and Nothingness* (2008: 27).

Heter also privileges Sartre's *Notebooks for an Ethics* because he holds that, in this text, Sartre is concerned with consciousness's practical freedom; whereas in *Being and Nothingness*, he is concerned with consciousness's ontological freedom. Heter's privileging of the *Notebooks for an Ethics*, his insistence that, in this text, Sartre holds that consciousnesses are ontologically entwined and that practical freedom should be privileged over ontological freedom, lead him to correctly argue that Sartrean authenticity requires that consciousness reflectively recognizes and respects the other's practical freedom because the realization of consciousness's practical freedom is dependent on the realization of the other's practical freedom (2008: 158).

However, *Being and Nothingness* and the *Notebooks for an Ethics* do not offer radically different analyses of consciousness's ontological structure; the two texts complement one another. *Being and Nothingness* describes the ontological characteristics of consciousness and the inauthentic mode of being consciousness will adopt if it does not reflectively understand that it is ontologically nothing. The *Notebooks for an Ethics* complements *Being and Nothingness*'s analysis by employing the same analysis of consciousness's ontological structure to: 1) show that consciousness's mode of being does not have to be inauthentic; and 2) outline what an authentic mode of being entails. Because of this, *Being and Nothingness* and the *Notebooks for an Ethics* do not disclose fundamentally different analyses of consciousness's ontological structure; they describe the different ways consciousness can choose to live its ontological nothingness as this choice is manifested in the pre-reflective fundamental project it chooses to live.

Secondly, Heter's insistence that consciousness's ontological and practical freedoms are radically distinct forms of freedom fails to understand that the two forms of freedom are intimately related: it is only because consciousness is ontologically free that it is able to choose how to express itself practically in the concrete world. The different modes of being described in *Being and Nothingness* and the *Notebooks for an Ethics* do not simply privilege either consciousness's ontological freedom or its practical freedom; they show that if consciousness fails to properly reflectively understand its ontological freedom, it will adopt an inauthentic mode of being that values its own practical freedom at the expense of others. It is only if consciousness does reflectively understand its ontological nothingness that it will choose to adopt an authentic mode of being that affirms its own, and others, practical freedom.

It is, therefore, simply not the case that the *Notebooks for an Ethics* offers a radically new concrete, social ontology that privileges consciousness's practical freedom over its ontological freedom in contrast to *Being and Nothingness*'s abstract, monadic ontology that privileges consciousness's ontological freedom over its practical freedom. The *Notebooks for an Ethics* complements *Being and Nothingness*'s analysis of consciousness by showing that while consciousness has a tendency to adopt an inauthentic mode of being that privileges its own practical freedom at the expense of others, its ontological freedom means it can escape from this inauthentic mode of being and choose to adopt an authentic mode of being that affirms its own, and other's, practical freedom.

Heter arrives at his conclusions because he misunderstands the relationship between *Being and Nothingness* and the *Notebooks for an Ethics*; simply rejects aspects of Sartre's thought, such as his insistence that the other is not an aspect of consciousness's ontological structure, that do not accord with his own philosophical position; replaces Sartre's arguments with his own; and appeals to Hegel's thought to 'shore up' Sartre's position so that it accords with his own argument. Thus, we find that: 1) Sartre's dismissal of the constitutive impact that social habit/custom have on the formation of consciousness's ontological structure should be replaced with Hegel's recognition that social habit/custom are constitutive formative aspects of consciousness's ontological structure; 2) Sartre's criticisms in *Being and Nothingness* of Hegel's insistence that consciousness and the other exist in a relation of ontological entwinement should be rejected and Hegel's embraced; and 3) Sartrean ethics should follow Hegel's in placing the concept of mutual recognition at its core (2008: 33–34, 36, 40–41). While it may be the case that Heter's Sartre is more philosophically appealing than Sartre's own position, we have to recognize that Heter arrives at his position because he ignores or rejects Sartre's arguments and replaces them with Hegel's. As such, he does not give a true picture of Sartre's own position.

In contrast, if we pay attention to Sartre's own statements, and while recognizing they are not always clear, we will find that the other is *not* an aspect of consciousness's ontological structure; the other is an aspect of the objective facticity on, in, and through which consciousness defines and expresses itself. Heter's insistence that 'the Sartrean self [...] is inter-subjective, relational and role-based' (2006: 37) is, therefore, only partly accurate. It is true that consciousness's *experiences* are shaped by the actions of others and the pressure the other puts on consciousness to conform to specific values, norms, and roles (EH: 45); but it is not true that the other is a constitutive aspect of consciousness's ontological structure. This leads to somewhat of a paradox: while Sartre's consciousness is *ontologically asocial*, insofar as it is ontologically distinct from other consciousnesses, it is *experientially social*, insofar as the other shapes consciousness's concrete experiences and the possibilities open to it in its objective situation.

We will see what the consequences of this paradox are for Sartre's accounts of authenticity and ethics, but it is important to note that its ontological asociality means that, before discussing the various ways in which two consciousnesses can relate to one another, Sartre must first identify the primordial way in which the other is revealed to consciousness.

The look as the primordial social relation

While Sartre recognizes that communication plays a crucial role in social relations, he insists that language is dependent on a prior moment of disclosure called 'the look.' In the first instance, the look is ocular and describes the process whereby consciousness is seen and objectified by the other. But the look of the other does not have to be an explicit moment of perception. 'The look [is] given just as well on occasion when there is a rustling of branches, or the sound of a footstep followed by silence, or the slight opening of a shutter, or a light movement of a curtain' (BN: 281). Importantly, however, there does not need to be an actual consciousness behind the shutter; it is sufficient that it is only 'probable' (BN: 281) that there is another consciousness behind the shutter for consciousness to feel the presence of the other.

The sudden emergence of the other shocks consciousness. Suddenly 'when I hear the branches crackling behind me [I realize] that I am vulnerable, that I have a body which can be hurt, that I occupy a place and that I can not in any case escape from the space in which I am without defence' (BN: 282). This experience leads consciousness to 'experience a subtle alienation of [its] possibilities' (BN: 289) in which it understands that it is no longer simply free to determine itself; it recognizes that it is subject to the judgement and activities of others (BN: 291).

While the other's look objectifies consciousness, the relationship between consciousnesses is fundamentally different to the relationship between consciousness and an object. Put simply, 'the other cannot look at [consciousness] as he looks at the grass' (BN: 280). When consciousness looks at an actual object, it simply sees a passive object; but when consciousness looks at another consciousness, it experiences an 'absence' (BN: 280) and realizes that the object in front of it is somehow different.

Importantly, however, consciousness cannot *look-at-the-other* and *be-looked-at* simultaneously. A social relation grounded in the look can not be one where the subjectivity of both, as manifested in their *looking-at* the other, exists simultaneously. Consciousness 'can not perceive the world and at the same time apprehend a look fastened upon [it]; it must be either one or the other. This is because to perceive is to *look at*, and to apprehend a look is not to apprehend a look-as-object in the world (unless the look is not directed upon us); it is to be conscious of *being looked at*' (BN: 282). At their foundational level, social relations conform to a strict binary subject/object dualism. Either consciousness objectifies the other by looking-at it, or consciousness is looked-at and objectified by the other.

However, this objectification does not necessarily have to be reflectively experienced; in the first instance, the objectification of the other's look effects consciousness *pre-reflectively*. Following Yiwei Zheng's (2001: 20–21) interpretation of the pre-reflective consciousness as a 'feel,' we may say that, in the first instance, the look of the other leads consciousness to *feel* objectified. Through its initial experience of the other's look, consciousness becomes pre-reflectively aware that it is 'a defenceless being for a freedom which is not [its] freedom' (BN: 291). But, because the other is a condition of its experience, consciousness cannot stop living with the other; consciousness is destined to be subjected to the other's objectifying look.

Reacting to the other's look: shame and pride

The 'immediate shudder' (BN: 246) that runs through consciousness when it experiences the other's objectifying look affects it in one of two ways: 'it is shame or pride which reveals to me the other's look and myself at the end of that look' (BN: 284–285). But these do not exist as equal possibilities; when Sartre writes that 'it is on the ground of fundamental shame or shame of being an object that pride is built' (BN: 314), it is clear that shame is consciousness's fundamental pre-reflective reaction to the other's look.

The other's look initially causes consciousness to feel ashamed because the objectification that emanates from the other's look violates consciousness's initial pre-reflective sense of pure subjectivity. Understanding why this is the case requires that I once again engage with consciousness's relationship to its body.

As noted, while the Sartrean consciousness has a pre-reflective understanding of its body, *it* initially holds that its body is synonymous with the pure, subjective freedom it pre-reflectively understands itself to be (BN: 353). It is only once the other looks at it that consciousness comes to see its body as something objective. While consciousness initially pre-reflectively understands itself to be a pure subjectivity, its experience of the other's objectifying look discloses an aspect of its being that it alone does not initially recognize: its objective facticity. However, this disclosure causes consciousness to feel ashamed because it contradicts the pure, subjective freedom that constitutes its primordial sense of self (BN: 283–284).

But while shame is consciousness's primordial pre-reflective reaction to the other's look, Sartre does recognize that consciousness can subsequently become proud of itself. Rather than affirm its ontological freedom, the proud consciousness accepts the other's objectification of it and takes pride in its objective status. In this way, it becomes and takes pride in being good-looking, charming, and intelligent. However, this self-objectification contradicts consciousness's ontological nothingness. For this reason, pride is a form of bad faith (BN: 314).

But at the same time as the proud consciousness pre-reflectively understands itself to have a fixed ontological identity, it also affirms its subjective freedom by pre-reflectively judging and objectifying the other (BN: 314).

Unfortunately, while consciousness designs ruses and strategies to make the other remain an object, 'one look on the part of the other is sufficient to make all these schemes collapse' (BN: 320) and for consciousness to once more become an object to the other's subjectivity. If social relations take place through the look, they are conflictual and tense: either consciousness looks-at the other and objectifies it, or is looked-at by a subjective other and objectified. Sartre demonstrates exactly what this conflict means by describing a number of concrete social relations that conform to this conflictual, subject/object schema. I will briefly examine love.

Being and Nothingness's discussion of love takes place through the conflictual, subject/object dichotomy. The lover wishes to possess his beloved, not in terms of physical possession, but in terms of capturing his beloved's free consciousness. By this, Sartre means that 'the lover wants to be "the whole World" for the beloved' (BN: 389). By becoming the non-surpassable foundation of his beloved's world, the lover will shape and determine his beloved's existence.

Importantly, however, the lover cannot simply demand that he become the Archimedean point of his beloved's existence. The lover desires that his beloved freely and spontaneously choose to make his freedom the foundation of her freedom (BN: 389–391).

However, the beloved does not simply give her freedom to the lover. She resists by either spurning his advances or trying to make herself the Archimedean point of the lover's existence. The lover and beloved are engaged in a conflictual battle; each is trying to win the other's freedom while safeguarding their own.

There are two problems with this relationship: first, if the lover actually does manage to seduce his beloved into giving him her freedom, he would not win what he desires: his beloved's freedom. By making herself subordinate to his freedom, the beloved would forego the very 'thing' the lover desires: her freedom. Thus, the lover's desire is self-defeating: 'he wants to be loved by a freedom but demands that this freedom as freedom should no longer be free' (BN: 389).

Secondly, Sartre notes that the lover's attempt to obtain his beloved's freedom alienates him from his freedom. In order to seduce his beloved, the lover has to adopt this as his pre-reflective project. However, this project implicitly entails the recognition that he needs his beloved; or, as Sartre puts it, 'to love is in essence the project of making oneself be loved' (BN: 397). The lover's attempt to make his beloved's freedom subordinate to his undermines itself: it demonstrates that the lover is not free from his beloved, but is actually dependent on her. It appears, therefore, that the lover's attempt to possess the beloved's freedom is doomed to end in conflict, frustration, and alienation.

Interacting with the other: the 'we' and the role of language

Sartre's insistence that all social relations are grounded in the other's objectifying look, that 'the essence of the relations between consciousnesses is not the *Mitsein*; it is conflict' (BN: 451), and his description of concrete social relations that conform to the conflictual, subject/object opposition inherent to the look can quite easily make it appear that he maintains that *all* social relations are conflictual. This is not so.

Sartre recognizes that 'one could probably point out to us that our description is incomplete since it leaves no place for certain concrete experiences in which we discover ourselves not in conflict with the other but in community with him' (BN: 434). With this, Sartre discloses that not all social relations are experienced as conflictual. He discusses non-conflictual social relations under the title of the 'we.'

The we describes a social relation where 'nobody is the object. The "we" includes a plurality of subjectivities which recognise one another as subjectivities' (BN: 435). However, because, in this section of *Being and Nothingness*, Sartre is primarily interested in showing that the we-relation is not the primordial form of social relation, he downplays the value of the 'we.'

This ensures that the Sartre of *Being and Nothingness* holds that the we-relation does not actually allow consciousness to experience the other's freedom. 'The experience of the we-subject is a pure psychological, subjective event in a single consciousness. It corresponds to an inner modification of the structure of consciousness but does not appear on the foundation of a concrete ontological relation with others and does not realise any *Mitsein*' (BN: 447).

Because the experience of a we-relation arises when one consciousness subjectively interprets its relationship with the other to conform to the relation of subjectivities that defines the we-relation, the we-relation described is not actually a relationship in which both consciousnesses are free subjects. By designating their social relation as a we-relation, one consciousness usurps the freedom of the other and imposes its subjective interpretation of their social relation onto the other (BN: 363).

However, consciousness can only effect the subjective, psychological alteration that allows it to experience a we-relation if 'the other's existence [...] has been already revealed to [it]' (BN: 451) through the other's look. But how do the two consciousnesses come to understand that the other is another subject in the way that leads to the creation of a we-relation?

Steve Martinot argues that communication is crucial. Martinot does not, however, note or discuss *Being and Nothingness's* insistence that the subject/subject structure of a we-relation is an impossibility; he simply adheres to Sartre's later position in which the subject/subject social relation of the we-relation is an actual possibility. Thus, while Martinot maintains that social relations conducted through the look are conflictual, he argues that social relations take on 'a different character when articulated in terms of the spoken or "audible"' (2005: 46).

According to Martinot, language plays such a crucial role in the formation of a we-relation because it allows both consciousnesses to communicate with one another, interact with one another, and so learn that the other is not a threatening object, but another subject. Language overcomes the subject/object dichotomy of a social relation conducted through the look by allowing consciousness to express its subjectivity in a way that does not nihilate the other's subjectivity. As Sartre explains, 'language reveals to me the freedom (the transcendence) of the one who listens to me in silence' (BN: 396).

Language fulfils this role because the speech-act requires a speaker and a listener, each of which can only fulfil their role if the other understands and fulfils its role. Because the speaker is dependent on a listener and a listener dependent on a speaker, language requires and sustains a relation of mutual recognition of, and respect for, each other's freedom.

In *What is Literature?*, Sartre returns to this issue by examining the reader/writer relation. He explains that the primordial reason the writer writes, is to fulfil his desire to be 'recognised as *essential* to the totality of being' (WL: 45). This recognition can only be given by someone who reads his text; it can only be given by the reader. 'Thus, the writer appeals to the reader's freedom to collaborate in the production of his work' (WL: 34). Note that the author does not *demand* that the reader read his book; he merely *appeals* to the reader. This appeal means the author can never dominate the reader. The reader is free to determine whether he reads the work, how it will be read, and what he thinks of it. By virtue of their mutual dependency, the author/reader relation is one of mutual respect: 'the author writes in order to address himself to the freedom of readers, and he requires it in order to make his work exist. But he does not stop there; he also requires that they return this confidence which he has given them, that they recognise his creative freedom, and that they in turn solicit it by a symmetrical and inverse appeal' (WL: 38).

The author-reader relation appears to support Martinot's claim: while a social relation based on the look conforms to the conflictual, subject/object, looking-at/looked-at dichotomy, language allows consciousnesses to overcome this binary opposition and establish a non-conflictual relationship of equals.

However, while Martinot is correct to note that Sartre is aware that not all social relations are conflictual, we have to be careful how we interpret these non-conflictual relations. There are three reasons for this: first, we have to remember that the *primordial* manner through which consciousness comes to learn about the other's existence is not through language, but is through the look (which, as noted, does not necessarily have to be ocular). Consciousness cannot help but immediately shudder when the other suddenly appears to it through the look. Sartre explains that it is only 'later when we are in direct connection with the other by language' (BN: 288) that the conflict inherent to the subject/object, looking-at/looked-at opposition can be overcome. Thus, consciousnesses do not *initially* interact through language. It is only once they have been disclosed to each other through their respective looks that the two consciousnesses can decide how to proceed with the interaction. If the two consciousnesses continue to simply look at one another, they become locked in the conflictual relation inherent to the look. But if the two consciousnesses communicate with one another, they can learn about each other and develop a relation based on the mutual recognition of, and respect for, each other's freedom.

Secondly, Martinot fails to explicitly recognize the importance of conversion for the development of an authentic social relation. I will shortly return to this issue, but for now it is sufficient to note that language can only facilitate the creation of a we-relation in the way Martinot claims it does if both consciousnesses have undergone conversion.

Thirdly, while Martinot appears to claim that *all* forms of the look lead to conflictual relations, I think we need to be more discerning and recognize that consciousness's relation to the other's look is more subtle and nuanced. Martinot makes this claim because he fails to differentiate between the initial look through which the other appears to consciousness and the way consciousness can subsequently choose to experience the same other's look.

Conversion and social relations

It is true that, in *Being and Nothingness*, Sartre maintains that consciousness can only take two attitudes towards the other's look: I can 'recognise the other as the subject through whom I get my object-ness – this is shame; and that by which I apprehend myself as the free object by which the other gets his being-other – this is arrogance or the affirmation of my freedom confronting the other-as-object' (BN: 314). This appears to support Martinnot's claim that consciousness's reaction to the other's look is constrained within the logic of the conflictual subject/object opposition: either consciousness is a subject for an objectified, degraded other; or consciousness is a degraded object for another subject.

But when we turn to the *Notebooks for an Ethics*, we discover that the conflictual, subject/object social relation outlined in *Being and Nothingness* describes social relations 'before conversion' (NE: 20). Undergoing the conversion allows consciousness to form a new, *authentic* social relation with its other.

As Chapter 1 showed, conversion describes the process whereby consciousness alters its pre-reflective fundamental project (NE: 472, 479). Sartre maintains that consciousness's 'natural' (NE: 6) tendency is to adopt a pre-reflective fundamental project that leads it to try to synthesize with objectivity to become a being-in-itself-for-itself; or, as he provocatively puts it: God.

But Sartre argues that if consciousness chooses to adopt a pre-reflective fundamental project that seeks to fulfil its pre-reflective ontological desire to be God, it is destined to fail. Attaining the security of the fixed ontological identity inherent to being-in-itself-for-itself would annihilate the absolute freedom that defines consciousness's ontological structure.

But while Sartre maintains that consciousness has a tendency to adopt the futile pre-reflective fundamental project of becoming a being-in-itself-for-itself, he does note that the experience of its continuous failure to become a being-in-itself-for-itself may lead consciousness to question its existence (NE: 472). This questioning may lead it to alter its pre-reflective fundamental project.

Those that do choose to undergo the conversion will alter two different, but related, aspects of their being. First, conversion involves a specific alteration in consciousness's pre-reflective fundamental project; 'there is a conversion from the [pre-reflective fundamental] project to-be-for-itself-in-itself and appropriation or identification to a [pre-reflective fundamental] project of unveiling and creation' (NE: 482). Whereas the pre-converted consciousness understands that it *must* seek to become God, conversion leads consciousness to re-evaluate this understanding. Through this re-evaluation, consciousness comes to reflectively understand that it does not simply have to seek to become God; it realizes that its freedom is the source of this futile imperative. Sartre thinks that this recognition will lead consciousness to abandon its previous futile desire to be God and place the affirmation of freedom as the end towards which its existence is directed (Detmer, 1988: 177–186).

By adopting a pre-reflective fundamental project that has the affirmation of freedom as its end, the converted consciousness reflectively recognizes that it is free to choose itself and so undergoes a process of continuous, reflective self-creation. Continuously, reflectively recreating itself allows consciousness to reflectively express its freedom without actually becoming or reflectively understanding itself to be anything. Acting in this way is at the foundation of authentic being (NE: 475, 514–515).

Secondly, accompanying this alteration in its pre-reflective fundamental project is a radically new form of reflective, pure self-understanding (NE: 472). Whereas the consciousness of impure reflection thematizes its ontological nothingness, thereby reflectively understanding itself to be defined by a fixed, ontological identity, conversion is the process whereby consciousness, having been in the natural attitude of impure reflection, comes to reflectively understand that it is ontologically nothing. By reflectively understanding its ontological nothingness, the converted consciousness gains 'a thematic grasping of freedom' (NE: 474) that leads to 'a new, "*authentic*," way of being [it]self' (NE: 474).

This new authentic way of being leads consciousness to a new understanding of the role that objectivity plays in its existence. Whereas the pre-converted consciousness understands itself to be a pure subject confronting a threatening object, conversion brings consciousness to realize that objectivity is a necessary aspect of its existence (NE: 20), insofar as the converted consciousness reflectively realizes that it is not a pure, subjective freedom confronting a threatening, objective world, but is a subjective freedom that chooses how it will live a socially embedded body (BN: 530). Accompanying this realization is a re-evaluation of consciousness's relationship to the other.

While the social relations of the pre-converted consciousness described in *Being and Nothingness* are a 'hell of passions' (NE: 499), insofar as each consciousness maintains it is a pure subject confronting a threatening other, the converted consciousness recognizes that the other is a free subject (NE: 500) that plays a necessary and positive role in the disclosure of its objective facticity (BN: 246). This insight is the fundamental difference between pre and post-conversion social relations.

Sartre is aware that even if the converted consciousness alters its understanding of the other, this does not alter the fact that the other still sees consciousness as an object. But he notes that 'if [the other] makes me exist as an existing freedom as well as a *being/object* [...] he enriches the world and me, he *gives a meaning* to my existence *in addition* to the subjective meaning I myself give it' (NE: 500). While consciousness appears to the other as an object, if the other recognizes that consciousness is also a free subject, it can provide consciousness with objective 'feedback' on its existence. This 'feedback' does not alienate consciousness from its freedom; it opens consciousness to new perspectives and activities. Importantly, however, the other can only play this role if it has affected the conversion to a pre-reflective fundamental project that has the affirmation of freedom as its end. If the other has not undergone the conversion, it will fail to recognize consciousness's freedom and will continue to understand that consciousness is a threatening object to its pure, subjective freedom.

However, consciousness is not simply dependent on the other effecting a self-conversion. Once it has undergone the conversion, consciousness can 'appeal' (NE: 274) to the other to engage in a 'common operation' (NE: 274). This appeal is not a *demand;* consciousness extends a 'firm but not immutable [invitation to] the other's will to want what it wants' (NE: 274). The appeal reaches out to the other and invites it to choose to engage in a common operation that may lead to the development of a social relation in which each experiences a sense of solidarity with the other's freedom (NE: 479). Sartre is aware that, for one reason or another, the other may not respond to consciousness's appeal (NE: 275); but if the other does respond positively, the two can work with one another to achieve a common end and, hopefully, establish a relationship based on co-operation rather than conflict. This will bring the converted consciousness to reflectively realize and accept that the other can *extend* its freedom in the actual world (NE: 280).

The fundamental aspect of the appeal is that consciousness recognizes the other's freedom and invites the other to recognize its freedom. Thus, while *Being and Nothingness* appears to hold that consciousness cannot know or identify with the subjective freedom of the other, in the *Notebooks for an Ethics*, Sartre allows that consciousness can *comprehend* the other's freedom.

But Sartre maintains that this comprehension is not 'contemplative [...] it is *sympathetic*' (NE: 276). The experience of the other brings the converted consciousness to reflectively recognize and identify with the other's situated freedom. Sartre explains that 'in the pure interrelationship among freedoms, there is a recognition of the other's freedom as being my freedom in the other and a relation of reciprocity (if he comprehends me, I can comprehend him, if he appeals to me, I help him, if he looks at me, I can look at him)' (NE: 330). Rather than maintain that the other's look is an objectifying threat to its subjective freedom, the experience of empathy that emanates from its comprehension of the other's situated freedom leads the converted consciousness to alter its comportment towards the other. Rather than trying to negate the other to affirm its own freedom, the converted consciousness learns to *live with* the other in a way that reflectively recognizes and affirms the other's freedom. A social relation in which both consciousnesses reflectively recognize, respect, care for, and affirm each other's freedom is, according to Sartre, an *authentic* social relation.

But Sartre does not hold that authentic social relations are experiences of sheer bliss. As Adrian Mirvish points out, for Sartre, 'conflict of a positive sort is crucial for friendship and authentic relations in general' (2002: 267). Authentic social relations require some sort of *'tension'* (NE: 415) to allow each consciousness to challenge and push the other. Through this challenge, each is opened up to new aspects of its world. But this challenge must not go so far as to nihilate the other, belittle it, or generally usurp its freedom. It must coax the other into challenging its own assumptions and world-view.

In relation to the earlier discussion of love, conversion also creates a new form of the love relation. No longer is the love relation strictly conflictual. While Sartre maintains that the post-conversion love relation is one of tension, insofar as neither knows exactly what the other will do; this ambiguity is a crucial aspect of love. It keeps each lover interested in their beloved. But the post-conversion love relation also has another aspect to it: a 'deeper recognition and reciprocal comprehension of [the lovers'] freedoms' (NE: 414). The lover no longer simply seeks to reduce his beloved's freedom to his ends; he wants his beloved to freely express herself and is no longer so preoccupied with ensuring that her every action revolves around him. He cares for her freedom and supports her as she tries to achieve her own projects; in turn, she supports and cares for her lover's independent projects. Put simply, each lover in the post-conversion love relation is not so preoccupied with dominating their beloved; their relationship is more relaxed. It is more of a partnership than a battle.

Conversion, language, and the 'we'

From this, we can say that undergoing the conversion instantiates a form of social relation that conforms to the subject/subject structure of the 'we.' While *Being and Nothingness's* insistence that the we-relation is a purely subjective designation imposed by one consciousness onto its relation with the other appears to ensure that social relations actually always conform to the subject/object relation even if they are not always experienced as such, the we-relation described in the *Notebooks for an Ethics* is a social relation in which each consciousness spontaneously relates to the other in a way that reflectively recognizes, respects, and affirms its own, and the other's, freedom. Each consciousness reflectively affirms its own freedom and reflectively recognizes, respects, and affirms the other's freedom. The social relation created is not one in which one consciousness usurps the freedom of the other; the freedom of each is maintained and affirmed. Indeed, the we-relation is the highest form of social relation precisely because it allows each consciousness to freely exist and, by working with others in a way that affirms each other's freedom, achieve ends they would not otherwise be able to achieve (NE: 414–415, 508).

But while I have previously noted that there is an ambiguity in Sartre's position relating to the possibility of establishing a social relation that conforms to the subject/subject structure of the we-relation, insofar as *Being and Nothingness* appears to reject it while the *Notebooks for an Ethics* accepts it, there is another ambiguity in Sartre's account of the 'we,' in that he seems to vacillate between two positions regarding how it is achieved. In *What is Literature?*, Sartre appears to think that certain forms of social relation (for example, the author/reader relation) naturally conform to it, while, in the *Notebooks for an Ethics*, he insists the we-relation is only a possibility once both consciousnesses have undergone conversion.

On my understanding, Sartre's account in the *Notebooks for an Ethics* is more consistent with his overall claims. There are two reasons for this: 1) throughout the *Notebooks for an Ethics*, Sartre consistently claims that authentic social relations are dependent on both consciousnesses undergoing the conversion. In contrast, his statement in *What is Literature?* is confined to a brief comment on one relation; and 2) Sartre's discussion of the mutual recognition inherent in the author/reader relation confuses *mutually entwined social roles* with *mutual respect and recognition of the other's freedom.* Sartre appears to think that the author and reader recognize and respect one another simply by virtue of their roles as reader and writer. But just because the author is dependent on the reader and the reader on the author to fulfil their role does not necessarily mean that each recognizes and respects the other's freedom. For example, the reader may fundamentally disagree with the author to the extent that he loses respect for the author. Alternatively, the author may hold his audience in contempt. A relation of *mutual dependency* is not necessarily a relation of *mutual recognition*.

This is not to say that the reader and writer cannot transform their relation of mutual dependence into a relation of mutual recognition of each other's freedom. However, it is only after each has affected the conversion that the author and reader can reflectively recognize and respect each other's freedom.

But if the creation of the we-relation is dependent on each consciousness undergoing the conversion, does the positive role that Martinot insists communication can play in the development of authentic social relations also depend on each consciousness undergoing the conversion? In other words, does communication always create an authentic social relation or can communication only lead to the development of a non-conflictual, authentic social relation if both consciousnesses in the relation have undergone the conversion?

Martinot appears to think it is the former: for two consciousnesses to develop a non-conflictual, authentic social relation, it is sufficient that they communicate with one another. Through this communication, the two consciousnesses can learn that, while the other's look is objectifying, this objectification does not necessarily threaten its freedom. This allows both consciousnesses to learn about each other in a way that leads to the development of a relationship based on mutual respect, rather than conflict.

This, however, fails to understand that the development of an authentic social relation is dependent on more than mere communication; after all, two consciousnesses can talk to one another without respecting one another. The development of an authentic social relation requires that two consciousnesses communicate with one another *and* that the consciousnesses involved have undergone conversion.

This is because the pre-converted consciousness's pre-reflective fundamental project: 1) maintains that the other is an objectifying threat to its pure subjectivity; and 2) is in bad faith, an aspect of which is that consciousness interprets the other through a closed, preconceived schema (BN: 91). Rather than being open to the other in a way that allows the other to disclose itself to consciousness, the pre-converted consciousness pre-reflectively imposes its closed, preconceived schema onto the other and interprets it through this schema. Because its pre-reflective fundamental project insists the other's objectifying look threatens its subjective freedom, the pre-converted consciousness's pre-reflective fundamental project leads it to be wary of the other. No matter how charming or friendly the other is, if consciousness's pre-reflective fundamental project makes it wary of the other, the two consciousnesses can talk all they like, but their wariness will prevent them from trusting the other in the way necessary to establish a social relation in which each reflectively recognizes, respects, and affirms the other's freedom.

Consciousness will only open itself to, and interact with, the other in the way necessary to establish a we-relation once it has undergone the conversion to a pre-reflective fundamental project that is in good faith. Only the open-ness of the converted consciousness's pre-reflective fundamental project allows it to reflectively recognize and respect the other's subjectivity. Or, to return to the previous example, because the converted consciousness has no preconceived ideas about the other, when the two meet, they can talk, and each can form its opinion of the other based on each other's actual comportment. Of course, they may find that, for one reason or another, they do not want to take the relationship any further; but it is only if each consciousness is open to the other, in the way that only the conversion allows, that it will be possible to establish an authentic relation based on the mutual recognition, respect, and affirmation of each other's freedom.

Crucially, because a relationship involves at least two consciousnesses, consciousness's altered attitude to the other must be reciprocated by the other. As Sartre explains, 'one cannot be converted alone [...] ethics is not possible unless everyone is ethical' (NE: 9). Only when both consciousnesses undergo the conversion will their pre-reflective fundamental projects allow them to open themselves to the other in the way that brings them to comprehend and empathize with the other's situated freedom. Only then will they be able to develop the authentic form of social relation in which each reflectively recognizes and respects the other's freedom.

Thus, while communication plays a crucial role in this development, communication can only lead to the development of an authentic social relation if both consciousnesses have converted to a pre-reflective fundamental project that is in good faith. Only then will their pre-reflective norms and values allow them to openly communicate with each other in the way necessary to establish a we-relation.

But Sartre insists that the consciousnesses of authentic social relations do not simply recognize each other's freedom. Post-conversion, consciousness experiences a sense of 'solidarity' (NE: 479) with the other that leads it to care for the other's freedom. Sartre explains that 'I [...] make myself the guardian of [the other's] finitude. In my freedom his finitude finds safety: I am the one who watches his back and who deflects from his back the danger he cannot see' (NE: 508).

While the pre-converted consciousness tries to make the other's freedom subservient to its own freedom, conversion brings consciousness to the reflective realization and acceptance that, because the other is a free subject, it has an independent project of its own. Importantly, however, rather than try to impede the realization of the other's independent project, the converted consciousness 'contribute[s] to *its happening*' (NE: 279) by either helping the other realize its project or momentarily turning away from its own projects to allow the other to realize its (NE: 279).

But Sartre warns that this does not mean that consciousness's freedom is usurped by the other, nor that consciousness becomes an instrument for the realization of the other's project. By voluntarily helping the other achieve its end, the converted consciousness simultaneously retains its own freedom, while also contributing to the realization of the other's freedom (NE: 280).

As noted in Chapter 1, while consciousness is always ontologically free, it must realize its practical freedom. For this reason, Sartre insists that ethics should be directed towards the realization of this end (NE: 470; EH: 38, 51–52). But consciousness only comes to reflectively understand this after it has undergone the conversion. Only then will consciousness adopt a pre-reflective fundamental project that has freedom as its end.

It is because consciousness should focus on becoming practically free that the question of the freedom of others becomes an issue. If consciousness is to creatively and freely express itself in the actual world, it must not be constrained by the concrete activities of others; the other must also be practically free to express itself in the actual world (EH: 51–52). But why is consciousness's practical freedom dependent on the other's practical freedom? Surely, consciousness could be practically free by dominating the other?

Sartre recognizes this, but appears to think that the converted consciousness's comprehension of the other will bring it to work to secure its own, and others, practical freedom. While Sartre is not altogether clear on why this is the case, three related reasons can be gleaned from the logic of his argument and his explicit statements on the topic: first, by bringing consciousness to a pre-reflective fundamental project that recognizes and accepts that the experience of the other's objectifying look is necessary to disclose its objective facticity, conversion ensures that consciousness no longer simply perceives that the other is an objectifying threat to its subjective freedom; it reflectively understands that the other is a necessary aspect of its existence, insofar as the other discloses aspects of consciousness's existence that consciousness alone cannot disclose. For this reason, the converted consciousness no longer seeks to defend its subjective freedom from the other's objectifying look, nor does the converted consciousness seek to dominate the other's freedom to affirm its own.

Secondly, Sartre holds that the converted consciousness's comprehension of the other's situated freedom means it is able to reflectively understand and empathize with the other's un-freedom. Sartre thinks this will bring the converted consciousness to work towards the realization of the other's practical freedom; because thirdly, the experience of its own practical freedom will lead the converted consciousness to experience a concrete, ethical imperative that impels it to secure its own, and the other's, practical freedom. Sartre explains that while 'freedom as the definition of a man does not depend upon others, [...] as soon as there is commitment, I am obliged to will the liberty of others at the same time as mine. I cannot make liberty my aim unless I make that of others equally my aim' (EH: 52). In other words, while consciousness's ontological freedom is not dependent on the existence of others, when consciousness attempts to secure its practical freedom, it tends to encounter others who are not practically free. This encounter will bring the converted consciousness to spontaneously work towards the realization of its own, and others, practical freedom.

Conclusion

Sartre's ethical position is, therefore, somewhat ambiguous. Despite insisting that there are no formal, transcendent, universal, ethical rules, Sartre's entire argument is informed by the implicit assumption that consciousness is more ethical if it lives authentically than inauthentically. Sartre's conception of social relations also discloses a second ethical imperative, albeit one Sartre insists emanates from consciousness's *experience*, rather than from an abstract notion of the good: to be authentic, consciousness must not only secure its own practical freedom; it must also secure the other's practical freedom.

This complicates Sartre's accounts of authenticity and alienation. It means that for the individual to be authentic requires that the other also exist authentically. This, in turn, requires that the individual and the other create a bond whereby the individual cares for and affirms the other's practical freedom and the other cares for and affirms the individual's practical freedom. Thus, while the individual can be practically free by nihilating the other's practical freedom, the individual can only be *authentic* if: 1) it is practically free; 2) the other is also practically free; and 3) they establish a relationship where each reflectively cares for and affirms the other's practical freedom. This reaffirms my point: while Sartre insists that the other does not and cannot impact on consciousness's ontological freedom, he holds that the other's existence is a constitutive aspect of consciousness's concrete situation and plays a crucial role in its attempts to be practically free.

However, Robert Williams (1997: 373–380) provides two arguments to show that Sartre's description of consciousness's *ontological* relation to the other sits uneasily with his description of the *experience* of mutual recognition inherent to authentic, post-conversion social relations.

First, Williams claims that Sartre's insistence that consciousness can recognize and respect the other's ontological freedom contradicts his critique of Hegel. As noted, Sartre charges that Hegel is epistemologically optimistic for insisting that consciousness can know and respect the other's freedom. However, Sartre's account of post-conversion social relations accepts that consciousness can know and respect the other's freedom. Despite his criticisms, Williams charges that Sartre subsequently accepts Hegel's position.

Williams' second point is more fundamental because it maintains that Sartre's analysis of consciousness's ontological structure prevents consciousnesses from developing just this sort of social relation; that is, a social relation that recognizes and respects the other's freedom. Williams notes that because consciousness's ontological structure is defined by the pre-reflective nihilation of its other, it exists by virtue of pre-reflectively setting itself in opposition to its other. Because of this, Williams argues that it is not possible for two Sartrean consciousnesses to form a relationship of co-operation; 'in Sartre's ontology, recognition can have only a negative significance, namely, reciprocal exclusion. Reciprocal exclusion means that recognition of self in other is impossible' (1997: 376). According to Williams, the ontological level of Sartre's analysis means that 'no reciprocal recognition [of the other's freedom] is possible' (1997: 376).

However, Steve Martinot implicitly rejects Williams' criticisms by: 1) arguing that consciousness's ontological freedom ensures it is free to choose its relation to the other; and 2) accepting the radical division between the ontological and experiential levels of Sartre's analysis.

This leads Martinot to claim that while consciousness is ontologically opposed to its other, 'solidarity, whether against an enemy or toward a process of cultural transformation and community construction, resides at a different level of ontological praxis and presupposes a different moment of value' (2005: 46).

Martinot's argument appears to accept that the distinction Sartre makes between consciousness's ontological structure and its experience is a valid distinction, and that the two levels of his analysis are independent from one another and of equal status. In the first instance, however, it is questionable whether the ontological and experiential levels of Sartre's analysis are of equal status and independent from one another. To be able to choose its experiential mode of being, consciousness must exist, which requires that it fulfil the ontological condition of its being and pre-reflectively nihilate its other.

Furthermore, it must be remembered that an aspect of the standard against which Sartre judges an experiential mode of being is whether consciousness reflectively understands its ontological nothingness in its chosen mode of being. Thus, consciousness's ontological structure acts as part of the standard against which Sartre judges consciousness's mode of being; it is this that allows Sartre to maintain that certain modes of being are authentic and others inauthentic. Not only is there a crucial link between the two levels of Sartre's analysis, but the relation between the two is hierarchical: the ethical validity of consciousness's experiential mode of being is determined by whether it reflectively understands and affirms its ontological nothingness.

Secondly, Martinot's acceptance that Sartre's analysis of consciousness operates on two distinct levels (the ontological and experiential levels) simply leaves intact the contradictions that arise from the two levels of Sartre's analysis. Martinot simply asks us to accept that while the ontological freedom that Sartre insists defines consciousness's ontological structure ensures it is free to choose different pre-reflective fundamental projects with different *experiential* relations to the other, consciousness is not free to choose its *ontological* relation to the other because a condition of its existence is that it pre-reflectively sets itself in opposition to its other. Or, that while a condition of consciousness's existence is that it pre-reflectively nihilates its other, a condition of authenticity is that consciousness also chooses to adopt a pre-reflective fundamental project that leads it to care for and affirm the other's practical freedom. Similarly, we are asked to simply accept Sartre's insistence that while consciousness is experientially embedded in the world, consciousness's ontological structure is defined by a pre-reflective act that nihilates, and so sets itself in opposition to, the world.

Importantly, however, these contradictions do not necessarily occur between the reflective and pre-reflective levels of Sartre's consciousness; they are contradictions that occur at the *pre-reflective* level of consciousness. Thus, while a condition of consciousness's ontological structure is that it pre-reflectively nihilates being-in-itself, a condition of Sartrean authenticity is that consciousness not only pre-reflectively nihilates its other to fulfil the ontological condition of its existence, but also chooses to adopt a pre-reflective fundamental project that leads it to simply live with its other and, in the case of another consciousness, actually affirm the other's practical freedom. While Martinot appears to be unconcerned by such contradictions in the pre-reflective consciousness, Douglas Kirsner (2003: 175) is. For Kirsner, the contradictions that arise from the combination of the various conditions of Sartre's analysis of authenticity ensure that Sartre's authentic consciousness is, at the pre-reflective level, both unhappy and schizoid.

While I am more sympathetic to Williams' and Kirsner's conclusion that Sartre's analysis of consciousness is irreducibly and unsatisfactorily contradictory, comparing the work of Williams and Martinot supports Judith Butler's (1987: 105) contention that the reader that tries to reach a conclusion about the legitimacy and validity of Sartre's analysis of consciousness is ultimately faced with a philosophical choice: either Sartre's analysis of the authentic consciousness pulls in two irreconcilable directions; or, more sympathetically, is a perceptive account of the contradictions consciousness must struggle to deal with on an everyday basis.

Whichever conclusion is reached, however, it is important to note that Sartre recognized that the human being cannot simply be conflated with consciousness. This led him to develop his account of human being further to take into consideration the ways in which membership of certain group formations and the individual's social situation in general shape his capacity to practically express himself.

4
Sartre, Group Formations, and Practical Freedom

As noted in the preceding chapter, Sartre's account of the individual's relationship to the other is somewhat paradoxical. On the one hand, Sartre maintains that consciousness's ontological structure is defined by a pre-reflective act that distinguishes it from its other; while, on the other hand, consciousness is always embedded 'in' a social situation inhabited by others whose practical activities impact on both its self-understanding and capacity to practically express itself. While his early work discusses the implications of the later from the perspective of immediate relations between two consciousnesses, the discussion of social relations in the *Critique of Dialectical Reason* complements and extends this by discussing: 1) the way the concrete individual relates to others through membership of various different *group formations*; and 2) how these group formations constrain or enhance the individual's practical freedom.

By distinguishing between different group formations, Sartre recognizes that not all social formations allow the individual to freely express himself in the same way or to the same degree. In other words, certain group formations allow the individual to be more practically free than others. While the mass of individuals of seriality and the group formation called the institution constrain the individual's practical freedom, the democratic, organic, and spontaneous group formations called the group-in-fusion and the organized group enhance his practical freedom.

Contrary to Mary Warnock's (1970: 116) influential interpretation, therefore, not only does Sartre recognize that the individual can relate to others in a way that recognizes, respects, and affirms the other's practical freedom, but he also maintains that certain group formations can enhance the individual's practical freedom. To demonstrate this, I will start with the relationship between the *Critique of Dialectical Reason* and Sartre's early work.

The early and later Sartre: radical rupture or continuity?

According to Thomas Anderson (1993: 1), there is a radical rupture between Sartre's early so-called existential thought, best exemplified by *Being and Nothingness*, and his later Marxist-inspired *Critique of Dialectical Reason*. On Anderson's reading, the impossibility of founding an ethics out of the conflictual ontological dualism of *Being and Nothingness* led Sartre to rethink the ontological categories around which his thought was based. The conclusion drawn is that the *Critique of Dialectical Reason* places a far greater emphasis on the way the individual's social embeddedness impacts on his free creative self-expression. This leads Anderson to insist that the *Critique of Dialectical Reason* describes a completely new ontology of being from the one outlined in *Being and Nothingness*. Indeed, for Anderson, 'the human being of the *Critique* seems to be almost a different species from the human being of *Being and Nothingness* and earlier works' (1993: 89).

While it is true that Sartre's analysis of the other in the *Critique of Dialectical Reason* differs in a number of respects from his early thought, I do not follow Anderson's argument that *Being and Nothingness* and the *Critique of Dialectical Reason* are irreducibly different. While there are differences in the categories used, the orientation of his thought, and the overall argument, Sartre's *Critique of Dialectical Reason* complements his early existential analysis.

There are two reasons for this: first, despite maintaining that *Being and Nothingness* was describing the being of being-for-itself and being-in-itself, Sartre subsequently recognized that he had tended to conflate the being of being-for-itself with consciousness. This led him to recognize that, despite having pointed towards consciousness's facticity, he had, in fact, proposed a 'rationalist philosophy of consciousness' (BEM: 41). To overcome what he saw as his early idealism, Sartre came to highlight and emphasize the socially embedded nature of individual existence. Rather than focus on consciousness, in the *Critique of Dialectical Reason*, Sartre places the emphasis on the concrete living individual. This does not replace his earlier work on consciousness; it complements it by showing that the concrete living individual is embedded in a concrete world that impacts on and shapes his capacity to realize the pre-reflective fundamental project 'his' consciousness has chosen.

Secondly, while his early work focuses on the freedom of consciousness, the *Critique of Dialectical Reason* complements this by focusing on the various ways consciousness's concrete embodiment shapes, and is shaped by, its efforts to concretely express itself in the actual world. In his early work, Sartre tends to emphasize consciousness's *ontological* freedom while the *Critique of Dialectical Reason* complements this by emphasizing the ways the individual's social situation impacts on and shapes his efforts to actually express himself in the concrete world. The result is that the *Critique of Dialectical Reason's* discussion of freedom relates to the individual's practical freedom.

This leads to a subtle alteration in Sartre's thought. Whereas *Being and Nothingness's* discussion of the ontological structure of consciousness discloses that consciousness's ontological freedom is never constrained or determined by its social situation, the *Critique of Dialectical Reason's* focus on the individual's *practical freedom* leads Sartre to examine the ways in which the individual's attempts to practically express himself through his concrete embodiment are conditioned by, and in turn condition, his external world.

The practico-inert and the other

To understand how the individual's concrete world shapes and constrains his practical freedom, and indeed to identify why the other is important in this respect, it will be helpful to briefly discuss Sartre's concept of the practico-inert. As noted, the individual is not simply free to determine how he will exist in the actual world. The world encountered by the individual is the direct result of his own and other individual's *praxis* or practical activity. The combination of each individual's praxis creates a practico-inert field that impacts on and shapes the individual's concrete existential possibilities.

The practico-inert describes the objects that emanate from each individual's praxis. These objects combine to form an objective horizon within which the individual exists. As Joseph Catalano explains, 'the practico-inert is the ensemble of rules, laws, codes of behaviour as well as in the entire social complex that tends to keep us on the social level in which we are born' (2007: 51). This objective horizon is not a thought-out planned occurrence; the practico-inert unintentionally results from the combination of each individual's practical activity. The result is that the practico-inert 'proscribes in advance a mode of life, class membership, and economic prospects, which shrink the range of man's spontaneity to mere, insignificant deviations, and it reaches its apex where the individual gives expression to no spontaneity at all, but plays his socioeconomic role in a completely inert or routinised manner' (Yovel, 1979: 488).

But Sartre does not simply hold that the praxis of others constrains the individual's practical freedom. He also appears to hold that the objects created by the individual's own praxis will eventually appear to him as a counter-finality that impacts on his practical freedom. Sartre reaches this conclusion because he implicitly distinguishes between the *act of objectification* that he deems to be the expression of individual freedom and the *being of objectivity* which he insists is alienating. For Sartre, while the activity constitutive of the *act of objectification* allows the individual to express his individuality in objective form, the act of producing something cannot go on indefinitely; eventually, either the project is abandoned or an object is produced. If an object is produced, because it is a static entity, it does not reflect the individual's active back to him. 'In losing their human properties, human projects are engraved in being, their translucidity becomes opacity, their tenuousness thickness, their volatile lightness permanence. They *become being* by losing their quality as lived events; and in so far as they are being they cannot be dissolved into knowledge even if they are deciphered and known' (CDR I: 178). The result is that although the individual's praxis allows him to express his subject freedom, the object created as a result of his praxis must necessarily appear to him as an other that constrains his practical freedom. Individual praxis is, therefore, a double-edge sword: on the one hand it allows the individual to practically express himself; on the other hand, the objects created by his praxis will fold back on the individual to constrain his future practical freedom. Or as Sartre puts it, the object becomes a 'counter-finality' (CDR I: 183).

The concept 'counter-finality' describes the process whereby individual '*praxis* inscribes itself in inertia and inertia returns as inverted *praxis* to dominate the very group which has objectified itself in this worked matter' (CDR I: 336). Whenever the individual acts to overcome a counter-finality, he reorganizes the dynamics of the social field. New relations arise which produce alternative counter-finalities that impact upon the individual. But while he is acting so is every other individual. Each individual produces his own practico-inert structures thereby creating a 'practico-inert field' (CDR I: 324). This field is the objective social world that surrounds each individual. It is composed of individual objective entities such as roads, cars, buildings; collectives such as organizations; and instruments such as road signs, pavements and bus stops whose 'frozen voices [define] how they are to be used' (CDR I: 324).

The combination of these practico-inert structures produces a dynamic tightly integrated web of counter-finalities.

The individual cannot completely free himself from these counter-finalities; every action he produces alters his social environment, while even when he is passive he is being acted on and altered by the activities of other individuals. Thus, while the other may not directly impose himself onto the individual, 'his dispersed *praxis,* totalised by matter, turns back on me in order to transform me' (CDR I: 226). For this reason, 'man has to struggle not only against nature, and against the social environment which has produced him, and against other men, but also against his own action as it becomes other' (CDR I: 124).

But the individual is not simply constituted by his practico-inert field; the ontological freedom of his *consciousness* means he is free to choose the meaning of his world and free to try to actually change his world. Thus, we find the dialectical reciprocity pointed to earlier: the individual finds himself in a specific historical situation with specific structures and possibilities that shape and constrain his practical freedom. It is only by overcoming the constraining pressures of his social world in the form of objective structures, social norms, and the consequences of other's actions, that the individual is able to actually and practically express himself in the world.

The point Sartre is making is that the concrete individual does not and cannot simply choose to express himself in the world as and when he sees fit. The individual encounters resistance to his practical self-expression in the form of an already constituted social world. To secure his practical freedom, he must 'enter into conflict with the situation in which he finds himself' (CDR I: 253). He must overcome the external resistance that emanates from his situation's practico-inert field before he can practically express himself. As Sartre puts it, 'men make their history on the basis of real, prior conditions' (SM: 87)

But when the individual does overcome the constraints of his practico-inert field, he does not become unencumbered from that world; he simply alters the relationship between existing counter-finalities and/or creates new ones that shape and constrain his practical activity. In other words, an individual's practical activity *rearranges* the dynamics of his social environment.

From this it should be clear that following on from his early works' recognition that consciousness lives in relation with other consciousnesses that impact on its existence, the *Critique of Dialectical Reason* recognizes that the concrete individual lives with others that impact on his capacity to actually express himself in the world. For this reason, and because the *Critique of Dialectical Reasons* focuses on the way various group formations constrain or realize the individual's practical freedom, Sartre spends significant time outlining various group formations and what these group social relations entail for the individual's practical freedom. It is to this that I now turn.

Seriality

Sartre maintains that the primordial group formation is the atomized crowd; what he calls *seriality* (CDR I: 687). While each individual of the series directs himself towards the attainment of the same end, they do not consciously act together, nor is there is a common bond between individuals. Individuals of the series work independently from one another to achieve their own ends, which just happen to be the same as their neighbour. Thus, while each individual of the series may be working towards the same end, each is only concerned with whether he attains that end.

Sartre's phenomenological description of the bus stop queue highlights the type of relationship he envisages the series to entail (CDR I: 256–269). Sartre writes that there is a gathering of people at a bus stop outside a church. It consists of numerous individuals of different ages, social classes, and sex who engage with one another in a particular manner. 'These people do not care about or speak to each other and, in general, they do not look at one another; they exist side by side alongside a bus stop' (CDR I: 256). Because each individual is only concerned with his own situation, he comports himself towards the other with an attitude of indifferent coldness. Each worries only about his own being and the activities that he has to undertake to fulfil his work or family commitments.

But while he worries about his own project, each individual exists with others who are also trying to fulfil their own ends. To fulfil their independent projects, each just happens to be engaged in the same activity as others: they must each wait to catch the bus. But the various individuals do not engage with one another; they simply stand next to one another and await the arrival of the bus. It is because they are all engaged in the same activity that they become a collective defined by the activity of waiting for the bus.

While each directs himself to the bus stop and so is defined by his relationship to this externality, he also becomes just another individual waiting for the bus. Because of scarcity there are not enough places for everyone waiting. As was the custom in Paris of Sartre's day, everyone takes a numbered ticket and waits his turn. There is no attempt to determine whose journey is more important and necessary. Each individual loses his individual uniqueness and becomes part of an interchangeable number conforming to the dictates of the bus stop (CDR I: 266). Not only does the ticket ensure that each becomes a faceless being interchangeable with the next, but each comports himself in a manner that is dictated in advance by the rules of the bus stop. No longer is he a free being with his own unique history and purpose; the bus stop alienates him from himself and the other.

Thomas Flynn (1984: 95) rightly notes that series being shares many of the alienating characteristics of the conflictual subject/object social relations described in *Being and Nothingness*. There are three related aspects to the alienation of serial being: first, series being isolates individuals from one another. While the individual lives besides other individuals, he does not engage them in a purposeful common activity. While his activity may bring him into contact with others, the individuals of the series do not attempt to purposefully help each other undertake the common activity their independent projects lead them to.

Secondly, serial being objectifies the individual by making him an interchangeable objective unit: for example, the individual becomes number four in the queue. This strips him of his unique subjectivity. It also leads each to comport himself towards the other in a specific way. Because of scarcity, each individual comes to see the other as a threat to the attainment of their shared goal. For example, the individual that stands at number five in the queue views number four as a threat to the realization of his goal. Similarly, the individual at number four in the queue sees number five as a threat to his practical freedom. With this, each individual becomes alienated, both from himself by virtue of becoming an interchangeable objective unit and, because each sees the other as a threat to his practical freedom, from the other.

This discloses the third aspect of the alienation of serial being: the individual's passive relationship to a dominating external object. As described, serial being is grounded in an external object that externally unifies each individual's intentional activity without creating an organic common bond between the individuals. But this unity is only achieved because the subjective freedom of the individual is usurped and replaced by an interchangeable objectivity that usurps the subjective freedom and circumstances of each individual. Serial being does not take into consideration each individual; it makes each conform to the pre-established dictates of an external other. Through this process, the individual is alienated from his freedom. He is not only turned into an interchangeable object, but, because he adheres to the pre-established rules of the other, does not freely and spontaneously express himself in the actual world.

Alienation is an inherent aspect of serial being and, because Sartre insists this is the primordial way in which individuals exist in relation to each other, is always a potential aspect of the individual's social being. But while the alienation of serial being is the foundation of all group formations, it is not the only group formation possible. While Sartre insists that individuals do not necessarily have to overcome serial being, he does note that serial being *can* be overcome. However, this can only happen if certain material circumstances occur and the individuals involved react to these circumstances in a particular manner. Sartre maintains that an apocalyptic threat may serve as the focal point that unifies the individuals threatened in such a way that they form a free organic and spontaneous unified group (CDR I: 341–241, 357). Sartre calls this group formation the *group-in-fusion*.[2]

The group-in-fusion

The group-in-fusion is the name Sartre gives to an organic, spontaneous, group formation in which each member works towards the attainment of the same end: namely, survival in the face of an external apocalyptic threat. The common intentional activity that results from each individual reacting to the same external threat creates a unified common praxis. This allows each to spontaneously act in a manner that affirms his own subjective freedom without this being usurped or constrained by the activities of other group members.

Whereas the individuals of the series do not take an interest in the ends of the other individuals present but simply *passively* experience and conform to the structures of the external object that they each independently perceive to be necessary to realize their own independent projects, the individuals of the group-in-fusion form an organic unity that *actively* fights against a common external threat (CDR I: 382). Because each individual is spontaneously and freely asserting himself against the same common threat, their individual activities coalesce to form a spontaneous, organic, and unified social formation. This is possible because the relationship between individuals of a group-in-fusion is one of mutual reciprocity in which each recognizes that the other has the same end as it and is crucial to the attainment of their common end. With this, each recognizes that the activities of the other are crucial to the attainment of their shared common goal.

Sartre maintains that the mutual recognition of each other's freedom and the common intentionality of their action create a social relation that is without a fixed hierarchy. Each individual's spontaneous action instantly inspires, re-enforces, and directs the actions of others. As such, each is a leader.

As a form of collective *action,* the group-in-fusion is not a collective entity or consciousness. Sartre argues that to maintain that collective action creates, emanates from, or sustains a collective being that transcends individual praxis would place the individual under the being of an other. Rather than freely express himself, the individual would be subject to the dictates of the collective entity which would alienate him from his free praxis (CDR 2: 16). Instead, Sartre insists that the group-in-fusion is a collective that is grounded in the immanent praxis of each individual. The spontaneous collective action of the group-in-fusion emanates from the fact that the intentionality of each individual is directed towards the same external threat rather than from a unified being that transcends the individuals involved and directs their activities.

To make his point Sartre differentiates between *totalization* and *totality* (CDR I: 45–47). By *totalisation* Sartre means an ongoing process of becoming that is grounded in the spontaneous activity of each individual. By *totality* he means a fixed, self-contained being that directs the activity of each individual. Sartre insists that the group-in-fusion is a *totalisation* that is created and sustained by the continuous spontaneous activity of its individuals; it is not a transcendental totality that subsumes and directs the individual (CDR I: 382).

To account for the unity of individual praxis constitutive of the group-in-fusion without grounding it in a static transcendent entity, Sartre introduces an important concept: the mediating third. Sartre insists that the mediating third creates and sustains the group. However, importantly, the mediating third is not an external entity that glues the members of the group together. Sartre holds that the common focus of each individual and the role that each individual has as a mediating third ensures that the individuals involved spontaneously bind together to form a group.

Each individual of the group is a member of an immediate dyadic relation and a mediating third for another dyadic relation. Its immediate relation with another individual and its role as a mediating third for another immediate dyadic relation ensures that each dyad is united with another. This interlinking creates the unity of the group; or, as Sartre puts it, 'the third party is the human mediation through which the multiplicity of epicentres and ends (identical and separate) organises itself *directly,* as determined by a synthetic objective' (CDR I: 367).

While the mediating third unifies the various individuals under a common intentionality, it does it in such a way that the activity of each individual contributes to the spontaneous development of their collective action. Not only is each individual's activity a spontaneous response to an external threat, but because the collective activity is created and sustained by the activity of each individual, whether he is acting as a member of a dyad or as a meditating third, the activity of the collective group forms a spontaneous and organic unity that is dependent on the activity of each individual involved for its continued existence. As such, at no time does the activity of the group-in-fusion lead to the passive inertia or static being that constrains the activities of each individual and alienates him from his capacity to freely express himself.

Whereas serial being maintains a strict division between the individual and the other, the mediating third overcomes this binary opposition and binds each dyadic social relation together to form an organic cohesive whole. With this, relations between individuals in the group-in-fusion take on a new meaning. 'In the fused group, the third party is my objectivity interiorised. I do not see it in him as other, but as *mine*' (CDR I: 377). The spontaneous common activity of the group-in-fusion overcomes the other-ness of the other and allows the individual to determine that he and the other have the same interests. This allows each to identify with the other in a manner that leads each to trust that his action will be mirrored by the actions of the other. Because he trusts that the other has the same interests as himself, the individual perceives that he can count on the other's support.

But we should not think that just because each individual has the same interests and acts in the same manner that this reduces each to an interchangeable element in the same way that serial being reduces each to the same interchangeable part. While each individual sees himself mirrored in the activity and intention of the other, this does not usurp the unique independence of either individual. Because the activity of each is spontaneously directed towards the negation of the same external threat, it is not subject to predetermined schemas. Each individual's activity emanates from his spontaneous self-expression, which is directed against and thereby unified by the same common external threat.

Because the group-in-fusion allows each individual to freely and spontaneously express himself, while simultaneously overcoming the other-ness of the other, it is not marked by the alienation constitutive of serial being. However, it is important to note that while the group-in-fusion emanates from the alienation of serial being, it does not form in order to overcome this alienation. The overcoming of the alienation of serial being is a secondary, unintended consequence of the group-in-fusion's primary reason for forming: the desire of its members to combat an explicit external threat. As Sartre explains, 'the explosion of revolt, as the liquidation of the collective, does not have its *direct* sources either in alienation revealed by freedom, or in freedom suffered as impotence; there has to be a conjunction of historical circumstances, a definite change in the situation, the danger of death, violence' (CDR I: 401).

But because the group-in-fusion is grounded in exceptional historical circumstances, its demise is inevitable. The group-in-fusion can only exist as long as there is an explicit external threat to its members. Once that threat subsides so too does the group-in-fusion. The disappearance of the group-in-fusion's external threat can lead to one of two transformations in the structure of the group: 1) if the external threat simply disappears the individuals comprising it can simply fall back into the atomized crowd of serial being; or 2) if the threat continues to be *implicit* the members of the group-in-fusion can choose to alter their group formation so that it becomes a sovereign institution (CDR I: 676). However, before it reaches the form of a sovereign institution, and following Sartre's logical progression, it first becomes an *organized group* bound by the pledge.

The organized group

If the external threat becomes implicit, Sartre holds that the members of the group-in-fusion can put in place standing measures, such as a democratic organization structure and the promise to care for and affirm the other's practical freedom by means of 'the pledge' (CDR I: 418), that will enable them to rekindle the loose knit spontaneous organic unity of the group-in-fusion if the implicit external threat once again becomes explicit (CDR I: 412).

While the group-in-fusion is a spontaneous organic unity, the pledge of the organized group mediates the members of the group and binds each to the other. This creates a semi-permanent structure which is maintained by each individual's promise to all its members that he will protect them from an external threat. 'In the order: 'Let us swear,' he claims an objective guarantee from the other third party that he will never become other: whoever gives *me* this guarantee *thereby* protects me, as far as he is concerned, from the danger that *being-other may come to me from the other'* (CDR I: 421).

Sartre recognizes that the pledge can take numerous forms; it does not necessarily have to be a formal statement of intent (CDR I: 419). However, while the pledge can be explicit or implicit, each form is directed towards the same end: the promise to act together to protect and affirm the other's practical freedom from an explicit external threat. But Sartre is quick to warn that the pledge is not a social contract. Unlike the social contract, the pledge does not seek 'to describe the basis of particular societies' (CDR I: 420). The pledge is simply a *'practical device'* (CDR I: 420) which each individual uses to secure the other's guarantee that he will protect the individual from an external threat.

Importantly, the pledge does not constrain the individual's freedom by predetermining how he will act towards the other. The pledge simply allows each individual to promise the other that he will act in a way that cares for and affirms the other's practical freedom. It is up to the individual to decide the actual content of his actions as and when the external threat arises. By promising to care for and affirm each other's practical freedom, each pledged member becomes a brother or sister to other members (CDR I: 437).

By trusting the other to care for his practical freedom, the individuals of the organized group come to recognize that the other is not a threat to their practical freedom. Each recognizes that the other extends his practical freedom by: 1) helping him secure his practical freedom against their common, implicit threat; and 2) contributing to the realization of his independent projects by either volunteering to help him attain his end or purposefully not creating impediments that would prevent him from achieving his ends (NE: 279).

The pledge is not, therefore, simply a superficial verbal statement; through the pledge and the concrete acts of support it instantiates, each member of the organized group becomes confident that the other will support and affirm his practical freedom. The pledge brings each member of the organized group to recognize and express solidarity with the other's practical freedom. The result of this reciprocated solidarity is a close knit group in which each member comports himself freely in relation to the other, supports the other's independent projects, and perceives the other to be an extension of, rather than a constraint on, his own practical freedom. For this reason, 'members [of the organized group] act in concert as a "we"' (Boileau, 2004: 78).

While the individuals of the group-in-fusion support one another as they each act together to combat the same external threat, their common activity is contingent on the existence of this explicit external threat. Not only do members of the group-in-fusion simply focus on a unitary end (survival in the face of an external threat) which prevents them from choosing what end that they, as a group, will work together to achieve, but there is a sense in which the solidarity engendered by the common external threat encountered by each member of the group-in-fusion is not a voluntarily action but is one that is thrust upon each member by their contingent circumstance. In contrast, the pledge of the organized group provides a standing promise that each member will protect and care for the freedom of the other irrespective of whether there is an immediate, common, and explicit threat.

Furthermore, by voluntarily expressing solidarity with the other's practical freedom, and due to the open, democratic nature of the organized group, it would appear that members of the organized group are free to choose the end towards which their group activity is directed; their collective action is not so constrained by the need to fight an immediate, explicit, external threat. For these reasons, I understand that it is the organized group and not, as is frequently argued, the group-in-fusion that: 1) best allows individuals to form a common bond in which each expresses solidarity with the other's attempts to be practically free; and 2) facilitates the achievement of practical projects that express and extend the individual's practical freedom in ways that would not be possible if he acted on his own.

At this point, however, I want to suggest an important, if often ignored, relation between the pledge and the conversion. This will further validate my argument that the *Critique of Dialectical Reason* complements, and is dependent on, Sartre's early works. Because Sartre maintains that individuals can only come to reflectively recognize, respect, care for, and affirm the other's practical freedom in the way necessary for a social relation based on the pledge to exist, the logic of his argument would appear to suggest that the pledge and the organized group created as a result of it are only a possibility once all potential members of the organized group have chosen to undergo conversion.

Because conversion brings consciousness to reflectively understand that the other is another subject with its own independent project and is necessary for the full disclosure of its being, the converted consciousness no longer seeks to simply affirm its subjectivity in opposition to the other. Conversion brings consciousness to empathize and express 'solidarity' (NE: 479) with the other's situated freedom. This sense of empathy and solidarity manifests itself in consciousness's reflective support for and affirmation of the other's attempts to secure its practical freedom (NE: 279, 282, 330, 508).

This is important for Sartre's discussion of the pledge because, as noted, the pledge brings the concrete individual to express solidarity with the other and explicitly affirm that he will care for the other's practical freedom in the way that Sartre has previously argued is only a possibility for the converted consciousness. Thus, while Sartre never explicitly makes this connection, I want to suggest that, because it is only the social relations of converted consciousnesses that allow each individual to reflectively recognize, respect, care for, and affirm the other's practical freedom in the way necessary for the creation and continuation of an organized group, it is only once all potential members of the group have chosen to undergo the conversion to a pre-reflective fundamental project that has the affirmation of freedom as its end that each member can open himself to the other in the way necessary for the pledge and the organized group it instantiates to exist.

But sustaining its loose but integrated structure requires the pledged group to organize itself into different functions. This organization allows the group to maintain a permanent structure that allows each to express his subjectivity, while also being sufficiently closely knit that, should it be required, the members can recreate the dynamics of a group-in-fusion. The notion of an organization has two functions: 'the word "organisation" refers both to the internal action by which a group defines its structures and to the group itself as a structured activity in the practical field, either on worked matter or on other groups' (CDR I: 446). The organization defines the group members to external non-members, while also providing each individual with a particular differentiated function. This differentiation unifies the organization while also allowing practical problems to be solved.

However, Sartre maintains that fulfilling a specific function does not constrain the individual's practical freedom because: 1) each voluntarily fulfils the activities of his function; 2) the common activity of the organized group protects him from the external threat's annihilation of his practical freedom; and 3) being a member of an organized group allows him to work together with others to achieve ends he would not be able to achieve if he worked on his own (CDR I: 467). While it may appear that fulfilling a fixed function alienates the individual from his practical freedom, Sartre explains that 'this alienation (at least at this level) is only apparent: my action develops, on the basis of a *common power*, towards a *common objective*; the fundamental moment which is characteristic of the actualisation of the power and the objectification of the *praxis* is that of free individual practice' (CDR I: 458).

From this, we see that the organized group is not a transcendent other that simply imposes itself on its members and alienates them from their practical freedom; the organized group is so structured that the individual contributes to its common praxis by freely fulfilling his specific function. This creates a fundamental difference between the internal structure of the group-in-fusion and the organized group. Because all members of the group-in-fusion are spontaneously focused on the same immediate end (the overcoming of an immediate threat), it lacks a coherent organizational structure; each individual simply acts in the way he thinks is most appropriate to his immediate situation. In contrast, the semi-permanence of the organized group creates an effective organizational structure that co-ordinates each individual's praxis and allows each to freely express himself within the limits of his function. This co-ordination allows each member of the organized group to contribute to the common activity that realizes his own and other's practical freedom.

Furthermore, each member of the organized group reflectively understands that the organized group is grounded in his own individual praxis. Each realizes that it is he who directs the group, shapes the group, and determines the common praxis of the group; the group does not appear as an other than directs his activity. As Sartre explains, 'the only direct and specific action of the organized group, therefore, is its organization and perpetual reorganization, in other words, its actions on its members. By this, of course, I mean that common individuals settle the internal structures of the community rather than that the group-in-itself imposes them as categories' (CDR I: 463).

But while the organized group allows each individual to effectively combat an external threat, the goal of each individual's praxis is not the group; it is the common threat that necessitates the creation of the organized group. To privilege the group would be to risk turning it into a transcendent totality that dictates how each individual is to act. This would alienate the individual from his practical freedom because his actions would be predetermined by the group. For this reason, Sartre insists that the organized group exists to further the individual's practical freedom; the individual does not exist to serve the ends of the organized group.

The organized group is, therefore, emblematic of the sort of spontaneous, organized, democratic, and fundamentally open group formation T-Storm Heter (2008: 121) sees Sartre as defending in the *Critique of*

Dialectical Reason. It is precisely because the organized group enhances rather than constrains the individual's practical freedom that Sartre implicitly holds that each individual's practical and political activity should be directed towards becoming a member of an organized group.

However, while being a member of an organized group enhances the individual's practical freedom, Sartre recognizes that the organized group will, logically, give rise to structures that will subsequently constrain the individual's practical freedom. The different functions of the organized group help establish a permanent unifying common bond between all its members. But while the organized group privileges the individual's praxis over the function, the reification of these functions will constrain the individual's practical freedom. Rather than focusing on the organized group as a form of common praxis in opposition to an external threat, the function of the group can become reified and valued for itself. Put differently, because the organized group is maintained by each individual fulfilling his specific function, it may come to be that the function is perceived to be the essential aspect of the group and the individual taken to be the inessential aspect. When this occurs, the individual is taken to be an interchangeable monad in an overarching *totality*. Sartre calls this atrophied group formation *the institution*.

Institutions

Institutions constrain the individual's practical freedom because the function of the institution becomes more important than the individual fulfilling that function (CDR I: 600). Two consequences arise from this: 1) the individual is no longer perceived to be unique; he is seen to be a mere object capable of being replaced by another individual; and 2) the individual is prevented from freely expressing himself in the actual world because his activity is predetermined by the dictates and norms of the function he fulfils in the institution. Contrary to the function of the organized group, the function of the institution does not allow the individual to freely and spontaneously choose how to fulfil the tasks constitutive of his function; it dictates in advance how he is to act.

Furthermore, the privileging of the function over the individual ensures that individuals do not spontaneously and freely interact with one another. Each individual recognizes that he is working towards a common goal with other individuals, but is prevented from freely interacting with others because their interaction is mediated by the formal functions, structures, and norms of the institution. Because the institution constrains the individual within predetermined boundaries, rules, and structures, while also dictating how each individual will interact with the other, it does not affirm, but constrains, the individual's practical freedom. It is, therefore, a 'degraded group' (CDR I: 600).

The specialization inherent to the activities of each member of the institution means that each individual is not only segregated from other members of the institution that do not engage in his specialization, but also tends to adopt a specific manner constituted by specific predetermined mannerisms, behaviours, actions, and ways of being. He becomes what Sartre calls an 'organisation man' (CDR I: 605).

Organization man defines himself in terms of his function in the organization. His existence revolves around freely subordinating himself to the role he fulfils in the organization. However, while the individual of the *organized group* freely adopts the behaviours and activities required by his role, there is still a direct and recognized relationship between his privileged position and his function. This ensures that the ways the activities of the function of the organized group are fulfilled is freely determined by the individual. In contrast, the function of the institution predetermines how the individual is to act to a greater degree. Because of this, the institution alienates the individual from his free spontaneity, constricts his actions, and makes him impotent in regard to the content of the function he fulfils.

But there is another aspect to the way the structure of institution alienates the individual from his practical freedom. According to Sartre, the different functions of the institution form a hierarchy headed by a sovereign. The sovereign has overall authority; he is the focal point that directs and orientates individual's actions (CDR I: 607–609).

Rather than choosing how he will live, organization man orientates his being around the dictates of another: the sovereign. As Sartre explains, 'provided that the goal of the sovereign really is the common object of the group, no one will have any aim other than serving the sovereign himself, and everyone will pursue the common aim, not because it is common, but because it is the object of free sovereign *praxis*' (CDR I: 631). By fleeing from his freedom, organization man is the epitome of someone who lives in bad faith.

The institution alienates the individual from his practical freedom because the sovereign alone determines the content of the objective structures and predetermined behavioural schemas that pre-define the individual's actions. Alienation is, therefore, a constitutive aspect of the individual's experience of the institution. Not only does his immediate function alienate him from his practical freedom, but the overall structure of the institution compounds this by predetermining how he is to live, what he is to do, and when he is to do it.

While the isolation inherent to the institution shares certain similarities with that of series being, in many ways the alienation of the institution is worse. While both the series and the institution are ways of being that constrain the individual's practical freedom, it becomes clear through Sartre's description that the institution creates far more insidious and complete forms of alienation, domination, and constraint than are found in the series. While series being directs individual activity, it still leaves the individual with the option of directing himself towards the external object in certain non-determined ways. For example, the individual at the bus stop could alter his attitude towards others, or he could engage them in conversation. However, Sartre implicitly insists that such is the constraint and domination found in the institution that its structures severely constrain each individual's attitude towards the other *and*, more importantly, each individual's capacity to interact with the other. Because the way of being instantiated by membership of an institution is more pervasive, constrained, and debilitated than the ways of being found in other group formations, it is membership of an institution that most constrains an individual's practical freedom.

But it must be remembered that Sartre's criticisms of the constraints imposed on the individual's practical freedom by the structure of the institution do not apply to all group formations. Other group formations, most notably the group-in-fusion and the organized group, do not constrain the individual's practical freedom; they contribute to its realization. Indeed, given that his entire *oeuvre* is concerned with the affirmation of the individual's ontological and practical freedom, it is not controversial to say that Sartre is implicitly defending those group formations that enhance the individual's practical freedom. While he recognizes that it is up to the individual to choose to affirm his own practical freedom, Sartre holds that membership of an organic, democratic, and open group formation, such as is found in the group-in-fusion and especially the organized group, is essential if the individual is to become practically free.

Importantly for later chapters, however, it is critical to remember that while Sartre maintains that membership of certain group formations can enhance the individual's *practical freedom*, his insistence that consciousness is ontologically monadic ensures that being a member of certain group formations is not a necessary or constitutive aspect of consciousness's *ontological freedom*. While Sartre maintains that being a member of certain group formations can enhance the individual's *practical freedom*, he maintains that consciousness is ontologically free irrespective of whether it belongs to these groups. This is a subtle but fundamental difference to Hegel. As will be outlined in subsequent chapters, Hegel maintains that membership of certain groups is necessary to not only secure the individual's practical freedom, but to also realize the ontological potential implicit to the individual's ontological structure. For this reason, Hegel maintains that membership of certain groups has *ontological* importance for the individual.

However, before I turn to engage fully with Hegel, it may be helpful to provide a summary of Sartre's conception of authenticity. According to Sartre, being authentic requires that the individual, and everyone he practically engages with, fulfil the following conditions: 1) he must effect the conversion to a pre-reflective fundamental project that leads him to reflectively understand that he is ontologically nothing/free; 2) he must reflectively affirm his ontological nothingness by reflectively understanding that he lacks a fixed ontological identity and is not constrained by predetermined moral rules; 3) he must reflectively understand and accept that he always lives an objective body in a concrete situation; 4) he must reflectively accept responsibility for his situation and previous actions; 5) he must reflectively live with the anguish that arises when he reflectively understands that his ontological nothingness means he is free; 6) he must reflectively choose a mode of being that reflectively affirms his own, and the other's, practical freedom; 7) he must reflectively understand that, because he must continuously affirm his chosen pre-reflective fundamental project, he will ultimately fail no matter what he does; and 8) he must reflectively affirm his freedom despite reflectively knowing that whatever he does, he will ultimately fail. Sartrean authenticity is, therefore, no small feat; consciousness is alienated when any one of these conditions is not met. With this in mind, it is time to turn to Hegel.

5
Hegel's *Phenomenology of Spirit*

Hegel's ontological analysis of human being differs significantly from Sartre's. This ensures that, while both thinkers recognize that alienation is a significant existential problem, they differ in terms of how it arises and the ways in which it impacts on human being.

Both do agree, however, that understanding the human being first requires an understanding of consciousness. It is in his *Phenomenology of Spirit* that we find Hegel's views on the relationship between alienation and consciousness. In this text, Hegel describes the logical process consciousness must go through to fully understand its ontological structure. Prior to arriving at this point, Hegel holds that consciousness is, in some way, alienated.

However, the *Phenomenology of Spirit* is a notoriously difficult book to understand. Such is its difficulty that it has been subject to numerous, sometimes contradictory, interpretations. Many of these emanate from a failure to understand the purpose and method of this difficult text. The purpose of this chapter is to correct these misinterpretations by showing what Hegel's phenomenological development of consciousness is, and is not, trying to achieve.

Hegel and phenomenology

Hegel starts by recognizing that philosophical thought usually begins by insisting on a specific understanding of consciousness and developing an argument from this understanding. Sartre employs this method to develop his argument from the foundational claim that consciousness is ontologically nothing. However, Hegel argues that the problem with undertaking philosophy in this manner is that, because each argument fails to justify its assumptions or foundational claim, each is ultimately unable to justify its conclusion(s).

For Hegel, the philosophical consciousness cannot simply assert that its conception of the truth is superior to the truth outlined by natural science, religion or art; it must demonstrate this (LA: 27). Only then can the philosophical consciousness be certain that its conception of the truth is legitimate. *Phenomenology* is the method Hegel uses to justify his account of consciousness and show the non-philosophical, natural consciousness that it is only the philosophical consciousness that is able to truly understand the issue under discussion. But what does Hegel understand by phenomenology?

While Sartre maintains that *phenomenology* is a *method* of *philosophy* and so collapses phenomenology into philosophy, Hegel maintains that *phenomenology* and *philosophy* are very different forms of inquiry. If we are to accurately understand Hegel's thought, it is necessary to understand the difference and, indeed, the relationship between Hegel's phenomenology and his philosophy.

The fundamental difference between Hegel's phenomenology and his philosophy lies in their different *purposes*. While Hegel's *philosophy* outlines the truth of a specific issue, the purpose of his *phenomenology* is to show that in order to know the truth of an issue, that issue must be thought about in a specific way. It will turn out that it is only the philosophical consciousness that allows consciousness to think about the issue under discussion in the way that discloses the truth of that issue, but consciousness only realizes this after it undertakes a specific journey. For Hegel, *phenomenology* legitimizes the need for *philosophy*, while also showing the manner in which the *philosophical* consciousness must think about an issue to fully understand that issue.

But it may be objected that in Hegel's *Philosophy of Mind* there is a section on *phenomenology* (PM: 153–158). Does the discussion of phenomenology in this philosophical text not invalidate my claim that phenomenology and philosophy are, for Hegel, distinct forms of inquiry? Darrel Moellendorf addresses this point by arguing that there is a constitutive and complementary link between Hegel's phenomenological description of consciousness and the *psychological* description of consciousness undertaken in the *Philosophy of Mind*. Moellendorf explains that whereas Hegel's phenomenological analysis describes consciousness's experience of its object, the psychological analysis described in Hegel's *Philosophy of Mind* 'accounts for the mental processes constitutive of that experience' (1992: 7). Thus, while Hegel's phenomenological analysis discloses consciousness's experience of its object, the *Philosophy of Mind*'s psychological description complements and deepens Hegel's phenomenological analysis by disclosing the complex mental processes involved in that phenomenological experience.

Because Hegel insists phenomenology demonstrates and justifies the need for philosophy, contra Sartre, he does not simply assert that his philosophical view of the topic under discussion is true. He justifies his *philosophical* argument by using the certainty gained from his *phenomenology* to show that the issue under discussion can only be fully understood if it is thought about in the way he does.

However, Hegel's phenomenology only legitimizes the need for philosophy; it does not provide it with content. Hegel's *philosophy* is grounded in the certainty the philosophical consciousness won from the phenomenological development of consciousness and shows, by starting with the most abstract and minimalist conception of the concept under discussion, that it *logically* leads to his understanding of that concept. For example, Hegel's *Science of Logic* starts with pure, abstract being and shows, through a long process, how this turns into the concrete, Absolute Idea. Similarly, Hegel's discussion of freedom in the *Philosophy of Right* starts with the most abstract conception of freedom and demonstrates that for freedom to be fully realized requires that the individual comport himself in a specific way in a specific state.

While Hegel's phenomenological development of consciousness and general philosophy have a predetermined end, insofar as, in the former, Hegel aims to legitimize the need for philosophy, while, in the latter, he explicitly argues for a position, Hegel does not legitimize these ends by simply appealing to an external standard or a presupposed foundation. The phenomenological development of consciousness shows that it is consciousness's own experience that legitimates the need for philosophy, while Hegel's philosophy shows that unfolding the issue under discussion in-line with the logic of its concept leads to his understanding of the issue. The important point is that Hegel's phenomenology and philosophy legitimate themselves through recourse to their own development, rather than through recourse to presuppositions, an external foundation, or subjective intuition.

While Sartre maintains that consciousness's ontological structure is defined by nothingness and uses this definition of consciousness as a transcendent standard against which to compare and judge whether consciousness reflectively affirms this in its actual mode of being, Hegel's analysis of consciousness's ontological structure discloses that consciousness has an implicit, historically sensitive, ontological potential that unfolds and develops to full realization in and through consciousness's concrete experiences. Thus, whereas Sartre separates consciousness's *ontological structure* and its *experiences*, Hegel maintains that it is only through its concrete experiences that the ontological potential implicit to consciousness's ontological structure is, and can be, fully realized.

We will see what this means as we develop, but it is perhaps helpful to return to Hegel's *Phenomenology of Spirit* and note that its purpose is three-fold: 1) to defend and legitimize philosophy as *the* form of consciousness that has privileged access to the truth; 2) to show that, contrary to popular opinion, philosophy cannot simply be immediately undertaken by all; there is a developmental process that consciousness *must* undertake if it is to think about an issue in the manner that will allow it to know the truth of that issue; and 3) to demonstrate the path that consciousness must traverse if it is to bring itself to the form of self-understanding that will allow it to fully understand itself and its object. As we will see, this journey involves a process of self-development that culminates in the overcoming of consciousness's self-alienation. To achieve its aims, Hegel uses a particular method. Failure to understand this method, or the various actors involved, will ensure his thought is misunderstood.

The method of Hegel's *Phenomenology of Spirit*

The *Phenomenology of Spirit* describes the *logical* movement consciousness must make to fully understand its ontological structure. Contrary to Sartre's assertion (CDR 1: 24), the process is not a history and so does not describe the actual movement that consciousness has made; although this is not to say that it does not allude to historical examples to illuminate the discussion.

The initial problem Hegel has, however, is that, because he aims to show the need for philosophy, he is unable to use philosophical thought to construct a predetermined schema or presuppose any external standard with which to legitimize the need for, or the content of, his philosophy. As William Maker notes, Hegel cannot simply appeal to the passions, God, the being of beings, economics, tradition, biological reproduction, or the will to power to justify or legitimize his philosophical thought. 'Hegel's systematic philosophy rejects all such foundations, and his critique of foundationalism opens the way for the creation of an alternative conception and system of reason, one whose claim to authority rests solely on its character as having articulated concepts and principles which can be seen to be the exclusive determinations of autonomous reason' (1994: 37). Hegel recognizes that consciousness cannot justify its argument by simply stating it is correct or appealing to an arbitrary, external, foundational source; consciousness itself must legitimize the need for the philosophical consciousness.

To achieve this, Hegel starts with the most abstract and minimal shape of consciousness and traces the movement consciousness must *logically* make if it is to fully understand its ontological structure. It is important to note, however, that the developmental process necessary for consciousness to fully understand itself need not *actually* be completed. Actual consciousness may not be willing to develop itself any further than a specific point, it may lose faith in the process, or it may simply die (PS: 51). Nevertheless, while the *actual* attainment of the philosophical consciousness may not be achieved, Hegel demonstrates that it is a *logical* possibility (Pinkard, 1996: 12).

As noted, however, Hegel's understanding of consciousness's ontological structure is very different to Sartre's. While Sartre insists that consciousness is always consciousness-of-something and so recognizes a link between consciousness and its object, he is very clear that its object is not part of consciousness's ontological structure. Consciousness is ontologically opposed to all forms of objectivity. In contrast, Hegel insists that consciousness's ontological structure consists of two aspects. 'Consciousness is, on the one hand, consciousness of the object, and on the other, consciousness of itself; consciousness of what it is for the True, and consciousness of its knowledge of its truth' (PS: 54). Put differently, there is a subjective and an objective aspect to consciousness's ontological structure. Because consciousness consists of a subjective and an objective aspect, it is, in actuality, not ontologically opposed to its object; consciousness and its object are ontologically entwined.

Contrary to Sartre's understanding (NE: 498), however, this does not mean that Hegel collapses the object into the subject. While Hegel maintains that consciousness's ontological structure is composed of a subjective *and* an objective aspect, its object is both an aspect of consciousness's ontological structure and a real object that exists independently from consciousness. Initially, however, consciousness does not realize this, takes its object to be purely other than itself, and so is alienated from itself.

Secondly, the different ways that Hegel and Sartre conceptualize consciousness's ontological structure lead to very different understandings of consciousness's relationship to its intentional object. While Sartre argues that consciousness is always consciousness-of-something, his insistence that consciousness is ontologically nothing discloses that its intentional object is always ontologically opposed to consciousness. In contrast, while Hegel agrees that consciousness is intentional, insofar as it is directed towards an ontologically independent object, he maintains that, because consciousness is dependent on a relationship to objectivity, its intentional object is an aspect of its ontological structure. Put simply, while Hegel and Sartre agree that consciousness is intentionally directed towards an object, Sartre argues that consciousness remains *ontologically* independent from its intentional object, whereas Hegel holds that, because consciousness's existence depends on an intentional relation, its intentional object is an aspect of consciousness's *ontological* structure.

Thirdly, the two thinkers conceptualize the fundamental relation between consciousness and its object differently. While Sartre's analysis maintains that objectivity is *ontologically* prior to consciousness and so insists that a condition of consciousness's existence is that it pre-reflectively nihilates being-in-itself, Hegel's insistence that consciousness is a synthetic unity of subjectivity and objectivity ensures that, for him, consciousness and its object exist in a relationship of dialectical entwinement where consciousness cannot exist without an intentional relationship to an independent object and objects are only ever objects for a consciousness. Thus, whereas Sartre's analysis of consciousness's ontological structure is grounded in the subject/object dichotomy, Hegel's maintains that consciousness and its object exist in a relation of ontological entwinement.

The different ways Hegel and Sartre conceptualize consciousness's *ontological* relation to objectivity also lead to different understandings of consciousness's relation to its objective situation. While Sartre recognizes that consciousness is always embodied in an objective situation, he does not maintain that its objective situation is an aspect of consciousness's ontological structure. Consciousness's ontological nothingness allows it to choose how it will live its objective situation. Because consciousness is ontologically nothing, it always remains *ontologically* other than its objective situation, despite always being *experientially* embedded in an objective situation.

While Hegel agrees with Sartre that consciousness is always embedded in a social situation, he rejects the distinction Sartre makes between consciousness's experience and its ontological structure and instead holds that consciousness's ontological structure develops through its experience. As such, Hegel maintains that consciousness's objective situation is a constitutive aspect of its *ontological structure*.

However, Hegel does not reduce consciousness to its objective situation; he agrees with Sartre that the subjectivity of consciousness ensures it is always different from its objective surroundings. Thus, while Sartre insists that consciousness is always *ontologically* other than its concrete situation, Hegel traverses a thin line that maintains that while consciousness is ontologically embedded in an objective situation, it is not synonymous with its objective situation.

The difference between the two thinkers on this issue seems to be that while Sartre's consciousness is a subjective freedom that chooses how it will live its situated body, Hegel's insistence that consciousness is a living synthesis of subjectivity and objectivity means that, for him, consciousness is ontologically entwined with its body and world in a way that is missing from Sartre's account. The consequence is that Hegel holds that consciousness's ontological structure is shaped by its world to a greater degree than Sartre recognizes.

The crucial difference between both thinkers is that Sartre maintains that, irrespective of its experiences, consciousness's ontological structure is always the same, in that it is defined by nothingness and is structured around the pre-reflective/reflective division, whereas Hegel maintains that consciousness's experiences form, shape, and develop its ontological structure. Thus, while Sartre recognizes that it is necessary to identify and analyse consciousness's objective situation when seeking to understand its *experiences*, he insists it is not necessary to understand consciousness's facticity to understand consciousness's *ontological structure*; irrespective of its actual situation, consciousness is always ontologically nothing. In contrast, because Hegel maintains that consciousness's *ontological structure* alters and develops with and through its *experience,* he insists that consciousness's ontological structure can only be understood if its objective situation is understood. By understanding consciousness's situation to be an aspect of its ontological structure, Hegel understands that consciousness is *ontologically embedded* in its world; it is not the ontologically unencumbered monad Sartre insists it is.

Because Hegel maintains that objectivity is an aspect of consciousness's ontological structure, and while he recognizes that consciousness must come to explicitly understand this, he is able to insist that consciousness and its object are not simply opposed to one another. Hegel's phenomenological development of consciousness shows that the way consciousness comes to truly understand itself is by experiencing the failure that comes from trying to understand itself, and its relation to its object, through the subject/object dichotomy. The experience of the failure that comes from understanding its relation to its object in strictly oppositional terms brings consciousness to understand that its object is an aspect of its ontological structure.

Thus, while the paradox of Sartre's analysis reveals the tension at the heart of his account insofar as the *experiential* level of his analysis recognizes that, if consciousness is to be authentic, it must overcome the subject/object opposition and recognize that it's other can extend its practical freedom, the ontological level of his analysis undermines this by being structured around the subject/object opposition. In contrast, Hegel demonstrates the fallacy of this dichotomy and shows that for consciousness to fully understand its ontological structure requires that it overcome this dichotomy and understand that it and its object are ontologically, not just experientially, entwined. However, Hegel insists that no external entity, predetermined schema, or a priori imperative can make consciousness understand this. Only its own activities can bring consciousness to understand itself.

Consciousness's initial failure to understand that it is ontologically entwined with its intentional object leads Hegel to insist that there is, initially, a distinction between the object as it appears *for-consciousness* and the object as it is *in-itself*. While this distinction results from consciousness's failure to properly understand itself, it also contains the means that will allow it to judge for itself when it has fully understood both itself and its object. Because the object as it appears *for-consciousness* and the object as it is *in-itself* belong to the same consciousness, consciousness itself is able to determine 'whether its knowledge of the object corresponds to the object or not' (PS: 54). It does this by comparing whether the way the object appears *for-consciousness* corresponds to the way the object is *in-itself*.

Because each shape of consciousness *initially* maintains that the two correspond, there must be a mediating aspect that allows consciousness to determine whether the two aspects of each shape of itself do actually correspond. Hegel calls this mediating aspect 'experience' (PS: 55). Thus, consciousness initially understands that its object, as it is *in-itself*, takes on a particular form. However, the experience of its object reveals to consciousness that what it previously took its object to be in-itself was only *for-consciousness*. There is, therefore, a discrepancy between the way consciousness initially understood its object and the way consciousness's experience of its object discloses its object to actually be. If consciousness is logical, it alters its understanding of the object to accord with the way its experience of the object discloses the object to be. This continues until consciousness's experience brings it to the shape of itself where its experience discloses that the way its object appears *for-consciousness* corresponds to what its object is *in-itself.*

It is not the case, therefore, that, if there is a discrepancy between its understanding and experience of its object, 'consciousness must [simply] alter its understanding of the object' (PS: 54). We must not think that Hegel is describing a process where there is a transcendent object that consciousness gradually gains a better understanding of. By insisting on a constitutive link between consciousness and its object, Hegel is able to maintain that when consciousness alters its self-understanding, this also alters its object. Thus, when the experience of its object discloses that a particular form of self-understanding fails to allow it to fully understand its object, consciousness alters its self-understanding, which also alters its object, to accord with its experience. 'Hence it comes to pass for consciousness that what it previously took to be the *in-itself* is not an *in-itself,* or that it was only an in-itself *for consciousness*' (PS: 54).

Consciousness now has *two* objects; 'one is the first *in-itself,* the second is the *being-for-consciousness of this in-itself*' (PS: 55). Consciousness now knows that the way it initially understood its first object did not disclose what that object actually was. However, consciousness does not simply stop here. Because consciousness must have an object before it in order to be consciousness, it is driven to adopt a new relation to an object. This transition is not simply a random occurrence; consciousness builds on the understanding it has gained from its previous experience. 'This is the moment of transition from the first object and the knowledge about it, to the other object [...] [K]nowledge of the first object, or the being-*for*-consciousness of the first in-itself, itself becomes the second object' (PS: 55).

This movement from the first object to the second occurs through the process of '*determinate negation*' (PS: 51). While negation simply involves consciousness negating its object so that while it once was, it no longer is; determinate negation is more complex. It describes the process whereby consciousness negates, preserves, and builds on the truth of its past experiences. This allows consciousness to gradually learn about and so gain a better understanding of its object. For this reason, Hegel explains that the later 'stages are more concrete. They presuppose the characters of the preceding stages and develop them further. Each following stage in a development is thus richer, augmented in virtue of these characters, and accordingly more concrete' (HP: 82).

While Hegel and Sartre agree that consciousness's ontological structure is intimately and constitutively tied to negativity, they differ in terms of what this negative is and means for consciousness. For Sartre, consciousness's act of nihilation is purely negative; its nihilating activity allows consciousness to remain free from its intentional object. Hegel's determinate negation, however, is a process of negation that simultaneously allows consciousness to develop its self-understanding. The developmental aspect of determinate negation is crucial to the journey that Hegel shows consciousness must go through to fully understand its ontological structure. By understanding that consciousness's act of negation is not simply a negative act, but can contribute positively to its existence by allowing it to learn something about itself, Hegel's account of negativity recognizes and goes beyond Sartre's (Butler, 1987: 132).

Determinate negation allows Hegel to show that, if it is logical, consciousness will not repeat its past mistakes by re-adopting shapes of itself that its experience has taught it do not allow it to fully understand its object; its experience allows it to gradually obtain a better understanding of its object. Consciousness then sees if its experience of this new understanding of its object allows it to fully understand its object. But it must be remembered that, because consciousness and its object are ontologically entwined, an alteration in consciousness's understanding of its object also entails and requires an alteration and development in consciousness's self-understanding. This continues until consciousness does discover the shape of itself that allows it to fully understand itself and its object.

Thus, Hegel does not *deduce* the movement from one shape of consciousness to the next as Robert Pippin (1989: 94–99) maintains, nor are the various shapes random, nor are they, as Philip Kain (2005: 11) contends, strategically chosen by Hegel to support his overall attempt to legitimize the philosophical consciousness. Consciousness engages in a journey in which it learns the route along the way by building on the partial truth of each of its previous forms of self-understanding in each of the subsequent shapes of itself it adopts. It is exactly this process that Hans-Georg Gadamer points towards when he explains that 'strictly speaking, the new content is not deduced, but has proven itself already to be that which endures the severity of contradiction and maintains itself as one therein, namely, the self of thought' (1976: 20).

It is only by passing through numerous shapes of itself that do not allow it to fully understand itself and its object that consciousness will arrive at the shape of itself that does allow it to fully understand itself and its object. The knowledge gained from its experience of a particular shape of itself can be *positive* knowledge, insofar as it allows consciousness to better understand itself and its object immediately. Alternatively, it can be *negative* knowledge, insofar as while the shape of consciousness did not provide consciousness with positive knowledge of its object as it actually is, consciousness now knows that what it and its object truly are, is not disclosed by that shape's self-understanding. While each failure of consciousness may not immediately lead it to fully understand its ontological structure, each failure does allow consciousness to learn something about itself. Jean Hyppolite is, therefore, perfectly correct to emphasize that Hegel 'takes seriously the pain, the work, and the patience of the negative' (1997: 103). This is perhaps one of the most original, forceful, and too often overlooked insights of his analysis: the experience of the negative is not necessarily simply negative; it can positively contribute to our self-understanding.

But this process is not *logically* infinite; there is an end point. Daniel Berthold-Bond explains that 'thought is not simply motion, but *directed* motion, a teleological development from potentiality to actuality, from the implicit and immediate and abstract to the explicit and mediated and concrete' (1989: 104). Hegel explains that 'the *goal* is as necessarily fixed for knowledge as the serial progression; it is the point where knowledge no longer needs to go beyond itself, where knowledge finds itself, where Notion corresponds to object and object to Notion' (PS: 51). Logically, consciousness's failed experiences will lead it to develop in such a way that it finally adopts a shape of itself where its experience shows that the way the object appears to it corresponds to the way the object is in-itself. At this point, consciousness fully understands the ontological structure of its object, and by extension, itself.

However, while it is consciousness that 'provides its own criterion from within itself' (PS: 53), thereby ensuring that it is its own activity that allows it to fully understand itself and its object, the movement between the various shapes of itself appears to *consciousness* as contingent and random. Consciousness does not recognize the process of determinate negation that allows it to learn what it and its object truly are. The logical movement between the different shapes of consciousness is made explicit by the 'we.'

The we describes the perspective of two actors: Hegel the phenomenologist and us, the reader. Because consciousness is busy living its life, it is not able to see the *logical* connection between the various shapes of itself. It is only the phenomenologists of the *we*, who are looking at the overall phenomenological development of consciousness, that recognize the overall *logical* movement. But it should not be thought that we direct or lead consciousness to the conclusion of its journey. We simply observe the movement that consciousness itself makes.

There are, therefore, numerous actors at work in the *Phenomenology of Spirit*: 1) consciousness that is working through the various shapes of itself as it tries to fully understand its ontological structure; 2) the phenomenologists of the we, who are able to see the overall movement that consciousness is making; and 3) Hegel in his capacity as a member of the we, and as the author of the *Phenomenology of Spirit* who is trying to justify the need for philosophy and show the manner in which consciousness must think to fully understand itself and its object. Failure to understand the existence and, indeed, the relationship between these actors will ensure that the *Phenomenology of Spirit* is misinterpreted. While 'Hegel the author' defends an argument, insofar as he tries to demonstrate the need for philosophy, he does so by showing that *consciousness* itself does *not* presuppose the need for philosophy, but must discover it as a result of its own experiences. But, importantly, it is only if consciousness itself discovers the need for philosophy that the philosophical consciousness will be justified. Contrary to Martin Heidegger's (1988: 30) and Philip Kain's (2005: 11–13) understanding, therefore, the crucial actor in Hegel's phenomenological development of consciousness is not Hegel, it is *consciousness*.

The end comes when consciousness realizes that its object is not an alien entity ontologically opposed to it, but is, in actuality, a constitutive aspect of its ontological structure. By coming to see that its intentional object corresponds to its thought and that its thought corresponds to its intentional object, consciousness comes to identify with its intentional object. At this point, consciousness fully understands its ontological structure because it realizes that it is, at one and the same time, 'consciousness of the object, and [...] consciousness of itself' (PS: 54). Recognizing that it exists in a relation of ontological entwinement with an independent object brings consciousness to understand that it is a spiritual synthesis of subjectivity and objectivity. With this, consciousness overcomes its self-alienation.

However, consciousness cannot come to this recognition in isolation from its object; consciousness only develops its self-understanding if it interacts with independent objects. Georg Lukács makes this clear when he explains that 'what is common to the different levels of consciousness manifested is that it is everywhere confronted by an already established, alien world (nature and society). By coming into conflict with this world, and interacting with it, consciousness gradually ascends to its higher forms [of self-understanding]' (1975: 472). Consciousness does not and cannot overcome its self-alienation by simply choosing to look at the world differently; fully understanding its ontological structure requires that it undergo a specific developmental process in which it interacts with independent objects in a particular manner.

Consciousness and the objective world

Hegel and Sartre both agree, therefore, that consciousness exists in a world of independent objects. Sartre's theory of intentionality explicitly rejects the reduction of the objective world to consciousness and the phenomenological development of consciousness demonstrates that Hegel explicitly rejects the notion that the world is synonymous with, or reducible to, consciousness. Hegel would also agree with Sartre that, while its object is ontologically independent from consciousness, what its object means *for consciousness* depends on the way consciousness subjectively interprets its object. They differ in terms of: 1) consciousness's ontological relation to its object; and 2) what its object is *in-itself.*

I have already noted that while Hegel and Sartre agree that consciousness has an intentional relation to its object, they disagree as to consciousness's *ontological relation* to its intentional object. While Sartre insists consciousness remains *ontologically* opposed to its intentional object, Hegel maintains that, because consciousness's existence depends on its intentional relation to its object, its intentional object is an aspect of consciousness's ontological structure. This is important because it means that while Sartre maintains that consciousness is 'a synthetic, individual totality, completely isolated from other totalities' (TOTE: 7), Hegel holds that the relation between consciousness and its object is one of ontological entwinement.

Hegel and Sartre also differ in terms of what the object that consciousness confronts actually is *in-itself.* While both recognize that the independent objects of the world are subjectively interpreted by consciousness, they differ in terms of what the object consciousness confronts is, prior to consciousness's subjective interpretation of it. This is important because it discloses aspects of their respective understandings of consciousness's ontological structure, the ontological structure of the objects of consciousness's world, and the way consciousness shapes its world.

While Sartre's analysis of consciousness's ontological structure discloses that consciousness exists in *ontological* opposition to a world of different objects, these objects share common ontological characteristics; namely, the ontological characteristics of being-in-itself. As noted in the first chapter, the defining ontological characteristics of a being characterized as being-in-itself are that it is solid, inert, passive, and undifferentiated. A particular object only becomes differentiated if and when consciousness differentiates its ontologically undifferentiated mass of being. When discussing consciousness's perception of an object that appears in the form of a tree, Sartre adopts the first-person perspective to explain that when 'persuaded that something is a *tree,* I generate a tree on that *something* [...] This means that I mime the vision of the tree, I retain each element of the vision in an organization called *tree.* I create what it is. If the in-itself *allows itself to be seen* as tree, it organizes itself within my view in such a way that it answers the questions that my eye asks of it, so that my attempt to "see" this obscure mass "as branches" is crowned with success and suddenly a *form* constitutes itself that I can no longer undo' (TE: 23–24). While consciousness intentionally relates to an ontologically undifferentiated, particular object (in this case, a particular tree), what its ontologically undifferentiated, intentional object means for consciousness in terms of its shape, colour, consistency, and feel depends on consciousness's subjective interpretation of the ontologically undifferentiated, particular object it intentionally relates to. The important point is that, for Sartre, consciousness exists in a world of *different objects* that are, in-themselves, *ontologically undifferentiated.*

In contrast, and while Hegel agrees that consciousness exists *in relation* to a world composed of *different objects,* he insists that these different objects are *ontologically differentiated* (HP: 84). Hegel explains that 'things in nature present themselves to us at once as concrete. A flower e.g., has various qualities, colour, smell, taste, shape etc., but they are all in *one.* None of these qualities may be missing. They are not here and there, smell here, colour there; on the contrary, colour, smell etc. are built together with one another into one thing, although as differences' (HP: 84). For Hegel, the differentiated properties of an object are not wholly created by consciousness's subjective act of differentiation; its differentiated properties are an actual part of the object's ontological structure.

Hegel is able to provide a more subtle and complex interpretation of the ontological structure of objects than Sartre because he holds that the ontological structure of objects is differentiated. Whereas Sartre's analysis of consciousness's experience of objectivity discloses that consciousness experiences a differentiated, particular object, this differentiation is, strictly speaking, grounded in consciousness's subjective interpretation of its intentional object; the objects of its world are not *ontologically* differentiated. For Sartre, while objects can be *experienced* as differentiated, *all* objects are, in-themselves, *ontologically* undifferentiated. This ensures that Sartre's analysis of the ontological structure of objectivity holds that objects that exist in the same ontological genus have exactly the same ontological structure.

For example, strictly speaking, Sartre's analysis of the ontological category 'being-in-itself' prevents him from identifying that red and blue lamps are ontologically different to one another. According to Sartre's analysis of the ontological characteristics of being-in-itself, the properties red and blue are not aspects of the lamp's *ontological structure*; the lamp is only described as blue or red if consciousness interprets it as blue or red. For Hegel, however, there is no generic, ontologically undifferentiated lamp that consciousness differentiates through its subjective interpretation; lamps are always a particular shape, size, and colour. A lamp that is a particular shape, size, and colour is *ontologically* different to another lamp that is another shape, size, and colour.

This issue also relates to another: the possibility of consciousness gaining objective knowledge of its object. For Sartre, particular objects are only *ontologically* differentiated by virtue of belonging to one ontological category in opposition to another; they are not *ontologically* differentiated in relation to other objects of the same ontological category. Objects of the same ontological category are only differentiated from one another by virtue of consciousness's act of differentiation. To return to the example of the lamp once again, because the way the lamp appears to consciousness depends on consciousness's subjective interpretation of it, each consciousness *experiences* a different lamp; for one consciousness, the lamp may be red, for another black. When Sartre's insistence that consciousness's *experience* of a lamp is a subjective interpretation of an ontologically undifferentiated, particular object is combined with his rejection of a priori, transcendent standards against which to legitimize a subjective interpretation as objectively true, it is difficult to see how Sartre can avoid maintaining that each consciousness's subjective *experience* of a lamp is as valid as any other. As long as each consciousness recognizes its object, in this case a lamp, actually is a lamp, the consciousness that insists its lamp is black is just as valid as the consciousness that insists its red. There does not appear to be any way to compare or evaluate different subjective interpretations of the object to determine their validity.

This is not the case for Hegel. Because his analysis of the ontological structure of objects recognizes that objects that belong to the same ontological category are also ontologically distinct from one another by virtue of having a distinct, particular content, his analysis is able to determine whether subjective interpretations of different objects do actually accord with what the object is *ontologically*. For example, if consciousness is confronted with a blue lamp, the consciousness that identifies the lamp as blue, rather than the consciousness that identifies it as yellow, is more valid. In contrast to Sartre's analysis of the ontological structure of objectivity, Hegel's understanding provides an *objective* standard against which to compare consciousness's subjective interpretation of the object before it.

The ontological development of consciousness

Furthermore, one of the crucial differences between the two thinkers relates to the relationship between consciousness's experience and its ontological structure. Sartre's analysis maintains that consciousness is 'always the same' (EH: 50). Consciousness is always ontologically nothing 'facing a situation which is always changing, and choice remains always a choice in the situation' (EH: 50). This leads him to hold that consciousness is an ontologically independent monad 'laid siege to by the world' (NE: 315). It is by overcoming the resistance from its world that consciousness exists and is able to freely determine what it will be experientially (BN: 528; WD: 37). Thus, Sartre holds that consciousness's experience never alters the fundamental relationship between pre-reflectivity and reflectivity nor its ontological nothingness; consciousness lives its ontological nothingness in its world by choosing how it will experience its world.

For Hegel, however, consciousness is not ontologically independent from its world, nor does it simply exist in the same fundamental manner; consciousness's ontological structure is defined by an implicit *ontological potential* that must be *developed* and is only developed through its activities in its world (HP: 71–86). While Sartre derides this understanding as nothing more than 'myth' (NE: 483), Hegel holds that the full realization of consciousness's implicit ontological potential takes place through numerous stages, with each stage in the development of its implicit ontological potential also entailing a development in its self-understanding. When consciousness understands itself in one way, it takes on the specific *ontological structure* that corresponds to that form of self-understanding; when consciousness adopts a new form of self-understanding this also alters its ontological structure. This continues until consciousness gets to the ontological structure and form of self-understanding in which its experience discloses that its understanding of its object corresponds to how the object is in-itself. But, because consciousness's understanding of its object corresponds to its own self-understanding, when consciousness adopts the shape of itself that allows it to fully understand its object, it also fully understands itself.

Sartre's understanding of consciousness's ontological structure is, therefore, far narrower than Hegel's (Williams, 1992b: 12). For Sartre, consciousness's ontological structure is defined by the pre-reflective nihilation of its other which ensures that consciousness exists as nothing. Consciousness's ontological structure does not include the particular manifestations of each concrete consciousness, such as its particular race, body, social class, nationality, and social relations (BN: 535). These are relegated to consciousness's facticity which, as I noted in Chapter 1, is the area of happening in, on, and through which consciousness chooses how it will live and experience the ontological freedom that emanates from its ontological nothingness.

For Hegel, however, consciousness's social class, race, body, nationality, and social interaction with other consciousnesses are all aspects of its ontological structure. Whereas Sartre maintains that all consciousnesses are the same *ontologically*, insofar as the ontological structure of consciousness is defined by nothingness and is structured around the pre-reflective/reflective division, but are distinguished from one another by virtue of how each chooses to live its ontological nothingness *experientially*, Hegel insists that not only do consciousness's experiences alter and define its ontological structure, but, because each consciousness has different experiences, each consciousness's *ontological structure* is, strictly speaking, different.

Hegel also rejects Sartre's insistence that consciousness is always pre-reflectively aware of what it is ontologically. For Hegel, consciousness is not immediately aware of what it truly is ontologically; it must develop this knowledge. Hegel maintains that a development in consciousness's self-understanding also entails: 1) an alteration in its ontological structure; and 2) a development in the realization of the ontological potential implicit to its ontological structure. This is crucial because it means that while Sartre insists that consciousness is *always* ontologically free, Hegel maintains that consciousness only becomes free if it *develops* the potential for freedom implicit to its ontological structure. To demonstrate the way this difference manifests itself, it may be helpful to discuss the way Hegel and Sartre conceptualize the ontological structure of a child's consciousness in relation to the ontological structure of an adult's consciousness.

While to my knowledge, Sartre does not provide an explicit or extended discussion of this topic, the limited statements he makes on the child and the *logic* of his argument would appear to hold that the ontological structure of the child's consciousness is no different to the ontological structure of the adult's consciousness: both are ontologically nothing. The difference between the adult and child emanates from the degree to which the consciousness of the adult and child can *reflectively under-stand* its ontological nothingness. It would appear that while the adult is able to reflectively understand its ontological nothingness and the free-dom that accompanies this, the child either simply cannot reflectively understand that it is ontologically nothing or cannot understand this to the same degree as the adult. For this reason, Sartre thinks the child is more susceptible to external influence in terms of its values, norms, and pre-reflective fundamental project. This is why Sartre emphasizes the way society imposes itself onto, and so shapes, the child's experi-ences and self-understanding (SG: 35–36).

For Hegel, however, the child and adult do not simply tend to have a different form of self-understanding; the ontological structure of a child's consciousness is different to that of an adult's consciousness. While Sartre would appear to maintain that the consciousness of an adult and child are both ontologically defined by nothingness, Hegel's understanding of the ontological structure of consciousness recognizes that a child's consciousness tends to be ontologically different to an adult's consciousness. The difference manifests itself in the degree to which the reason that is implicit to all human consciousness tends to be developed in a child's consciousness when compared to the conscious-ness of an adult.

On the one hand, Hegel thinks the child's capacity to reason tends to be less developed than the adult's. But, on the other, he notes that the actual degree to which the adult and child are capable of rational thought tends to be different with the former's ontological capacity to reason being greater than the latter's. This does not simply mean, as it does for Sartre, that the adult and child have different *epistemological* capabilities with the adult being capable of greater self-reflexivity; for Hegel, the difference between the adult's and child's reasoning capabil-ity is indicative of different ontological structures.

Furthermore, whereas Sartre insists that whether consciousness over-comes its alienation is, in the first instance, dependent on it choos-ing to adopt a pre-reflective fundamental project that allows it to reflectively recognize its ontological nothingness, Hegel insists that whether consciousness fully understands itself is not simply depend-ent on whether consciousness simply chooses to *recognize* what it truly is ontologically. Hegel's insistence that consciousness must develop its self-understanding to fully understand itself ensures that whether consciousness overcomes its alienation depends on whether it chooses to *develop* its self-understanding in a particular way. Importantly, however, this developmental process is *not* something consciousness can do on its own in isolation from its world. Consciousness can only overcome its alienation if it interacts with its external world in a specific way.

Thus, whereas Sartre holds that consciousness's journey to authenticity is primordially an *individual* one, insofar as consciousness must first choose to undergo the conversion before going on to develop the authentic social relations possible post-conversion, Hegel holds that the process whereby consciousness overcomes its self-alienation is a thoroughly *social* one. Whether consciousness overcomes its self-alienation is, for Hegel, dependent on a number of factors and events beyond its control. The conclusion drawn is that Sartre's primordially individualistic account of self-revelatory recovery drastically underestimates the social struggle consciousness must go through to overcome its self-alienation.

Thus, while Hegel and Sartre agree that consciousness must *become* authentic/non-alienated, they differ in terms of what this becoming entails. But before discussing this further, I want to respond to a potential criticism; that is, that while Sartre uses the term 'authenticity,' Hegel does not.

In response, we should remember that being 'alienated from something presupposes the existence of an opposite state of non-alienation' (Baxter, 1982: 3). In other words, the concept 'alienation' only gains its meaning when contrasted to an alternative state of non-alienation or, as I will call it, authenticity. While alienation and authenticity are, in one sense, opposed, insofar as they describe opposed ways of being; they are, in another sense, constitutively related, insofar as to describe one, also discloses the other. If we understand what it is to be *alienated*, we also, at least *implicitly*, understand what it is to be authentic. Similarly, if we understand what it is to be *authentic*, we, at least, *implicitly* understand that if we lack those aspects of being that constitute an authentic way of being, we are alienated.

Therefore, while Hegel never explicitly uses the term, his analysis of the different ways consciousness's self-understanding is alienated *implicitly* points towards a non-alienated or *authentic* form of self-understanding. Thus, in each shape of consciousness prior to Absolute Knowing, Hegel shows that consciousness is alienated because it fails to properly understand its ontological structure. Because consciousness only fully understands its ontological structure in Absolute Knowing,

Hegel *implicitly* holds that the self-understanding of Absolute Knowing is the authentic form of self-understanding.

While Sartre holds that for consciousness to become authentic requires that it become reflectively aware of the ontological nothingness it always is, this becoming is a purely *epistemological* becoming, insofar as consciousness *becomes* reflectively aware of its ontological nothingness.

For Hegel, however, the process through which consciousness comes to fully understand its ontological structure is not simply, nor is it fundamentally, an *epistemological* becoming of what it is ontologically. For Hegel, the process through which consciousness comes to the authentic self-understanding of Absolute Knowing entails: 1) an *epistemological becoming*, insofar as consciousness comes to fully understand its ontological structure; and 2) an *ontological becoming*, insofar as consciousness becomes what it can potentially become *ontologically*.

This is because whereas Sartre's analysis of consciousness's ontological structure is grounded in the subject/object dualism, Hegel's is not. Hegel's analysis of consciousness's ontological structure recognizes that while a being's ontological structure is defined by its membership of a specific ontological category, the concrete beings that exist within this ontological category do not necessarily have the same ontological structure. Each specific category of being delineates *ontological parameters* that define what the individual beings that exist within that ontological category of being can *potentially* achieve (PN: 352–353).

But it should not be thought that the ontological potential of the human being is static and ahistoric; Hegel recognizes that the ontological potential of the human being is historically sensitive. In other words, the parameters that delineate the ontological potential of each individual will differ according to his historical period. For this reason, what is ontologically possible for one individual living in one historical period will differ from the ontological possibilities open to another individual living in a different socio-historical setting. Because a being's ontological *potential* must be individually developed, and because each being's capacity to develop its ontological potential is dependent on a number of contingent factors, each being that exists in that ontological category will, strictly speaking, exist with a different *actual* ontological structure.

To put this reasoning in less abstract terms, we can say that each individual human being belongs to the universal ontological category 'human being' that delineates a universal, socio-historically sensitive ontological structure constituted by an implicit ontological potential unique to each particular individual. But, for Hegel, the concrete human being does not simply exist with its particular ontological potential fully realized; each concrete individual must develop itself so that its implicit ontological potential is fully realized (PN: 370). The extent to which an individual's ontological potential can be developed depends on a number of contingencies out-with his control, such as his material wealth, socio-historical situation, and the activities of others. This ensures that some individuals will be able to develop their implicit ontological potential to a greater degree than others. Within the ontological category 'human being,' therefore, each concrete individual will, strictly speaking, have a different ontological structure by virtue of the degree to which that particular, concrete individual has realized his unique, socio-historically sensitive, ontological potential.

But as the concrete human being develops its ontological potential, Hegel insists that this *ontological* development also involves an *epistemological* development that allows consciousness to develop a better understanding of its ontological structure and what it is capable of achieving. The difference between the two thinkers on this crucial point is that while Hegel recognizes that *consciousness's ontological structure* undergoes a historical development in-line with developments in its self-understanding, Sartre holds that, while consciousness is socially embodied, its ontological freedom means that its fundamental ontological structures remain distinct from, and unaffected by, it's socio-historical situation (Roth, 1988: 59).

Hegel's phenomenological development culminates when consciousness comes to the realization that it exists in a relation of ontological entwinement with its object. However, this does not mean that consciousness usurps the independence of its object or that its object usurps the independence of consciousness. While the exact relationship between the subjective and objective aspects of the Hegelian conception of consciousness is a topic of much scholarly debate, what is important for our purposes is that consciousness overcomes its self-alienation when it realizes that it is a differentiated unity of subjectivity and objectivity. But this does not mean that the independence of either aspect is usurped by the other; importantly, 'while each opposed moment contains the meaning of its other, the incommensurability of these moments is nevertheless preserved' (Ludwig, 1989: 19).

This difference in unity is possible because Hegel recognizes that the two aspects of consciousness are mediated by spirit. Spirit is able to unify fundamental differences because 'the defining feature of spirit [is its] ability to be "both itself and the other to itself." Spirit is characterised by self-differentiation, in the sense that spirit is able to make itself an other to itself and, from there, return to itself' (Honneth, 2005: 31).

Because Sartre's strict subject/object ontological dichotomy cannot accept mediation, he holds that the mediation of spirit usurps the ontological distinction between subject and object and reduces two distinct ontological substances to one. It also means he interprets Hegel's notion of spirit as an entity that usurps the independence of both consciousness and its object. For Hegel, however, mediation does not usurp two relational terms; it unites them while maintaining their independence. This allows Hegel to insist that spirit is the mediating aspect that unites, without negating the difference between, consciousness's subjective and objective aspects. Indeed, because spirit mediates the two aspects of consciousness's ontological structure, consciousness is, fundamentally, spirit. Consciousness, however, must develop its self-understanding to realize this.

Spirit

Hegel's notion of spirit is, however, notoriously difficult to understand. Indeed, its difficulty has led to contradictory interpretations. What I aim to do here, is briefly examine four different conceptions of Hegel's notion of spirit to show where they go wrong and how we must conceptualize spirit to truly understand the crucial role in plays in Hegel's analysis.

The first interpretation of Hegel's notion of spirit I will look at is, in many respects, the traditional interpretation of Hegel. It interprets Hegel as a thinker of an absolute, transcendent entity called spirit. This interpretation has many proponents including Karl Popper (2003: 24), Martin Heidegger (1988: 30), and, given our focus, Sartre. These thinkers interpret Hegel's notion of spirit as an all-important metaphysical entity that transcends consciousness and the world. This leads them to insist that Hegel not only establishes a metaphysical duality between this world and the world of the transcendent entity called spirit, but, importantly, makes this world subservient to the transcendent world. Interpreting Hegel in this strict dualistic manner leads Sartre to cast Hegel as a thinker of an absolute totality, Heidegger to reject Hegel as a mere metaphysical thinker, and Popper to insist that Hegel sowed the seeds for political totalitarianism.

However, this interpretation simply does not fit with Hegel's own comments. Interpreting Hegel as a strict dualistic thinker completely fails to understand that Hegel's dialectical method goes to great lengths to show that existence is far more complex, dynamic, and organically unified than can be captured by a system of binary oppositions. Portraying Hegel as a metaphysical dualist greatly betrays both the content and spirit of his thinking.

This brings me to the second interpretation of Hegel's notion of spirit; an interpretation that is fundamentally opposed to the first interpretation insofar as it maintains that Hegel's notion of spirit is thoroughly non-metaphysical.

According to Terry Pinkard, Hegel's spirit is 'not a metaphysical entity but a fundamental *relation* among persons that mediates their *self-consciousness*, a way in which people reflect on what they have come to take as authoritative for themselves' (1996: 9). On this reading, spirit designates the social space that exists *between* individual consciousnesses that allows them to engage with and relate to one another.

While this interpretation correctly notes that spirit is not a metaphysical entity, it is ultimately inadequate because it fails to explicitly recognize that spirit is not simply a passive relation that is dependent on the activities of each individual consciousness for its creation; spirit is also the substance of consciousness. While Pinkard is correct to note that spirit emanates from the activities of consciousness, it must also be explicitly recognized that spirit does not simply designate the social relation *between* individual consciousnesses; spirit is what consciousness fundamentally is.

This leads me to Robert Pippin's interpretation. For Pippin, Hegel's 'spirit is not a "thing" (even "in-itself") or substance in any sense' (2008: 15). Spirit describes a 'fully realised state of norm-governed individual and collective mindedness' (2008: 39). While Pippin agrees with Pinkard that Hegel's spirit delineates a socio-cultural space, he goes beyond Pinkard's interpretation by also claiming that it entails the development of shared cultural norms. Pippin's understanding emphasizes and stresses that spirit is developmental, that this development is purely social, and that this social development creates common socio-cultural norms that bind consciousnesses together in a common social world that allows each to fully realize and express itself.

While Pinkard and Pippin are correct to note that spirit must be developed, with this development creating common social norms and a common cultural environment, spirit is not simply a social mindedness that creates socially accepted norms that bind consciousnesses together in a particular social formation. While this is an aspect of the developmental process that fully realizes spirit, on numerous occasions Hegel notes that spirit is more than socio-cultural norms and values; it is the *ontological substance* of existence: 'The spiritual alone is the *actual*; it is essence, or that which has *being in itself*; it is that which *relates itself to itself* and is *determinate*, it is *other-being* and *being-for-self*, and in this determinateness, or in its self-externality, abides within itself; in other words, it is *in and for itself*' (PS: 14), and 'spirit, being the *substance* and the universal, self-identical, and abiding essence, is the unmoved solid *ground* and *starting point* for the action of all, and it is their purpose and goal, the in-itself of every self-consciousness expressed in thought' (PS: 264).

But Hegel notes that 'everything turns on grasping and expressing the True [spirit], not only as *Substance*, but equally as *Subject*' (PS: 10). Spirit is not an inert substance; it is a dynamic substance that always exists, at least, in embryonic form, can and must be realized, and whose full realization is dependent on a socio-historical process that emanates from the existence of the beings it grounds. So, while Pippin insists that spirit 'should be considered in historical terms, not in terms of substance, and in some sense "practically," not ontologically' (2008: 55), I disagree, and understand that spirit *is* the ontological universal substance of existence. But this ontological substance must be developed to be fully realized and is only developed through the existence of the beings it constitutes. In relation to consciousness, the actions and interactions of consciousnesses create social norms and a common cultural environment that bind each consciousness together in an organic social union which, due to the social nature of consciousness's ontological structure, allows each to fully realize the freedom implicit to its ontological structure.

In a fundamental respect, Charles Taylor's (1975: 43–45) influential *essentialist* interpretation of Hegel's spirit is nearer the mark. For Taylor, Hegel's spirit is a 'cosmic spirit' (1975: 44) that is the essential ground of existence. But Taylor notes that while spirit is 'the spiritual reality underlying the universe as a whole' (1975: 45), it must be realized and is only realized through the actions of consciousness. According to Taylor, while spirit delineates a 'spiritual force' (1975: 44) that underlies the activities and existence of consciousness, it only gains its content from the activities and existence of consciousness. Once consciousness is fully developed, so too is spirit.

However, while Taylor is correct to maintain that spirit is an essence that must be socially realized, Paul Franco is right to insist that, in describing this essence, 'it is not necessary to import into this concept any dubious metaphysical or cosmic connotations.' (1999: 84). The problem with Taylor's insistence that spirit is a cosmic force that underlies the universe as a whole is that it creates a distinction between the actual world and the cosmic realm of spirit. Admittedly, Taylor does go some way to overcoming this division by recognizing that the cosmic force is dependent on the activities and understanding of the consciousnesses of the actual world for its content and development. However, we should go further and recognize that, rather than being a cosmic force existing in another realm underlying the actual world that is dependent on the activities and understanding of the consciousnesses of the actual world for its content and development, spirit is the constitutive ontological substance of the actual world that finds concrete expression, to various degrees and forms, 'in' the various beings of existence.

But spirit does not constitute each being as a fixed, inert substance. Spirit constitutes each being as 'a germ of infinite possibility' (PH: 57) that is shaped and made actual by the actions of the beings it constitutes. Put differently, the content, form, and development of each being's ontological potential is dependent on the social situation, activities, and understanding of that particular being. Because of this, Hegel holds that spirit 'is not a dead essence, but is *actual* and *alive*' (PS: 264).

Thus, while recognizing that Pinkard's, Pippin's, and Taylor's interpretations describe aspects of spirit, in true Hegelian fashion, we have to combine aspects of their interpretations to adequately understand Hegel's notion of spirit. While Pinkard and Pippin's *socio-cultural* interpretation is correct to emphasize that Hegel's 'spirit' is non-metaphysical and encompasses a social space that creates socially minded norms, spirit must be understood as being more than simply a social space imbued by a social mindedness; it must be understood in terms of the essential universality Taylor describes, albeit without the distinction Taylor makes between the actual world and an underlying cosmic realm of spirit. While Taylor's understanding of Hegel's spirit can be called *socio-cosmological*, insofar as it delineates the underlying *cosmological* force of existence that must be developed and realized, and is only developed and realized by the *social* activities of the consciousnesses it grounds, and while my understanding shares Taylor's insistence that Hegel's spirit delineates a substantial essence that is realized socially, we must remove all cosmological connotations and explicitly recognize that Hegel's spirit is *socio-ontological*, insofar as it delineates the *ontological substance* constitutive of all beings that, initially, finds concrete expression, to various degrees and forms, as an ontological potential implicit to the ontological structure of each particular being that must be, and is only, realized by the *social* activities and actions of the beings it constitutes.

As a spiritual being, consciousness's essence is defined in terms of spirit's essence: freedom (PH: 53, 55, HP: 75). Hegel explains that 'all men are rational, and the formal side of rationality is that man is free; this is his nature, inherent in the essence of man' (HP: 75). But again, this essence is only ever an *implicit* possibility that must be made *explicit* and is only made explicit by being made actual by the activities and understanding of consciousness. In other words, in the same way that 'a plant develops from its germ: [where] the germ already contains the whole plant within itself, but in an ideal way, so that we must not envisage its development as if the various parts of the plant – root, stem, leaves, etc. – were already present in the germ *realiter*, though only in a very minute form' (EL: 161A), consciousness also has an implicit *ideal* essence that defines its possibilities. While consciousness always has the *potential* to realize its ontological potential by becoming free, it is only if it *actually* realizes this implicit potential that it will fully realize itself by actually becoming free. Thus, whereas Sartre holds that consciousness is always ontologically free even when it is not practically free, Hegel's insistence that consciousness must become free, and his insistence that true freedom is practical, means that the distinction between consciousness's ontological and practical freedom found in Sartre's analysis is absent from Hegel's. For Hegel, consciousness only realizes the ontological potential implicit to its ontological structure when it becomes truly practically free.

But when Hegel says that the essence of consciousness is (practical) freedom, he does not mean that consciousness is *absolutely* free to determine what it will be; consciousness's essential possibilities are not limitless. Hegel thinks this because he recognizes that consciousness belongs to the ontological category 'human being,' which delineates specific ontological features and possibilities. As a consequence of these ontological parameters, individuals can only engage in activities that are ontologically possible for a human being to engage in.

Because Hegel's conception of essence delineates an *ideal* essence that must be realized and is only realized by the actions of the consciousnesses it constitutes, we can say that, for Hegel, spirit is the substance of consciousness that is, initially, manifested as an implicit, *non-determining* essence that delineates what consciousness, as a human being, can *potentially* become. As a non-determining essence, consciousness's spiritual essence does not determine its *actual* activities, nor does it determine that consciousness will *actually* become the free being it can *potentially* become. Whether consciousness fully realizes its ontological potential by actually becoming the free and creative being it can potentially become depends on its actions and socio-historic position. Importantly, however, even if consciousness does not realize its ontological potential, it still exists; it is just that it has not yet fully realized its ontological potential.

The notion that spirit delineates the ontological substance of consciousness that is, initially, manifested as an implicit ontological potential that must be realized and is realized by the actions of consciousness allows Hegel to differentiate between different shapes of consciousness, societies, and cultures in terms of the extent to which they allow the individual to fully understand, and freely express, himself.

While spirit, at least implicitly, exists in the shapes of consciousness called Sense-Certainty and Revealed Religion, it is Revealed Religion that provides it with a fuller sense of self-understanding. As such, Hegel values this shape of spirit/consciousness over Sense-Certainty. Similarly, in the *Philosophy of Right*, Hegel's insistence that spirit is the universal ontological substance that is, and must be, realized in the world by the activities and interactions of historical individuals, allows him to note that while spirit exists in societies grounded in the freedom of abstract right, it is only in societies shaped in accordance with the freedom of ethical life (*Sittlichkeit*) that spirit is fully realized and individuals can fully and freely express themselves. Furthermore, it is because spirit is the implicit, substantial essence of existence that must be developed and realized in the world through the actions and interactions of the historical individuals it constitutes, that Hegel, in the *Philosophy of History*, is able to argue that, while spirit exists in each stage of history, it is only modernity that fully realizes the freedom implicitly constitutive of spirit.

The important thing to remember at this stage is that the relationship between spirit and consciousness is dialectical: while spirit is the constitutive ontological substance of consciousness that is initially manifested as an implicit, non-determining potential, spirit is dependent on the activities of consciousness for its content and development. Contrary to Sartre's insistence, Hegel's spirit is *not* an abstract, metaphysical entity that dictates and impinges on the understanding and activities of consciousness; it is an embodied, ontological substance that animates, and is animated by, the activities of embodied consciousnesses.

Hegel and Sartre on freedom

Hegel and Sartre agree, therefore, on a crucial point: freedom is the essence of consciousness. They disagree on what this freedom is and how consciousness relates to it. While Sartre insists consciousness is always ontologically free, he maintains that consciousness alienates itself whenever it does not reflectively understand this. The first step towards overcoming its self-alienation is for consciousness to reflectively understand that its ontological nothingness means it is free. This realization comes about from a purely subjective choice; consciousness simply has to *choose* to adopt a pre-reflective fundamental project that has the affirmation of freedom as its end.

Hegel's notion of freedom and the way consciousness becomes free are different. Hegel starts by noting that, because freedom does not simply exist, it must be actualized in the world. While Sartre does not distinguish between consciousness and the will, instead holding that the two are synonymous with one another, Hegel's insistence that consciousness is an organic, differentiated, spiritual unity allows him to hold that while it is the will of consciousness that actualizes the freedom implicit to its ontological structure (PR: 4A), consciousness cannot simply be reduced to the will. Thus, while freedom is the non-determining, implicit essence of consciousness, not only is there no teleological necessity that makes its realization a foregone conclusion, but it is not something that happens to consciousness. Freedom needs to be realized and is only realized by the will of consciousness.

Hegel agrees with Sartre that the will is no-thing or, put into his language, indeterminate. Its indeterminacy allows it to dissolve 'every limitation, every content, whether present immediately through nature, though needs, desires, and drives, or given and determined in some other way' (PR: 5). Because of this, it is able to remain absolutely free from all determinacy. But Hegel notes that this limitless freedom comes at a price: the will's freedom is abstract. It is only the abstract freedom of 'pure thinking' (PR: 5).

This is clearly the freedom Sartre maintains is constitutive of consciousness's ontological structure; it is the freedom that emanates from consciousness's pre-reflective nihilation of being-in-itself. Hegel agrees with Sartre that the will is free because of its capacity to retreat from all determinate being. But while Hegel notes that the will's capacity to nihilate everything determinate describes an aspect of the will, he criticizes those, like Sartre, who insist it fully describes the will.

For Hegel, the problem with associating freedom with the will's subjective capacity to nihilate determinacy is that consciousness's freedom can only ever be a '*negative* freedom' (PR: 5R). If this freedom remains purely theoretical, it simply delineates a turn to 'pure contemplation' (PR: 5R) that achieves nothing actual. If, however, the consciousness defined by the act of nihilation tries to act practically, its practical activity can only ever be destructive (PR: 5R & 5A). In other words, this notion of consciousness has nothing *positive* to contribute to the actual world. While Sartre argues that the act of nihilation allows consciousness to create its world, Hegel would argue that this misunderstands the process of nihilation. An act of nihilation is purely destructive; without recognizing a positive correlate to the process of nihilation, Hegel would argue that if Sartre is to be logically consistent he cannot insist, as he does in his discussion of consciousness's practical freedom, that a consciousness defined by the act of nihilation can contribute anything positive or creative to the actual world.

Hegel overcomes this by recognizing that, while the act of nihilation describes an aspect of the will, it is not the only one. For Hegel, the will is also capable of positively contributing to actuality. The positive aspect of consciousness describes the process whereby the indeterminate, absolutely free will turns itself into a finite, determinate object.

Thus, while Sartre holds that consciousness's ontological structure is defined by the act of nihilation, Hegel recognizes two aspects to the will: a negative capacity that simply nihilates determinacy by affirming its infinite, abstract freedom *and* a positive aspect that allows it to create something concrete and finite. But Hegel's insistence that the positive aspect of the will 'constitutes the concept or substantiality of the will' (PR: 7) clearly discloses that he privileges the will's creative aspect over its negative aspect.

This relates to consciousness's ontological relationship to objectivity. While Hegel maintains that consciousness can only overcome its self-alienation when it comes to understand that it is an organic, spiritual unity of subjectivity and objectivity, this development can only occur if consciousness objectifies itself and 'remains with itself' (PR: 7A) in this objectification. If this happens, consciousness can come to see and recognize itself in objective form and so overcome the alien-ness of its objective world. At this point, it will be truly free because nothing in its actual world will be strictly other than itself; consciousness will see that its world is an extension of itself. Thus, freedom is not realized when consciousness sees itself as existing in strict opposition to its world; true freedom 'consists in cancelling [*aufzuheben*] the contradiction between subjectivity and objectivity and in translating its ends from their subjective determination into an objective one, while at the same time remaining *with itself* in this objectivity' (PR: 28).

Because seeing itself in object form allows consciousness to see its world as an extension of itself, Hegel argues that consciousness overcomes its individual standpoint, understands the importance of the universal perspective, and identifies with its world. This is important because 'when the will has universality, or itself as infinite form, as its content, object [*Gegenstand*], and end, it is free not only *in itself,* but also *for itself* – it is the Idea of its truth' (PR: 22). In other words, when the will sees its world as an extension of itself, it will have overcome all opposition to itself and become truly free in the world.

But while Hegel holds that consciousness becomes free when it recognizes that the determinate object it creates is an aspect of its ontological structure, he maintains that freedom does not consist in consciousness *arbitrarily* expressing itself in object form. While Hegel recognizes that the will is infinite in the abstract, he rejects the notion that the will should use this infinite, abstract possibility to simply do as it pleases when it pleases (PR: 15). There are two reasons for this: first, the will that arbitrarily determines itself immediately finds itself questioning whether its choice is the correct one. This doubt leads consciousness to rescind its previous choice and choose another; this, however, also ends in self-doubt. This self-doubt prevents the will from actually achieving anything in concrete reality.

Secondly, the will that acts arbitrarily insists on the division between its infinite freedom and the constraining finitude of concrete existence. This leads the will to maintain that its determinate activity contradicts its infinite, indeterminate freedom. To reconcile its infinite, indeterminate freedom with the constraints of its determinate existence, the will holds that it is the *process* of making itself indeterminate, as opposed to the status of *being* determinate, that allows it to freely exist in the world. In other words, the will holds that to remain as an indeterminate, free being requires that it express itself in opposition to determinacy. The problem with this understanding is that because the will *must* constantly negate determinate objects to remain wholly indeterminate, it finds that its subjective freedom is constrained by this necessity. As such, it is no longer free.

These criticisms lead Hegel to maintain that freedom is not won when consciousness acts in accordance with its own subjective whim; freedom requires consciousness to comport itself in a manner that is 'in accordance with the concepts of ethics' (PR: 15A). This means that consciousness must establish and act in accordance with the customs and norms of a *rational* community. While we will return to this issue in subsequent chapters, some aspects of Hegel's conception of a rational community include a community whose: 1) structures and ends are subject to reason rather than emotion, the passions, or arbitrary fiat;

2) structures interlink to integrate all members into a unified community; 3) laws and structures protect certain inalienable abstract rights, such as the individual's right to own private property; and 4) members recognize, accept, and affirm that being a member of a rational community is necessary for the realization of their own freedom.

While the creation of the objective structures necessary for the realization of freedom may require consciousness to limit its *immediate* activities, Hegel argues that this does not necessarily limit consciousness's freedom. Only certain objective structures will safeguard consciousness's freedom and co-ordinate the activities of every consciousness in such a way that each is able to freely express itself as far as possible, but not so far that their individual actions threaten the existence and/or freedom of the whole community.

The notion that the will must limit its abstract freedom to achieve anything concrete and become truly free is one of the cornerstones of Hegel's social philosophy. But we should not think that this means that consciousness must not dream, or aspire to create anything, nor that consciousness must simply adhere to the norms of its social world; it simply means that to achieve anything practical, consciousness must focus its attention and activity. It is for this reason that Hegel approvingly quotes Goethe's saying that 'whoever aspires to great things must be able to limit himself' (PR: 13A).

Hegel and Sartre have, therefore, very different understandings of consciousness's relation to objective structures. While earlier chapters showed that Sartre distinguishes between consciousness's ontological and practical freedom, he holds that both consciousness's ontological and practical freedom are won in opposition to objective structures. The ontological nothingness of consciousness's ontological structure ensures it is defined in ontological opposition to objective structures, while Sartre's insistence that consciousness can only be practically free once it has overcome the constraining resistance of the objective structures and social norms of its world means that consciousness's practical freedom is won in opposition to objective structures.

Admittedly, in the *Critique of Dialectical Reason*, Sartre does recognize that belonging to the group formations he calls the group-in-fusion and the organized group can enhance consciousness's practical freedom. This is because these group formations, to varying degrees, *co-ordinate* the practical activities of various consciousnesses in such a way that each is able to practically express itself without impinging on the practical freedom of others. However, membership of certain groups does not impact on, nor is it a necessary aspect of, consciousness's ontological structure. While Sartre recognizes that consciousness can come to reflectively accept and adhere to the social norms and identity necessary for it to be a member of group formations, such as the group-in-fusion and the organized group, that can enhance its practical freedom, the social identity conferred on it by membership of these groups is irrelevant to its ontological nothingness. Irrespective of the degree to which membership of certain group formations extends consciousness's practical freedom, consciousness is, and always remains, ontologically nothing.

In contrast, the *Philosophy of Right*'s detailed discussion of the objective structures necessary to realize consciousness's practical freedom discloses that, for Hegel, consciousness's ontological structure and identity is constitutively related to its social identity, that developing the ontological potential implicit to its ontological structure requires that consciousness exist within specific social formations, and that consciousness is not truly free when it sets itself in opposition to everything determinate and determines for itself what to do. For Hegel, consciousness is only able to realize the ontological potential implicit to its ontological structure and be truly free if it establishes a specific relation *with* objectivity where it identifies with a specific form of its objective world, is recognized as a free consciousness by other free consciousnesses, and becomes a member of a rational community.

The implications of this difference are two-fold: first, while Sartre maintains that reflectively understanding itself to have a social identity alienates consciousness from its ontological nothingness, Hegel insists that it is consciousness's social identity that defines its ontological structure. For this reason, consciousness's social role must allow it to fully understand its ontological structure and realize the ontological potential implicit to its ontological structure. In other words, whether consciousness fully understands its ontological structure and realizes its ontological potential is intimately connected to the freedom of its community.

While Sartre simply insists that being authentic requires consciousness to reflectively recognize, care for, and affirm the other's practical freedom, because Hegel recognizes that the individual exists in a relation of ontological entwinement with others, he is able to hold that the reason that the individual must reflectively recognize, care for, and affirm the other's freedom is not because of some arbitrarily introduced ethical imperative, but is because it is only if the other realizes its ontological potential that the individual can realize his.

Secondly, while Sartre insists that becoming authentic is a primordially subjective choice, insofar as consciousness must choose to undergo the conversion that subsequently allows it to create authentic social relations, Hegel maintains that whether consciousness becomes authentic by fully understanding its ontological structure and fully realizing its implicit ontological potential is not simply, nor is it primordially, dependent on a subjective decision. It requires that consciousness interact with its world in a specific way, develop a specific form of self-understanding in which it recognizes that it is essentially spirit, create specific objective structures, and relate to these objective structures in a specific way.

But before engaging with the objective structures and subjective ethical attitude that Hegel thinks are necessary to realize the individual's freedom, the next chapter complements and extends this one by discussing the role that alienation plays in the phenomenological development of consciousness.

6
Alienation and the
Phenomenology of Spirit

As noted in Chapter 5, Hegel maintains that consciousness does not immediately understand that it is composed of a subjective and an objective aspect and that these are unified by spirit. Because consciousness initially takes its object to be something strictly other than itself, it initially maintains that an aspect of itself is purely other than itself. It is, in other words, alienated from itself. While consciousness *can* overcome this alienation, it can only do so by passing through a specific developmental process where it experiences a variety of relations with its object that it, in some way, takes to be strictly other than itself.

While in each of the shapes preceding Absolute Knowing, consciousness fails, in some way, to fully understand its ontological structure, its constant failings lead it to a better understanding of its ontological structure. Because consciousness's failures teach it something about what it is *not,* and because consciousness learns from its failures, consciousness gradually learns what it actually is. As Hegel remarks, consciousness 'wins its truth only when, in utter dismemberment, it finds itself. It is this power, not as something positive, which closes its eyes to the negative, as when we say of something that it is nothing or is false, and then, having done with it, turn away and pass on to something else; on the contrary, spirit is this power only by looking the negative in the face, and tarrying with it' (PS: 19). It is the experience of being alienated from itself that drives consciousness to adopt a new shape of itself in the hope that this new shape will allow it to fully understand its ontological structure. Consciousness's experience continues to lead it to adopt new shapes of itself until it reaches Absolute Knowing, where its experience discloses that this form of understanding does allow it to fully understand itself.

But while the movement between the different shapes of itself is a necessary one if consciousness is to fully understand its ontological structure, the movement itself is not an easy one. Each new shape adopted requires that consciousness forego the certainty that its previous shape gave it. While consciousness can exist in a state of estrangement, and indeed can find a degree of satisfaction in its estrangement, fully understanding its ontological structure requires that consciousness alter its self-understanding. This takes courage. It is not easy for consciousness to let go off its understanding of the truth. However, consciousness will only learn what it truly is, if it is willing to alter its self-understanding to accord with its experience (Houlgate, 1991).

But discerning the role that alienation plays in this development is not easy. Hegel never provides an analytic of the concept. We cannot look to a passage or a definition from which to start the discussion. We must tease out its meaning, work through the various shapes of consciousness to determine where it occurs, where it does not, and why it occurs in this shape and not in another. As Hegel reminds us when he famously writes that 'the True is the Whole' (PS: 11), we cannot understand consciousness's relation to alienation until we understand the whole phenomenological development of consciousness. Only once it has reached the certainty of Absolute Knowing can consciousness look back to determine why its previous understandings were partial. This looking back discloses that consciousness is alienated whenever it does not explicitly recognize that it is a living synthesis of subjectivity and objectivity and that, because spirit both grounds and mediates the various aspects of itself, it is, fundamentally, spirit.

This is not to say that consciousness's alienation emanates from the same relation or is manifested in the same way in each of the shapes it adopts. The descriptions of the various shapes of consciousness show that consciousness understands itself and its object differently in each shape it adopts. The unique deficiency of each of these shapes ensures that alienation enters the life of consciousness from a variety of different angles, perspectives, and relations. Importantly, however, consciousness's experience of the alienation constitutive of the various pre-Absolute Knowing shapes discloses that it is the experience of being alienated that is crucial to the process that allows it to overcome its alienation. This is necessarily so, because, as Hegel explains, 'it is the nature of spirit, of the Idea, to alienate itself in order to find itself again' (HP: 80).

Numerous commentators have failed to realize the complexity and multi-dimensionality of Hegel's analysis of alienation. Stanley Rosen

(1974: 173) is correct to maintain that alienation occurs when consciousness fails to understand that the objects it creates are externalizations of its own subjectivity, but fails to understand other sources of alienation. Philip Kain (2005: 156–169) correctly identifies that an aspect of alienation occurs when consciousness experiences reified socio-cultural structures, but fails to understand that not only does alienation not need to be explicitly experienced by consciousness, but that there are other sources of alienation besides reified social structures. Louis Dupré maintains that 'alienation occurs [...] when consciousness is unable to recognise itself in a particular form which it *knows* to be its own' (1972: 220), and so fails to understand that alienation does not need to be explicitly experienced by consciousness. Eric von der Luft (1989: 90) insists on a tripartite division of alienation into 'cultural,' 'spiritual' and 'perceived' forms of alienation and so recognizes that different forms of alienation occur in different shapes of consciousness. However, not only is this tripartite division too schematic, but it does not explicitly engage with the role that alienation plays in the overall phenomenological development of consciousness.

What these commentators fail to appreciate is that the role alienation plays in the phenomenological development of consciousness is not one-dimensional, does not only occur in one particular shape of consciousness, and is not only significant when it is explicitly experienced by consciousness. Properly understanding the role alienation plays in the phenomenological development of consciousness requires that we remember the contextual nature of Hegel's comments. Abigail Rosenthal is one of the few commentators to explicitly recognize that 'to argue a point in Hegelian interpretation by stressing a term he used, without at the same time signalling the whole scope and tendency of his thought, is to abandon all hope of understanding Hegel as a consistent philosopher. The same term may be used in different senses, according to the stages of the knowing consciousness wherein it appears' (1971: 206n).

With this in mind, we must remember that the role alienation plays in the phenomenological development of consciousness is nuanced, multi-faceted, and contextualized. In some shapes of consciousness, alienation is explicit, in others, it is implicit. What constitutes a moment of alienation in one shape of consciousness takes on a different meaning in another shape. The way consciousness is alienated depends on the context, the shape of consciousness under discussion, and the way consciousness comports itself towards its alienation in that particular shape of itself.

Alienation as estrangement

But to fully understand the role that alienation plays in the *Phenomenology of Spirit* requires that we recognize that 'alienation' translates two German words: 'Entfremdung' and 'Entaüsserung.' 'Entfremdung' describes a process or state where consciousness is separated from, at least, one of the aspects that are required for it to fully understand its ontological structure. In contrast, 'Entaüsserung' describes the process whereby consciousness externalizes itself in object form and, through this objectification, develops a better understanding of its ontological structure. To clarify the following discussion, 'Entfremdung' will be translated as 'estrangement,' and 'Entaüsserung' will be translated as 'externalization.'

Estrangement (*Entfremdung*) refers to what I have previously called 'alienation.' It occurs whenever consciousness does not explicitly recognize that it is constituted by a subjective and an objective aspect, and that, because spirit grounds and unifies both aspects without negating their independence, it is, fundamentally, spirit.

In its immediate form, the estrangement of consciousness is negative because, when estranged, consciousness fails to fully understand its ontological structure. However, while estrangement is negative, this is not to say that consciousness always *experiences* it negatively, nor is it to say that it is always experienced at all by consciousness. If estrangement required that consciousness be explicitly aware of its estrangement, the moments of estrangement would be limited. We would be unable to identify those moments of estrangement that consciousness does not explicitly experience, but in which it is nevertheless estranged because it does not understand that it is a spiritual synthesis of subjectivity and objectivity.

The shapes of consciousness called the 'Unhappy Consciousness' (PS: 126–130) and the description of 'the heart of the matter' in the shape of consciousness called 'The Spiritual Animal Kingdom and deceit, or the "Matter in Hand" itself' (PS: 246–252) demonstrate that consciousness can, but does not need to, *explicitly* experience its estrangement.

The Unhappy Consciousness develops from consciousness's previous experiences. It understands that consciousness is a 'dual-natured, [...] contradictory being' (PS: 126). This duality takes the form of an essential, objective aspect called the 'unchangeable,' and a contingent, subjective aspect called the 'changeable.' But the duality of the Unhappy Consciousness is not a static binary opposition; it is a duality constituted by motion. Consciousness takes the unchangeable aspect to be the essential moment and the changeable aspect to be the unessential moment. Despite both aspects belonging to the same consciousness, consciousness does not explicitly recognize this; it takes each aspect to be completely alien to the other. Because it is aware of the essential, unchangeable aspect, consciousness takes itself to be the unessential, changeable aspect. Combining this with its privileging of the former aspect ensures that the Unhappy Consciousness attempts to set aside its changeable aspect.

However, because this shape of consciousness is constituted by a duality, to negate one aspect of itself is to immediately reaffirm its opposite aspect. Whenever consciousness seeks to affirm its unchangeable aspect by negating the changeable aspect of itself, it does not achieve its aim, but simply reaffirms its changeable aspect. This reaffirmation sets the whole process off again. This shape is 'unhappy' for the simple reason that it cannot reconcile the two aspects of itself in a peaceful and harmonious way.

While the Unhappy Consciousness explicitly experiences its estrangement, consciousness does not have to explicitly experience a sense of estrangement to be estranged. This is shown in the discussion of the 'heart of the matter' in the shape of consciousness called 'The Spiritual Animal Kingdom and deceit, or the "Matter in Hand" itself' (PS: 246–252).

This shape of consciousness arises from consciousness's previous experiences. The 'heart of the matter' emanates from a discussion of the role and constitution of work. Through work, consciousness expresses itself in object form. This act of objectification develops consciousness's self-understanding because it brings consciousness to realize that objectivity is an aspect of its ontological structure. Work also allows consciousness to create an object that contributes to the life of its wider community and so brings it to recognize that it is intimately connected to something greater than itself. At this stage in its development, consciousness still has to explicitly recognize that this 'something greater' is spirit, but work contributes to this realization.

However, when this shape of consciousness lets its work go into the world, it adopts a specific attitude towards it. The consciousness of 'the heart of the matter' maintains that its work is merely an impartial, objective contribution to the development of its social world. However, the reality of its effort belies this superficial proclamation. The work is created, not as a disinterested contribution to the life of its community, but as an expression of consciousness's individuality. 'While, then, it seems to him that his concern is only with the "matter in hand" as an abstract reality, it is also a fact that he is concerned with it as his own doing' (PS: 249). Consciousness deceives itself for it takes itself to be acting out of universal concern when it is, in fact, only concerned with its own particular interest. By not sincerely and explicitly working towards the development of its community, consciousness is unable to develop the explicit knowledge of its organic relation with its community that would enhance its self-understanding. Importantly, however, consciousness does not explicitly recognize that its actions prevent it from fully understanding itself. It does not, therefore, explicitly experience the estrangement that results from its actions.

Degrees of estrangement

While Sartre's insistence that 'authenticity is achieved en bloc, one either is or is not authentic' (WD: 219) discloses that his analysis of alienation is constrained within an either/or dichotomy, Hegel's is more subtle. Because it shows that consciousness develops different understandings of its ontological structure, some of which allow it to have a better understanding of itself than others, Hegel's analysis discloses that the various shapes of the developmental process that brings consciousness to the shape of itself that allows it to fully understand its ontological structure are constituted by different degrees of estrangement. The different degrees of estrangement emanate from the manner in which the shapes of consciousness form a hierarchy of development. An earlier shape of consciousness is more alienated than a later shape of consciousness because, in earlier shapes of consciousness, consciousness is further away from fully understanding its ontological structure. Put conversely, the closer consciousness gets to Absolute Knowing, the less its existence is constituted by alienation.

As such, 'Sense-Certainty' is a more estranged form of consciousness than 'Revealed Religion' because, while neither shape allows consciousness to fully understand its ontological structure, in the shape of itself called 'Sense-Certainty,' consciousness is further from fully understanding its ontological structure. Indeed, because it has a less developed understanding of itself than other shapes of consciousness, 'Sense-Certainty' is the most estranged form of consciousness.

This is not to say, however, that consciousness *explicitly* experiences a lowering in its estrangement level as it progresses through the various shapes constitutive of the developmental process that allows it to fully understand its ontological structure. As noted, consciousness does not need to *explicitly* experience its estrangement to be estranged. But whether explicitly experienced or not, the overall phenomenological development of consciousness demonstrates that consciousness is constituted by the greatest degree of estrangement when it adopts a shape of itself that is at the lowest levels of self-understanding.

However, while Hegel recognizes that being estranged is an undesirable experience, he holds that we should not think that the experience of estrangement is *wholly* negative. Because consciousness's experience of the various pre-Absolute Knowing shapes of itself discloses that, in these shapes, its object is other than it initially took it to be, consciousness's experience teaches it that it must alter its self-understanding to understand its object. If consciousness is willing to learn from its mistake, it alters its understanding of its object to accord with the improved understanding of its object that its experience discloses. This process continues until consciousness's experience discloses that its understanding of its object corresponds to how its object is in-itself. At this point, consciousness discovers what its object truly is and, because its object is an aspect of its ontological structure, what it truly is.

Estrangement contributes to this development because it is only if consciousness is estranged from what it truly is that it will be motivated to alter its self-understanding to try to discover what it truly is. Thus, while consciousness's journey to full self-understanding is not an easy or happy one, the experience of 'pain, [...] self-estrangement [and] homelessness in the world [...] are necessary moments to be lived through by the individual consciousness [so] that it may ascend to higher levels of self-consciousness and freedom' (Greene, 1966: 367–368).

Thus, while Sartre insists that alienation is a purely negative phenomenon, Hegel recognizes that while consciousness's self-estrangement is undesirable, being estranged from what it truly is plays a fundamentally positive and constitutive role in consciousness's efforts to overcome its alienation. As such, while Sartre simply insists that consciousness must seek to avoid being alienated, Hegel offers a subtler analysis that shows that while consciousness may not wish to be estranged from itself, it is only by being estranged from what it truly is that consciousness can come to fully understand itself.

Alienation as externalization

But while Hegel demonstrates that estrangement is an undesirable phenomenon that, ultimately, contributes to consciousness's self-understanding, the second sense of 'alienation' allows consciousness to develop its self-understanding *immediately*. It is the combination of estrangement and self-externalization that contributes to the development of consciousness's self-understanding.

Externalization (*Entaüsserung*) describes the process whereby consciousness externalizes itself in objective form and, through this self-objectification, develops a better understanding of its ontological structure. While the experience of the estrangement constitutive of the pre-Absolute Knowing shapes of itself motivates consciousness to alter its self-understanding, externalization is the means through which consciousness objectifies itself and learns that objectivity is an aspect of its ontological structure. As Hegel explains, consciousness must 'externalise itself, have itself as an object, so that it knows what it is, in this way [it] exhausts all its potentialities, becomes entirely its object, wholly discloses itself and plumbs and reveals its whole depth' (HP: 80–81). By externalizing itself in the world and seeing itself manifested through its object, consciousness learns that its object is not simply opposed to itself; consciousness learns that objectivity is an aspect of its ontological structure. This allows consciousness to overcome the strict ontological opposition it initially understands itself to have to objectivity. As we will see, however, externalization can lead to estrangement if consciousness does not subsequently recognize itself in the object its self-externalization creates.

Consciousness can come to understand that externalization plays a positive role in the development of its self-understanding because it *passively* undertakes the duties constitutive of a particular shape of consciousness. This can be seen through the transformative role that work plays in the master/slave relation (PS: 111–119). Alternatively, consciousness can come to *purposefully* externalize itself in objective form because its previous experiences have taught it that externalization can enhance its self-understanding. This can be seen in the shape of consciousness entitled 'Individuality which takes itself to be Real In and For Itself' (PS: 236–252).

The famous section that describes the master/slave relation emanates from the development of previous shapes of consciousness. Consciousness's experience teaches it that the negation of an inanimate object does not allow it to fully understand itself. Rather than annihilate its inanimate object to affirm its independence, consciousness comes to realize that its self-understanding is dependent on it being recognized as a free being by another living consciousness.

However, consciousness does not want to recognize the other's freedom because this contradicts its insistence that its freedom is secured at the expense of the other's freedom. This leads each consciousness to try to gain the other's recognition of its freedom without recognizing the other's freedom. This creates a life-and-death struggle which is only overcome in a way that develops consciousness's self-understanding if one consciousness foregoes its own absolute freedom and becomes a slave. In turn, the dominant consciousness must realize that it requires a living being to provide it with the standing negation that will ground its own self-certainty; it must let the other consciousness live. An asymmetric master/slave relation is established. Because the slave chose to live rather than be free, he does not exercise his own freedom; he carries out the orders of the master. The slave is the mediating aspect between the master and the world. While the master relaxes and enjoys the world as it is brought to him by the slave, the slave must work on the world to bring it to his master.

But while it appears that the slave is in a position of complete and unfettered bondage, the slave's work allows him to transcend the slave's self-understanding. By working on the world to satisfy his master's desire, the slave exercises his own subjectivity and alters the objects of the world. By shaping these objects in line with his own subjectivity, the slave learns that he is not simply opposed to his world; he learns that the world is the objective expression of his subjective freedom. As Hegel explains, the object the slave has fashioned

> does not become something other than himself through being made external to him; for it is precisely this shape that is his pure being-for-self, which in this externality is seen by him to be the truth. Through this rediscovery of himself by himself, the bondsman realises that it is precisely in his work wherein he seemed to have only an alienated existence that he acquires a mind of his own (PS: 118–119).

While this shows that consciousness's act of externalization can be *reactive* in that consciousness does not have to purposefully initiate the externalization, but can be led to externalize itself through the activities constitutive of the particular shape of itself it has adopted, externalization does not have to be a reactive process. As consciousness's self-understanding develops, it learns that the process of externalization can allow it to better understand itself. With this, consciousness seeks to purposefully and *proactively* externalize itself in objective form. The shape of consciousness entitled 'Individuality which takes itself to be Real in and for itself' demonstrates that consciousness can purposefully externalize itself because its previous experiences have taught it that this can allow it to better understand itself.

This shape of consciousness develops from consciousness's experience of previous shapes of itself. Consciousness's experience has taught it of its relationship to the wider community. However, consciousness realizes that its universal community does not have a content that is independent of its actions. Through work, consciousness purposefully expresses its subjectivity in objective form and so provides its community with concrete content. By expressing itself in this manner, consciousness learns that it provides the content of its reality, while also seeing itself in objective form (PS: 242). By identifying with the object it has created, consciousness begins to understand that it is not simply a particular subject, but is intimately connected to a community. Consciousness must develop further if it is to fully overcome its estrangement from objectivity, but the important point for the current discussion is that, in this shape of itself, consciousness explicitly understands that it must externalize itself in object form to understand what it truly is.

While there are more to these shapes of consciousness than I have outlined, discussing these aspects of these shapes of consciousness shows that, irrespective of whether it occurs from a specific decision by consciousness or incidentally as a result of the activities constitutive of a particular shape of consciousness, externalizing itself through work contributes to the development of consciousness's self-understanding. In the early shapes of itself, consciousness learns from its externalization as it externalizes itself. This ensures that, having learnt from these experiences, the more developed shapes of consciousness have a more explicit understanding of the ways in which the process of externalization allows it to gain a better understanding of itself. This enables consciousness to recognize the importance of externalizing itself in objective form before it actually does it. In a sense, in the early shapes of consciousness, the positive development that arises from the process of externalization emanates from the logic of that particular shape of consciousness; consciousness does not explicitly recognize that the process of externalization is a necessary aspect of its journey to full self-understanding. In contrast, in the more developed shapes of itself, consciousness realizes that the process of externalization can contribute to its self-understanding and so explicitly seeks to externalize itself in objective form.

Because consciousness comes to fully understand itself by engaging in the activities constitutive of each shape of itself it adopts, its self-understanding develops as a result of its experiences. Consciousness's experiences do not necessarily result from a conscious effort to exercise its freedom. This leads to an important difference with Sartre's understanding of the relation between consciousness's experience and its self-understanding.

Because Sartre insists that consciousness is, at the very least, always pre-reflectively aware that it is ontologically opposed to its object, he maintains that it must use this 'knowledge' to choose to either live authentically by reflectively understanding its ontological opposition to objectivity or be alienated by reflectively understanding itself in terms of a fixed, ontological identity. For Sartre, consciousness's experiences do not play a constitutive role in determining consciousness's ontological structure, even if its experiences shape the life situations consciousness finds itself in.

In contrast, and while Hegel recognizes that consciousness is free to choose whether it will learn from its experiences, because he insists that consciousness and its world exist in a relation of ontological entwinement, he maintains that consciousness is not simply free to choose its existence; its self-understanding is intimately connected to its situation and previous experiences. While Hegel maintains that consciousness is free to determine whether it will learn from the various situations it finds itself in, he argues that it is a combination of consciousness's experiences, choices, and situations, and not, as Sartre believes, simply whether it chooses to adopt a fundamental project that brings it to reflectively understand what it is ontologically that determines whether consciousness's self-understanding is alienated or not.

Consciousness's reaction to its self-externalization

But Hegel holds that consciousness's understanding can only develop from the process of self-externalization if it approaches the object created in a specific way. First, consciousness must be open to the process of self-objectification. It must not think of this process as negative, or as a threat to its own subjectivity. Externalization takes courage on the part of consciousness. It must be willing to lose itself by becoming the object it initially takes itself to be other than.

Secondly, consciousness's self-externalization can only contribute to the development of its self-understanding if consciousness subsequently identifies with the object that its self-externalization creates. If consciousness achieves this, it will come to recognize that its object is an objective expression and extension of itself. If, however, consciousness externalizes itself in objective form, but then fails to recognize itself in the object it creates, it will not realize that the object it created is an extension of itself. It will continue to see its object as somehow strictly opposed to itself. With this, consciousness will continue to be estranged because it will fail to understand that it is intimately and ontologically entwined with its intentional object.

But it is not simply consciousness's reaction to its self-externalization that determines whether its self-objectification allows it to better understand itself. The degree of self-objectification that consciousness undergoes also determines whether consciousness's self-understanding develops immediately as a result of its self-externalization. While consciousness must objectify itself to develop its self-understanding, it must continue to understand that it is also a living subject. To focus on either the subjective or objective aspect of itself to the detriment of the other estranges consciousness from the spiritual synthesis of subjectivity and objectivity it truly is.

The shape of consciousness called 'Stoicism' shows that if consciousness retreats from the actual, concrete world and understands itself in terms of pure subjectivity, it becomes estranged from the objective aspect of its ontological structure. By neglecting the objective aspect of itself, this shape of consciousness understands itself in terms of pure subjectivity and does not realize that it is constituted by both a subjective *and* an objective aspect.

In contrast, the shape of consciousness called 'Physiognomy and Phrenology' demonstrates that consciousness estranges itself if it tries to understand itself in terms of pure objectivity. By understanding that it is synonymous with the objectivity of the hands or head of its body, this shape of consciousness maintains that *'the being of spirit is a bone'* (PS: 208). By holding that it is essentially an object, consciousness neglects the subjective aspect of its ontological structure and so fails to understand that it is a spiritual synthesis of subjectivity and objectivity.

Hegel's understanding of consciousness's relation to objectivity and objectification is, therefore, nuanced and multi-faceted. This is not and has not always been appreciated. For example, Karl Marx fails to recognize Hegel's differentiated understanding of objectivity and objectification and their relation to consciousness when he maintains that Hegel simply holds that all forms of self-objectification estrange consciousness from its pure, abstract subjectivity. This misreading of Hegel led Marx to famously declare that, because Hegel turned thought on its head by subsuming the concrete world within the abstract world of spirit, we need to put philosophy on its feet by emphasizing the concrete, material conditions of human existence (1992: 386–387).

However, not only is Hegel aware that a form of self-objectification is a necessary aspect of the process that develops consciousness's understanding of its ontological structure, but he does not hold that consciousness is a pure subjectivity in the way Marx maintains he does. The phenomenological development of consciousness demonstrates that if consciousness is to fully understand its ontological structure, it must not privilege either the subjective or objective aspect of itself, ignore the concrete world, or make the concrete world subservient to another world called 'spirit.' Consciousness must come to understand and accept that it is a spiritual synthesis of subjectivity and objectivity, that it shares this (non-determining) spiritual essence with its world, and that a specific relationship with a reshaped concrete world is fundamental to the development of this understanding.

Marx's failure to realize this leads to a distorted interpretation of Hegel that fails to understand that: 1) while he recognizes that consciousness must come to realize this, Hegel maintains that consciousness is a spiritual synthesis of subjectivity and objectivity; it is not simply a pure, subjective consciousness confronting an alien, objective world; 2) Hegel's notion of spirit is not abstract or transcendent to this world; it delineates the ontological substance constitutive of all beings that, initially, finds concrete expression, to various degrees and forms, as an ontological potential implicit to the ontological structure of each particular being that must be, and is only, realized by the social activities and actions of the beings it constitutes; and 3) Hegel distinguishes between self-objectification that leads to the immediate development of consciousness's self-understanding and self-objectification that estranges consciousness from what it truly is.

This distinction is important because it discloses a fundamental difference in the way that Hegel and Sartre conceptualize consciousness's ontological structure. As I have argued, Sartre's analyses of consciousness's relation to objectivity and objectification are contradictory, insofar as he holds that, in terms of its ontological structure, consciousness is opposed to all forms of objectivity; while, in terms of his analysis of authenticity, he holds that being authentic requires that consciousness effect the conversion that brings it to reflectively understand: 1) the important and inescapable role that its objective body and situation play in embedding it in the concrete world; and 2) that developing a specific relation with objectivity can enhance, rather than constrain, its practical freedom.

But Sartre is also inconsistent in his remarks on the relation between consciousness and the object created as a result of consciousness's act of self-objectification. In the *Critique of Dialectical Reason* (CDR 1: 253), Sartre appears to hold that the objects created as a result of consciousness's creative act of self-expression *always* subsequently appear to

consciousness as obstacles that must first be overcome before consciousness can freely express itself practically. But, in *What is Literature?* (WL:
29), Sartre holds that, if consciousness undergoes the conversion, it
comes to see that the objects created as a result of its creative act of self-
objectification enhance, rather than constrain, its practical freedom.

Hegel's analyses of consciousness's relation to objectivity and objectification are more consistent, coherent, subtle, and multi-dimensional.
Because he maintains that consciousness is a spiritual synthesis of subjectivity and objectivity, he argues that fully understanding its ontological structure requires that consciousness reflectively understand
that objectivity is an aspect of its ontological structure. One of the ways
through which consciousness comes to recognize this is by externalizing itself in objective form and subsequently recognizing itself in the
object it creates. This allows Hegel to distinguish between relations with
objectivity that alienate consciousness from what it truly is ontologically,
relations with *objectivity* that allow consciousness to fully understand
its ontological structure, *self-objectification* that is alienating, *self-objectification* that enhances consciousness's self-understanding, *self-objectification* that consciousness purposefully does to itself that subsequently
alienates it, *self-objectification* that consciousness purposefully does to
itself that develops its self-understanding, and *self-objectification* that
results from the activities of a particular shape of consciousness, rather
than from any purposeful intent on the part of consciousness. By insisting that consciousness can, and must, have different relations with its
object to fully understand its ontological structure, Hegel's analysis of
consciousness's ontological structure is not only able to distinguish
between different forms of *objectivity* and *self-objectification*, but is also
able to produce a more nuanced and differentiated understanding of
the *ontological* relation between consciousness, objectivity, and the act
of objectification than that offered by Sartre's.

Concluding remarks

Previous chapters have, I hope, made it clear that Hegel and Sartre
have different conceptions of alienation and authenticity with these
differences grounded in the different ways they conceptualize consciousness's ontological structure. Throughout, I have argued that it is
Hegel's analysis of consciousness's ontological structure that is able to,
and indeed does, provide the more subtle, nuanced, and multi-dimensional analysis of a range of topics. To further develop my argument,
it may be helpful to examine how each thinker justifies his analysis of

consciousness's ontological structure. This will disclose whether it is simply a matter of philosophical choice, or whether there is something in their philosophical method that supports my argument that Hegel's analysis of consciousness's ontological structure is capable of providing the more subtle and multi-dimensional account of alienation and consciousness's relation to alienation than Sartre's.

Sartre's account of authenticity is complex and multi-dimensional. It seeks to combine numerous, sometimes contradictory, arguments in a way that discloses not only what being authentic is, but what consciousness must do to exist authentically. The problem Sartre has, however, is that of justifying his account. Sartre's method is to describe the ontological structure of two categories of being and then, in the case of consciousness, describe the various ways consciousness can live its ontological structure. It could be thought from this that Sartre justifies his account of authenticity by insisting that authenticity requires that consciousness be true to what it is ontologically. In other words, consciousness is authentic if it reflectively understands that it is ontologically nothing. This is an aspect of Sartre's account of authenticity, but he goes beyond this by arguing that authenticity requires that consciousness also fulfil certain experiential conditions, such as being practically free *and* reflectively recognizing, caring for, and affirming the other's freedom. The question is: how does Sartre justify these ethical demands?

As I argued in Chapter 2, Sartre justifies his philosophical conclusions through an appeal to intuition (Detmer, 1998: 186–202). In other words, Sartre maintains that contemplation of the concept 'authenticity' brings him to *see* or *feel* that authenticity requires that consciousness act in the manner he describes.

However, the problem with simply insisting that consciousness act in a certain way is, as Hegel notes, that '*one* bare assurance is worth just as much as another' (PS: 49). Because Sartre simply insists on specific conditions of authenticity, there appears to be no reason why other conditions are not equally justified. Sartre simply leaves us with a philosophical choice: either we accept his argument or we do not.

In contrast, Hegel attempts to justify his account of the authentic self-understanding of Absolute Knowing by showing that it is consciousness's experience that brings it to this form of self-understanding. This is important for two reasons: first, it means that whereas Sartre insists that authenticity relates to the way consciousness chooses to live its ontological freedom, Hegel holds that the achievement of the authentic self-understanding of Absolute Knowing is not simply a matter of individual choice; it is dependent on a specific developmental process that occurs as a result of consciousness's reaction to its *experiences*. In other words, it is Hegel's analysis of consciousness's ontological structure and not Sartre's that depends on consciousness's experiences to disclose what consciousness's ontological structure truly is.

Secondly, it means that whereas Sartre defines authenticity by simply insisting on specific conditions consciousness must meet, Hegel justifies his insistence that Absolute Knowing constitutes the authentic form of self-understanding by demonstrating that consciousness's experience of other conceptions of self-understanding fail on their own terms. Contra Sartre, Hegel does not impose his own conception of authenticity onto consciousness and simply insist that consciousness conform to it; he shows that consciousness's own experiences demonstrate the truth of Absolute Knowing.

Furthermore, as I have noted, an aspect of Sartre's account of the authentic consciousness is that it reflectively understands and affirms its ontological freedom by reflectively affirming its ontological opposition to objectivity. According to Hegel, however, the problem with this formulation is that, rather than freeing consciousness from determinate being, it locks consciousness within a constraining necessity: the necessity that it *must* set itself in opposition to all forms of determinate being. This necessity violates consciousness's desired freedom. For this reason, Hegel insists that consciousness is only truly free if 'it is at home with [it]self in the other' (HP: 82). Rather than understanding that it exists in strict ontological opposition to its object, Hegel holds that consciousness will: 1) only fully understand its ontological structure if it accepts that objectivity is an aspect of its ontological structure; and 2) be truly free if it comes to see a particular form of its world as an extension of itself.

Of course, it may be objected that Sartre holds that authenticity requires that consciousness reflectively understands that objectivity is a necessary and potentially positive aspect of its practical experience. However, it is only at the *experiential* level of his analysis of the authentic consciousness's relation to objectivity that Sartre draws close to Hegel's insistence that being truly free requires that consciousness come to understand that developing a specific relation with objectivity can extend, rather than constrain, its freedom. Ontologically, Sartre holds that a condition of consciousness's existence (whether authentic or not) is that it pre-reflectively nihilates the objectivity of being-in-itself. But Sartre's insistence that authenticity requires that consciousness adopt a pre-reflective fundamental project that leads it to reflectively understand that developing a specific relation with objectivity can enhance, rather than constrain, its practical freedom does not sit well with the *ontological* level of his analysis that holds that consciousness exists in strict opposition to objectivity.

In contrast, Hegel's insistence that consciousness's ontological structure is composed of a subjective and an objective aspect, and that consciousness comes to realize this through its experiences means that: 1) his account of the authentic consciousness is not split between two levels of analysis; consciousness's ontological structure and its self-understanding develop through its practical experiences; and 2) developing a specific relation with objectivity, in which consciousness sees its object as an extension of its freedom, is not simply necessary because consciousness's practical activity depends on objectivity. It is necessary because the development of the ontological potential implicit to its ontological structure requires that consciousness interacts with its object in a specific way. Thus, while the reconciliation of consciousness to its object that takes place in Sartre's analysis occurs at the superficial level of practical experience leaving untouched consciousness's *ontological* opposition to objectivity, Hegel holds that consciousness can only fully understand its ontological structure and realize the potential implicit to its ontological structure if and when it understands that objectivity is an aspect of its *ontological structure.*

But there is a further difference between the two thinkers relating to what being authentic entails. For Sartre, being authentic is defined by the *process* whereby consciousness reflectively understands and affirms its ontological and practical freedom. In contrast, the phenomenological development demonstrates that, for Hegel, consciousness overcomes its alienation when it reaches the authentic self-understanding of Absolute Knowing. For Hegel, therefore, the authentic self-understanding of Absolute Knowing is a *state of being* to be realized. But this does not mean that there is a simple difference between the two thinkers in that while Sartre thinks authenticity delineates a specific way of living constituted by a specific process consciousness must constantly reflectively engage in, Hegel thinks the authentic self-understanding of Absolute Knowing describes a state of being to be attained.

While Sartre insists that an aspect of authenticity describes the process whereby consciousness continuously reflectively nihilates its object to reflectively affirm its ontological non-identity, Hegel insists that the authentic self-understanding of Absolute Knowing is a state of being to be attained, with this state of being only attained because consciousness engages in a specific developmental process.

While Sartre's thought is grounded in a binary opposition that privileges, what he sees, as the activity of becoming authentic over the passivity of being authentic, Hegel's phenomenological development of consciousness demonstrates that consciousness only overcomes its alienation by engaging in a specific process that brings it to fully understand itself, its object, and their ontological entwinement.

However, Hegel recognizes that once consciousness achieves the authentic self-understanding of Absolute Knowing, its battle against alienation is not over. When the authentic self-understanding of Absolute Knowing is *attained*, consciousness must continually fight to *maintain* it. Attaining the state of being that allows it to fully understand its ontological structure is, for Hegel, a continuous process of becoming.

But while Hegel and Sartre recognize that authenticity involves a process of becoming that needs to be constantly recreated, they differ in terms of what this means. For Sartre, consciousness is continuously thrown back into the same fundamental choice: whether to adopt the *inauthentic* pre-reflective fundamental project of bad faith or whether to adopt the *authentic* pre-reflective fundamental project that has the affirmation of freedom as its end. The Sartrean consciousness never escapes this fundamental choice. But neither does it seem that there is a reason why consciousness should choose the *authentic*, pure form of self-reflection over the *inauthentic*, impure form of self-reflection (NE: 357). Indeed, as noted in Chapter 1, the existential anxiety that results from the adoption of the authentic, pure form of self-reflection surely provides consciousness with a valuable reason to choose the inauthentic, impure form of self-reflection?

While it is unclear why the Sartrean consciousness would choose to explicitly experience the failure *and* anxiety of the authentic, pure form of self-reflection as opposed to the mere failure of the inauthentic, impure form of self-reflection, Hegel provides, at least, three reasons why consciousness will strive to overcome its alienation and be authentic. First, the developmental nature of consciousness's journey to the authentic self-understanding of Absolute Knowing is so structured that, if it is *rational*, its various experiences will provide the impetus that leads consciousness to develop its self-understanding to the shape of Absolute Knowing.

Furthermore, while Sartre holds that consciousness is constantly returned to the same fundamental choice, Hegel maintains that this is not necessarily consciousness's fate. If it is undertaken *logically*, consciousness's journey to the authentic self-understanding of Absolute

Knowing is one where consciousness's experience gradually *reduces* the number of choices it faces until it comes to the form of self-understanding in which its experience of itself corresponds to what it understands itself to be. Thus, while Hegel recognizes that consciousness must choose to follow it, he maintains that there is a *logic* to its phenomenological development that drives consciousness to make specific choices that, ultimately, bring it to the authentic self-understanding of Absolute Knowing.

Secondly, while Hegel and Sartre agree that reflectively understanding its ontological structure is a necessary condition of authenticity, they disagree as to what consciousness's *experience* of the authentic form of self-understanding entails. Whereas Sartre holds that the authentic form of reflective self-understanding causes consciousness to experience *failure* and *anguish* as opposed to the mere *failure* of the inauthentic, impure form of self-reflection, Hegel understands that consciousness's experience of the authentic self-understanding of Absolute Knowing is inherently *fulfilling* (PS: 492). Hegel argues that, because the experience of the authentic self-understanding of Absolute Knowing is inherently fulfilling, consciousness will continue to strive for it.

But this does not mean that the existence of the consciousness of Absolute Knowing is perfect or without difficulties, challenges, and struggles. Hegel recognizes that the fulfilled consciousness will still encounter difficulties and challenges. However, by fully understanding its ontological structure, he holds that consciousness will not be overcome by its difficulties. Its self-certainty will allow consciousness to better understand its capabilities and situation which, in turn, will allow it to more easily deal with the difficulties and struggles it encounters.

Thirdly, Hegel insists that consciousness will follow the logic of the phenomenological development because its ontological potential 'has the urge to develop, to exist, to change into the form of existence' (HP: 77). In other words, consciousness has an implicit ontological desire to realize its implicit ontological potential which shapes its choices towards those that will allow it to realize what it can potentially be.

Hegel and Sartre do, however, agree that while consciousness is free to choose to adopt a particular form of self-understanding, once it does, the *logic* of its choice crystallizes over it and shapes its worldview. In other words, when consciousness adopts a specific form of self-understanding, it becomes embedded within the *logic* constitutive of that form of self-understanding. The logic of each form of self-understanding consciousness adopts *implicitly* shapes the *explicit* choices it makes. So if, in Sartre's terms, consciousness's pre-reflectively chosen fundamental project is to be a doctor, its reflective choices will subsequently be directed towards the fulfilment of this fundamental project. In Hegelian terms, once consciousness chooses to enter a shape of consciousness, the logic of that specific shape of itself leads consciousness to think in a specific way.

However, while both thinkers agree on this point, the different ways they conceptualize consciousness's ontological structure ensure that they differ in terms of the degree to which consciousness's chosen form of self-understanding shapes its existence and self-understanding. While Sartre recognizes that its society shapes consciousness's initial choice of *fundamental project* and *can* shape its *reflective* self-understanding, he holds that consciousness's ontological nothingness ensures it is not synonymous with either of these; consciousness can always simply choose to alter its pre-reflective fundamental project.

While Hegel agrees with Sartre that subjective choice is an aspect of the process through which consciousness alters its self-understanding, because he maintains that consciousness's ontological structure and self-understanding are shaped by its social interaction to a greater degree than Sartre recognizes, Hegel holds that consciousness cannot simply choose to be other than it is at that moment. The dialectical entwinement between consciousness and its social world ensures that, for Hegel, it is far more difficult for consciousness to alter its self-understanding than it is for the Sartrean consciousness that simply has to choose to effect the conversion to the authentic, pure form of self-reflection.

Furthermore, while Sartre recognizes that consciousness can learn from its past failures and so effect the conversion that allows it to *live with* objectivity in a way that enhances its practical freedom, this learning only affects consciousness *experientially;* it never affects consciousness's ontological structure: consciousness is, and can only ever be, *ontologically* opposed to objectivity.

In contrast, because Hegel holds that consciousness's intentional object is an aspect of its ontological structure, and because he recognizes that consciousness must *learn* what it is ontologically, he is able to show that while the subject/object binary opposition of Sartre's analysis of consciousness's ontological structure describes one potential ontological relation consciousness can have to its object, it is not the only one. Indeed, Hegel's analysis of consciousness's ontological structure insists that consciousness will only truly understand its ontological structure if it learns to *not* think of itself in terms of the subject/object dichotomy and, instead, realizes that it is a spiritual synthesis of subjectivity and objectivity. Importantly, however, by insisting that a development in its self-understanding also entails an alteration in its ontological structure, Hegel shows that the learning process consciousness goes through as a result of its decision to follow the logic of the phenomenological development effects it to the very depths of its being.

But, because its intentional object is an aspect of its ontological structure, when consciousness achieves the shape of itself that allows it to fully understand itself, it also achieves the form of understanding that allows it to think about its object in the manner that discloses what its object truly is. Because consciousness's phenomenological development demonstrates that only the *philosophical* consciousness can allow it to fully understand itself and its object, it follows that it is the job of *philosophy* to describe the content of its object.

With this, Hegel can claim that his *phenomenology* has: 1) defended and legitimized philosophy as *the* form of consciousness that has privileged access to the truth; 2) showed that, contrary to popular opinion's insistence that *philosophy* can be immediately undertaken by all, there is, in fact, a developmental process that consciousness *must* undertake if it is to think about an issue in the manner that will allow it to know the truth of that issue; and 3) demonstrated the path that consciousness must traverse if it is to bring itself to the form of self-understanding that will allow it to fully understand itself and its object.

By grounding his philosophical thought in the self-grounding certainty gained from the phenomenological development of consciousness, Hegel offers a justification for his philosophical thought in a way that Sartre does not. Of course, it may be objected that this relies on the truth of the phenomenological development. But even if the truth of the phenomenological development is questioned, we have to agree that even by raising the question of how to justify philosophical thought, Hegel goes beyond Sartre for whom the issue of philosophical justification does not appear to have been of any concern.

But while the phenomenological development shows the process that will allow *consciousness* to fully understand itself and so overcome its self-alienation, Hegel recognizes that the *concrete individual* cannot simply be associated with *consciousness*. What we need, therefore, is a further analysis that demonstrates the means through which the concrete individual can overcome his alienation from the actual world.

Hegel's *Philosophy of Right* uses the certainty the philosophical consciousness has won from the phenomenological development to expound and elaborate on the objective social structures and ethical disposition necessary to allow the individual to overcome his alienation from the objective world. But we must not think that the division identified here between Hegel's discussion of consciousness's relation to alienation and his discussion of the concrete individual's relation to alienation is a strict separation. For Hegel, consciousness's concrete situation impacts on its capacity to fully understand itself and consciousness's self-understanding impacts on the content of its concrete situation.

Thus, despite their differences in terms of how consciousness achieves this, and what it entails, Hegel and Sartre agree that while fully understanding its ontological structure is a condition that consciousness must fulfil to overcome its alienation, it is not the only one. Both agree that, for it to overcome its alienation, consciousness must also be able to freely and creatively express itself in the actual world. Their different understandings of 'freedom' do, however, mean that they disagree as to what is required for this to be realized. We have already discussed the individual and collective actions Sartre thinks are necessary to realize the individual's practical freedom so, in the next chapter, it is time to see what Hegel says about these matters. This will disclose the objective structures and subjective ethical disposition he thinks are necessary for the individual to overcome his social alienation and be truly free.

7
Hegel's Social Philosophy: Abstract Right and Morality

While Hegel's *Phenomenology of Spirit* describes the process that allows consciousness to fully understand itself and so overcome its alienation, Hegel's social philosophy uses the certainty the philosophical consciousness has won from its phenomenological development to describe the conditions required to allow the concrete individual to overcome his alienation from his social world.

But the individual does not simply achieve this by deciding that his world is no longer alien to him or by subsuming the world within his own subjectivity. The individual overcomes his alienation from the external world when he recognizes it as a home and, crucially, when that home realizes the universal freedom Hegel insists is necessary to secure individual freedom. This requires that the individual develop a particular form of self-understanding and that he live 'in certain (ultimately institutional, norm-governed) relations to others' (Pippin, 2008: 4). But, crucially, Hegel's social ontology means that the individual does not first understand himself before developing the objective relations that will allow him to overcome his social alienation. For Hegel, the individual's reflective self-understanding is dialectically entwined with his social world.

This is different from Sartre for whom, as we saw, the individual's sense of self-reflection is grounded in a purely subjective decision as to the form of pre-reflective fundamental project he will adopt. While others impact on his practical freedom, the extent to which the individual understands his ontological nothingness/freedom is primarily dependent on whether he is willing to simply choose to undergo the conversion that subsequently allows him to develop the relationships with others that enhance his practical freedom. For Hegel, however, coming to fully reflectively understand himself requires that the individual's social world be so structured that it facilitates the form of self-understanding that realizes this end. For Hegel, the individual's sense of self is intimately bound up with and connected to his social world in a way that is lacking in Sartre's account.

The aim of Hegel's social philosophy is to identify the objective social structures, cultural norms, and subjective ethical comportment that will allow the individual to overcome his estrangement from the world. Thus, contrary to the claim that 'the *Philosophy of Right* does not expound a specific theory of the state' (Marcuse, 1996: 184), Hegel's social philosophy is a piece of normative political theory that sets out to describe the structures of the state that are required for a universally free society. But, because Hegel notes that philosophy 'must distance itself as far as possible from the obligation to construct a *state as it ought to be*' (PR: Preface, 21), the normative aspect of his thought must be properly understood.

While the *Philosophy of Right* sets out the objective structures of the state that are necessary for the realization of freedom, Hegel does not simply impose his own abstract conception of the state onto actuality. Because he thinks that the modern world contains, at least in embryonic form, the necessary structures for the full realization of freedom, and because he recognizes that no actual state contains *all* of these aspects, he combines aspects of the various actual states of his time to describe what the rational fully free-state would look like. This ensures that 'Hegel's political philosophy is non-utopian insofar as it focuses upon a comprehension of existing arrangements. But neither is it conservative, for [it] provides an implicit critique [of] the contradictions and limitations in these arrangements and thereby looks beyond them to developments they imply' (Ware, 1999: 148).

However, even though his account of ethical life combines various aspects of the political systems of his own time, this does not mean that Hegel's rational state is simply relevant to his own time, nor does it mean that because some of the objective structures of the rational state are no longer a part of our social world that it is somehow incorrect or has nothing to teach us. Because Hegel insists that his conception of the state is fully rational, and because an aspect of rationality concerns itself with universality, he insists that, irrespective of whether these objective structures actually exist or whether they appear as strange and antiquated relics of the past, his conception of the rational state does describe the universal structures, cultural norms, and subjective ethical comportment that are necessary for the individual to overcome his estrangement from the world and be fully free.

But Hegel's insistence that true freedom requires the individual to live in a state has not been universally endorsed. For example, while Charles Taylor maintains that 'Hegel's political theory is quite without precedent or parallel' (1998: 81) and Stephen Houlgate argues that the *Philosophy of Right* is 'one of the greatest works of social and political theory ever written' (2005: 181), Karl Popper (2003: 24) associates Hegel's conception of freedom with totalitarianism. On this reading, not only is it a political philosophy without merit, but it is one that should be condemned in the strongest possible terms.

However, while Hegel notes that the full realization of freedom requires the individual to live as a member of a state, the next chapter will show that Popper is wrong to associate this with the notion that the individual must conform to *any* state *and* even that Hegel's rational state usurps the independence of the individual. Not only does Hegel make the realization of freedom dependent on the realization of a *specific* state, namely one that is rational, whereby rationality delineates a state that is subject to rational analysis *and* conforms to Hegel's understanding of the concept 'freedom,' but the relationship the individual is to have to the state is not one in which the individual's freedom is usurped by the demands of the state. The architectonic of Hegel's theory of the state is so structured that each individual's freedom is safeguarded in a way that contributes to the realization of every other individual's freedom.

But the *Philosophy of Right* does not simply define the concept 'freedom' and then describe the state that will realize it. Rather than simply assert his definition of freedom, Hegel takes the time and effort to justify it by considering the inadequacies of other conceptions of freedom. In the same way that the phenomenological development of consciousness uses the process of *determinate negation* to build on the various experiences of its various shapes of itself until consciousness fully understands itself, so too does Hegel's social philosophy use the process of determinate negation to build on the partial account of freedom constitutive of abstract right and morality. This allows Hegel to then describe what the fully realized freedom of ethical life entails. There are, therefore, three conceptions of freedom at play in Hegel's *Philosophy of Right*: the freedom of abstract right, the freedom of morality (*Moralität*), and the fully realized freedom of ethical life (*Sittlichkeit*) (Neuhouser, 2000: 5).

Importantly, however, the less developed forms of freedom are not simply *replaced* by another conception of freedom; the partial truth(s) of the less developed conceptions of freedom are *incorporated* into the more developed forms of freedom. This ensures that the most developed form of freedom (ethical life) contains the partial truth(s) of the less developed forms of freedom (abstract right and morality). This allows Hegel to show what the fully realized freedom of ethical life entails *and*, by identifying the inadequacies of alternative conceptions of freedom and showing that they logically require the structures constitutive of ethical life, justify why the freedom of ethical life is the fullest realization of freedom.

But as outlined in Chapter 5, Hegel has a particular, and somewhat unique, understanding of the concept 'freedom.' To understand his social philosophy and the role alienation plays in this philosophy, we have to understand his particular understanding of freedom. As such, in the first section of this chapter, I briefly return to Hegel's conception of freedom to show why he believes that individual freedom is dependent on a particular form of social world. In section two, I engage with the freedom of abstract right; and, in section three, the freedom of morality. I do not pretend that this discussion will engage with every aspect of Hegel's thinking; my aim is more modest in that it aims to reveal the general outline of Hegel's argument that will allow the next chapter to show why he believes that individual freedom is only truly realized in ethical life.

The sociality of individual freedom

While Hegel recognizes that the will is infinite in the abstract, he rejects the notion that the will should use this infinite abstract possibility to simply do as it please when it pleases. First, the will that arbitrarily determines what it is to do immediately finds itself questioning whether its choice is the correct one. It therefore rescinds its previous choice and chooses another; this, however, also ends in self-doubt. This self-doubt prevents the will from actually achieving anything in concrete reality.

Secondly, the will that acts arbitrarily insists on the division between its infinite freedom and the notion that finite existence limits this freedom. As such, the will insists its determinate activity contradicts its infinite freedom. This leads the will to insist that it is the *process* of making itself determinate as opposed to the status of *being* determinate that allows it to freely exist in the world. In other words, to remain as an indeterminate being requires that the will constantly exert itself in opposition to determinacy. The problem with this activity, however, is that, because the will *must* constantly negate determinacy to remain indeterminate, it finds its subjective freedom constrained by this necessity. As such, it is no longer free.

Applying this argument concretely means that individual freedom is not won when the individual simply asserts himself against others. Freedom requires the individual to act in a manner that respects and affirms the other's freedom. Only this action will allow each to: 1) win the recognition from another free being that is necessary to validate and re-enforce his own freedom; and 2) be free from the necessity of having to protect his freedom from other's attempts to become free.

Thus, for Hegel, freedom is not won when the individual acts in accordance with his own subjective whim; freedom requires the individual to comport himself in a manner that is 'in accordance with the concepts of ethics' (PR: 15A). In short, he must act in a way that respects and affirms the freedom of all. This, however, requires that he overcome the sense of self-identity that maintains a distinction between himself and others and, instead, comes to see that he is ontologically entwined with the other. This is crucial because 'the will which has being in and for itself is *truly infinite,* because its object [*Gegenstand*] is itself, and therefore not something which it sees as *other* or as a *limitation*; on the contrary, it has merely returned into itself in its object' (PR: 22). Or, put differently, freedom is not realized when the individual secures his indeterminate freedom in opposition to his world; true freedom 'consists in cancelling [*aufzuheben*] the contradiction between subjectivity and objectivity and in translating its ends from their subjective determination into an objective one, while at the same time remaining *with itself* in this objectivity' (PR: 28).

By seeing and recognizing himself in his other, Hegel insists the individual will overcome the alien-ness of his objective world and recognize that his social world is an extension and expression of himself rather than something that limits his activity. It is for this reason that Hegel defines freedom as 'being at home with oneself in one's other' (EL: 24A2; see also HP: 79–80).

Importantly, however, it is not the case that the individual must come to reconcile himself to any socio-cultural formation. For Hegel, individual freedom is dependent on him existing within and consciously affirming objective structures that allow him to express himself and achieve his own ends, while doing so in a way that facilitates and supports the freedom of others. This does not mean that each is sacrificed to the well-being of others; each individual's freely chosen actions express his intentions in a way that also contributes to the freedom of others.

Furthermore, the objective structures of ethical life must not simply dictate how the individual is to act. While they provide guidelines for his action, the objective structures of his social world must leave the individual with sufficient scope to freely and creatively express himself. As such, to freely act in the world requires objective structures that allow each individual to freely express himself as far as possible, but not so far as his actions threaten the overall freedom of his community, which, it will be remembered, would also undermine his own freedom.

But again, getting each individual to limit his activity to that which facilitates and supports the freedom of others is not something that is simply imposed on each individual from an external source. A free society requires the cultivation of a particular community-orientated social culture manifested 'in' each individual as a community-orientated mentality. Such a culture/mentality will bring each individual to spontaneously and *voluntarily* act in a manner that contributes to the freedom of others. The instantiation of this community-orientated culture/mentality will ensure that each individual's activity and sense of self is spontaneously and un-reflectively aligned to the freedom of his wider community.

There is, in other words, an objective and a subjective aspect to ethical life. 'The objective side of ethical life is the ethical order, a rationally articulated system of social institutions. The subjective side is the ethical disposition or attitude (*Gesinnung*) [of the individuals of the community]' (Wood, 1995: 209). Each aspect plays an important role in getting individuals to realize that their own freedom is dependent on the freedom of others. Thus, rather than value the individual's freedom over that of the wider society or the wider society over the individual, Hegel aims to describe those objective structures and the subjective ethical comportment necessary to reconcile the individual's actions to those that facilitate and support the freedom of all citizens. As such, neither the individual nor the state will be primary; instead, the creation of a number of interlocking structures and the development of a specific community-orientated culture will bring each to recognize that his freedom is dependent on the freedom of others. In turn, this will bring each to voluntarily comport himself in a way that facilitates and supports the other's freedom.

But before getting to the objective structures and subjective comportment that will secure the freedom constitutive of ethical life, and because Hegel justifies the freedom found in ethical life by demonstrating the limitations inherent to other conceptions of freedom, it is necessary to first discuss the freedom of abstract right and morality.

Abstract right and private property

The first form of freedom Hegel examines is the least developed form: it is the purely abstract, formal freedom of abstract right. Abstract right values the individual's capacity to abstract from everything concrete and so remain free from the contingencies of concrete existence. By privileging the abstract sense of self instantiated by his abstract rights, the individual thinks he manages to remain free from all determinate being. However, because 'indeterminacy itself, when opposed to the determinate, takes on the determination of being something determinate' (PR: 34A), his privileging of indeterminacy does not, in actuality, allow him to escape a determinate identity. By insisting that he is an indeterminate being, he actually attains a (negative) determinate identity in the form of: 'I am not anything determinate.' With this, he attains the 'abstract identity' (PR: 34A) of a *'person'* (PR: 34A).

By thinking of himself as an 'abstract I' (PR: 35R), the individual gains certain universal rights. But, because these rights are purely formal, they do not take into account particular circumstances or contingencies (PR: 37); they simply delineate the minimum universal rights necessary for an individual to be a person. As Hegel explains, 'in formal right, therefore, it is not a question of particular interests, of my advantage or welfare, and just as little of the particular ground by which my will is determined i.e. of my insight and intention' (PR: 37). Abstract right simply delineates the minimum formal conditions that will allow the individual to be considered a free being.

But securing his own abstract rights in a world full of other persons requires that each individual treat others as he would wish to be treated. With this, abstract right achieves two goals: 1) it delineates the minimum universal rights necessary to define an individual as a person; and 2) it establishes universal guidelines that dictate how individuals should act in relation to others. Because the commandment of this form of right 'is [...] *be a person and respect others as persons'* (PR: 36), these guidelines take the form: the individual is defined by certain inalienable rights and is to be able to freely express himself in accordance with these rights, but only to the extent that his actions do not violate the abstract right of other individuals.

Because abstract right delineates an abstract 'I,' the individual of abstract right takes himself to exist in opposition to his concrete world. However, his abstract subjectivity contradicts the wills conception of itself as 'infinite and universal' (PR: 39). To overcome this contradiction and fully conform to the universality of its own self-conception, the will of abstract right seeks to possess objective things. By designating objects as his, the person is able to: 1) maintain and affirm his conception of himself as an absolutely free being; while 2) incorporating objects into his life. By determining how he will use objects, the person affirms his independence from objects and so re-enforces his sense of identity as an absolutely free being. In other words, possession of property secures the individual's sense of self and his freedom. In fact, Hegel goes on to say that possessing property is so important to the individual's sense of self that it is 'not until he has property [that] the person exist[s] as reason' (PR: 41A). In other words, the individual can only be free if he possesses private property.

Thus, whereas Sartre maintains that property is important because it allows the individual to satisfy his material needs, Hegel maintains that this is not the true significance of property. If property is simply understood as being that which allows individuals to fulfil their material needs, it becomes a means to another end. For Hegel, however, property is important in-itself because 'property, as the first *existence* [*Dasein*] of freedom, is an essential end for itself' (PR: 45R). In other words, property is important because it is the first expression of the individual's sense of self as a substantial, concrete, free being.

Importantly, however, the abstract right to own property is purely private. Common property undermines an individual's freedom because his will is constrained by the arbitrary will of another and is prevented from determining for himself what to appropriate or how to use what he does appropriate (PR: 46).

Property becomes private when an individual imbues an object with his will by either taking possession of it or designating it as his (PR: 50). Only once he has taken possession of it can he use it to express himself. But because property is dependent on the will of the individual, the individual is able to freely dispose of his property if and as he sees fit. This, however, only applies to external property; the individual is not justified in disposing of his own body whether through suicide or by consenting to slavery because this would contradict what he truly is: a free being (PR: 66R).

But while the individual cannot dispose of his own body or choose to enter into slavery, he can justifiably hire his labour out for a limited time (PR: 67) because, in this action, he retains and recognizes his right to the abstract rights that delineate him as a person. Of course, this assumes that the work does not violate the individual's abstract right, but, I think, the point Hegel is making is that there is a difference between slavery and paid labour. In the former, the individual has no abstract rights, while, in the latter, he does.

Due to our interest in the role alienation plays in Hegel's thought, however, it must be noted that Hegel describes this disposal of property as the alienation [*Entaüsserung*] of property. As previously noted, *Entaüsserung* primarily refers to the process whereby the individual objectifies himself and remains with himself in this objectification. But there is another meaning of the term: when it is used in the context of Hegel's discussion of property, *Entaüsserung* is used in the traditional legal sense of the term meaning to dispose of or transfer property. While this understanding of alienation requires that the individual be separated from his object, it is not a separation in the negative sense of the term; the separation meant here is not a wrenching apart nor is it a negative form of separation. It is simply a voluntary transfer of property from one individual to the next.

But because the individual owns property by virtue of subjectively appropriating it, it is possible that others will not recognize it as his and so will try to appropriate it. To protect and preserve each individual's property and, by extension, his personality, an objective contract is created that recognizes each individual's status as a property owning person (PR: 71R).

Contract and its violation

Contract is a formal arrangement where each will, while remaining independent, recognizes the other's claim to an object. While the individual was previously *subjectively* certain of his ownership of the object, contract allows his subjective claim to the object to be recognized by others. With this, the individual's subjective claim gains objective validity.

The problem with formal contract, however, is that because a contract requires at least two individuals to enter into agreement with one another, it 'has not yet progressed beyond the stage of arbitrariness, and [so] remains susceptible to wrong' (PR: 81A). In other words, because it is merely a formal arrangement, it is quite possible that either of the parties may not uphold their end of the bargain. Importantly, wrong is not imposed on the contract; wrong is a possibility inherent within the very notion of contract itself (PR: 81). This is because contract is composed of two aspects: the *subjective* particular will of the individual based on his consenting to an agreement with another, and through this act of consent, the creation of an *objective* universal agreement based on the mutual recognition of the others right to property. The contract conforms to right when both individuals willingly consent to the creation of a contract *and* accurately adhere to its content. Wrong arises whenever the universal agreement of the contract is not adhered to. But, by distinguishing between unintentional wrong, deception, and crime, Hegel recognizes that not all wrongs are equally serious.

Unintentional wrong is the least serious form of wrong. It occurs when an individual aims to uphold the contract, but fails to accurately understand its requirements. While he insists his activities conform to the requirements of the contract, the manner in which he understands the contract does not actually conform to the contract's requirements. The crucial point is that 'each person wills what is right, and each is supposed to receive only what is right; their wrong consists [*besteht*] solely in considering that what they will is right' (PR: 86A). There is, in other words, a discrepancy between the actual requirements of the contract and the individuals understanding of it. This wrong is unintentional because the individual does not aim to hurt the other; he aims to uphold the contract but fails to accurately understand what that contract actually entails.

The second form of wrong is deception. Whereas unintentional wrong respects the objective universal right of the contract, but misunderstands what is actually entailed in the contract, deception purposefully does not aim to uphold the universal right of the contract. However, the deceiver does not simply break the contract; the deceiver aims to give the other the illusion that he is upholding the contract by giving the other what the other believes is contractually owed to him. In actuality, however, the deceiver fails to respect the others right by failing to give him what is contractually owed to him. In other words, deception arises when the individual rescinds his agreement to uphold the contract while feigning adherence to this agreement. This is a more serious matter than unintentional wrong because the universal right of the contract has been *intentionally* broken. It is for this reason that while unintentional wrong does not elicit punishment, deception does.

The most serious form of wrong is coercion and crime. While the individual's property expresses his will in objective form, and because his property interacts with other wills, it can be unjustly appropriated by them. Because the individual's will is embodied in his property, when his property is wronged so too is he. While unintentional wrong aims to uphold the right of the contract but fails to properly understand what this entails, and deception violates the right of the other while pretending to affirm his right, crime does not even pretend to uphold the right of the other. Crime simply violates the other's universal and particular right. To fully understand why this is case requires that we understand the relationship between the will and the body.

For Hegel, the individual is composed of both a will and a body. While these two aspects exist independently from one another, they also form an organic union. Thus, while the individual's body can be forced to do something against his will, coercion only occurs if the individual's will consents to coercion (PR: 91–92). But Hegel notes that, because the body and will are organically united, to coerce the body is also to impact on the will's freedom.

Therefore, while Sartre insists that the individual's capacity to effect the pre-reflective nihilating withdraw from determinate being allows him to be ontologically free, because Hegel insists that the true meaning of freedom describes the individual's capacity to freely act in the world, he insists that while the individual can always withdraw from his world, when he does so, and while it allows him to escape coercion and remain free, this freedom is an abstract debased form of freedom. When consciousness withdraws from the concrete world, this does not allow it to be truly free; it merely prevents it from being fully coerced.

The basic point Hegel is making is that while the negative aspect of the will allows it to withdraw from the world and so escape coercion, because coercion of the body effects the wills capacity to express itself in the world, and because practical freedom is a higher version of freedom than the abstract freedom achieved when the individual withdraws from the world, coercion of the body also violates the wills freedom. Because crime coerces the body of the individual, it also constrains his will. By usurping the individual's freedom, both in terms of his particular right to freely express himself *and* in terms of his universal right as a person, crime is the grossest violation of the individual's freedom.

But the criminal act is simply a violation of right; it does not set up a new notion of right in opposition to that which it violated (PR: 97). Despite thinking that his criminal act allows him to freely express himself as an individual, crime's violation of other's rights actually violates a condition of true freedom (i.e. that he actually affirm his own and others freedom) and so estranges the criminal from the freedom he thinks he has realized.

But crime does not simply *lead to alienation*; for Hegel, crime is also *caused by alienation*. It is because the criminal does not recognize that freedom contains an objective aspect, in the form of universal right, that he affirms his subjective will in a way that violates the universal right upon which his individual right is dependent. In other words, it is because the criminal does not properly understand what it is to be free that he acts in a manner that violates the very condition that would allow him to be free: affirming his own and other's rights. This demonstrates two aspects to Hegel's understanding of alienation: 1) alienation arises when the individual does not explicitly understand what is required for him to overcome his alienation and be free; and 2) alienation is a crucial concept when seeking to understand crime because it provides us with insight into both the causes and consequences of crime.

But crime does not simply violate universal right. Because crime is parasitical on universal right, and because universal right is a condition of freedom, the wrong of crime must be corrected. It is punishment that corrects crime's wrong (PR: 97A). But, for Hegel, punishment is not an externality to crime; punishment is inherent to the very structures of crime itself. Because crime is parasitical on right, crime recognizes the existence of right and, indeed, its dependence on right. In recognizing the existence of right, the criminal recognizes the primacy of universal right and so accepts that his negation of universal right must itself be negated. If this were not the case, the criminal's wrong would be established as right which would invalidate the ethical validity of right (PR: 99–100). But we should not think that the punishment of wrong develops freedom; punishment simply rights the wrong of crime.

However, Hegel argues that the correction of wrong must take a certain form. Punishment cannot be mere revenge. Revenge fails to correct the wrong of crime on two accounts: first, revenge is grounded in the judgement of the individual wronged. The problem with this, however, is that the individual who was wronged 'may go too far in his retaliation, which will in turn lead to further wrong' (PR: 102A). The wrong of revenge then needs to be made right by the one wronged. In turn, he uses revenge to right his wrong which then needs to be made right and so on.

Secondly, because revenge is grounded in the subjective whim of the one wronged, it does not re-establish the universality of right. Revenge simply pits one subject against another. This does not enable the criminal to overcome his wrong by recognizing the universality of right; as noted, it simply leads him to think he has been wronged. This sets off the whole punishment/revenge process described above (PR: 102).

To overcome the failings of revenge, punishment must recognize and reaffirm the universality of right. To achieve this, punishment must be *retributive* and must be determined by an objective third party. It is only if the punishment is determined by 'a justice freed from subjective interest and subjective shape and from the contingency of power'

(PR: 103) that it will avenge the wrong committed in a way that is without subjective prejudice and restore the universal objectivity of right. Because the punishment of the third party is fair and aims to re-establish the primacy of right, and because the criminal's parasitical relation to universal right ensures he recognizes the need to be punished for his transgression, the criminal will recognize both the necessity and objectivity of retributive punishment. As such, the universality of right is restored by 'a will which, as a particular and *subjective* will, also wills the universal as such' (PR: 103). This, however, requires a will that knows and affirms the universal aspect of right. The subjective will that has universal right for its content is not the will of abstract right, which, it will be remembered, is focused on the individual's abstract, formal rights; it is the moral will. As such, abstract right is dependent on the freedom of morality.

Morality

While abstract right affords the individual certain inalienable, formal, abstract rights and insists that he is free when these rights are not infringed, morality goes further and insists that the individual must also promote the freedom of others. This does not replace the formal rights afforded to the individual by abstract right; it complements and re-enforces them by showing that, while the freedom of abstract right describes valid conditions for freedom, this freedom is only secured if the other's rights are also affirmed.

Thus, while adherence to abstract right is purely negative in that it insists that freedom is achieved when the individual's formal rights are not infringed, the universal right of morality is positive in that it takes into consideration and aims to enhance the general 'welfare of others' (PR: 112A). While the universal right of the moral will is grounded in subjective will, it is not a subjective will that acts only in accordance with its own self-interest. The subjective will is moral because it chooses to *act* in the universal interest.

The essential aspect of the moral will is, therefore, action. But not all acts are equally ethically valid. There are three aspects to a moral act (PR: 114). First, the individual must purposefully engage in that act. Second, the individual must intend to act morally. For this reason, the individual cannot be *morally* responsible for the consequences of his actions that he did not intend. Third, the individual must act in accordance with the good of universal right. In other words, an act is moral if it purposefully intends to enhance the welfare of all.

But, according to morality, the specific content of the good is defined by the subject's conscience. As Hegel puts it, the good is the '*essential character of the subject's will*' (PR: 133). As its essential character, the moral will has a duty to adhere to the good. But, initially, the subjective will takes the good to be something other than itself and, because it knows itself to be a concrete particular will, understands the good to be the '*universal abstract essentiality*' (PR: 133) of duty.

However, duty itself is empty. It does not describe what doing one's duty actually requires; 'all that is available so far is this: to do *right*, and to promote *welfare*, one's own welfare and welfare in its universal determination, the welfare of others' (PR: 134). The subjective will is, therefore, left with the '*empty formalism*' (PR: 135R) of doing one's '*duty for duty's sake*' (PR: 135R). To overcome this formalism, the moral will must delineate what duty entails. But morality does not achieve this by defining itself in comparison to an abstract, universal law; as noted, it turns to the individual's, subjective conscience (PR: 136).

Conscience is subjectivity that is absolute certainty of itself. Its absolute self-certainty allows it to use its subjective judgement to determine what is universally right and, by extension, what the abstract notion of duty actually entails. However, this does not mean that conscience arbitrarily determines what duty entails. 'True conscience is the disposition to will what is good *in and for itself*; it therefore has fixed principles, and these have for it the character of determinacy and duties which are objective for themselves' (PR: 137). In other words, conscience wills and adheres to universal fixed principles. But, importantly, these fixed principles are not external to conscience; it is conscience itself that wills them.

In many respects, morality delineates the ethical outlook of Sartre's authentic consciousness. It will be remembered that a crucial aspect of post-conversion social relations is that consciousness no longer simply looks after its own freedom in opposition to others, but experiences a universal imperative to help the other realize his practical freedom. This imperative does not appear to be socio-historically contingent; instead, Sartre maintains it is a transcendent, universal, ethical imperative that the individual experiences as a result of choosing to alter his pre-reflective fundamental project to one that has freedom as its end. The result is that Sartre's authentic consciousness no longer works solely to achieve his own practical freedom, but also actively works to further the practical freedom of others. However, this ethical outlook only occurs for Sartre because of a subjective decision by consciousness. In other words, it is only because consciousness chooses to undergo the conversion that it subsequently experiences this ethical imperative.

Furthermore, beyond a vague, general imperative that the individual help others become practically free, Sartre does not spell out what exactly this requires and entails. The implication is that what action the individual should take to help others become practically free is left up to each individual to decide. As such, the ethical outlook of Sartre's authentic consciousness is grounded in consciousness's own subjective decision to not only will the universal interest, but to also determine how each will contribute to the realization of this end.

However, Hegel points out that the problem with this is that while morality correctly outlines that the individual should act in the universal interest, it fails to outline exactly what form that action should take. Leaving each individual to simply choose how to further the freedom of others in-line with his own subjective understanding risks not only contradiction, but, more seriously, conflict as each individual's understanding of what is necessary to further the practical freedom of others comes into conflict with others. Rather than promoting a harmonious freedom, the empty subjective universality of morality risks a war of all against all.

For this reason, Hegel maintains that genuine freedom is not found in morality, but in ethical life. Whereas morality leaves it to the individual to decide how to fulfil its empty, formal ethical imperatives, ethical life embeds each individual within objective structures that interlock with one another to secure and affirm the freedom of others. The objective structures of ethical life not only secure the individual's freedom, but also *co-ordinate* the activities of each individual to ensure that they realize and enhance the practical freedom of others. By also instantiating a social culture that brings each individual to recognize the importance of being recognized by others, ethical life overcomes the sterile, universal formality of morality and replaces it with an organic, universally orientated culture that values and promotes the freedom of all. Whereas the individual of morality must reflectively choose to promote the freedom of others, the individual of ethical life un-reflectively affirms the other's freedom because his concrete, socio-historical cultural norms and values bring him to spontaneously act in this manner.

Morality and the problem of evil

We will see exactly what this means in the next chapter, but, for now, let us return to morality. The fundamental problem with leaving ethical choice to conscience is that conscience can just as easily choose one of two options: either conscience can be moral and affirm the welfare of all or conscience can be immoral by making universal right contingent on 'the *arbitrariness* of its *own particularity*' (PR: 139). When it chooses the former it acts morally, when it chooses the latter it is *'evil'* (PR: 139).

But while evil is always a possibility of individual existence, it is a possibility that must be chosen by the individual. For Hegel, the individual is composed of two aspects: his 'natural will' (PR: 139R) composed of his natural drives, desires, and inclinations *and* a rational will composed of the capacity for reasoned thought. The realization of his freedom requires that he develop in such a way that his natural drives become subject to and dominated by reason. While the individual's natural will gives content to his rational will, his rational will is not to be determined by his natural will; his rational will chooses how he will live his natural will. The rational will can, therefore, choose to 'be either good *or* evil' (PR 139R). While good arises when the individual lives his natural will in a way that affirms the welfare of all; evil arises when 'the will lets its content be determined by these desires' (PR: 139R).

Evil is, therefore, an inherent possibility of human existence, but it is a possibility that only becomes actual if the individual chooses to follow his own natural drives to the detriment of the rational acts that further the universal good. Now, of course, Hegel recognizes that while evil is a possible human choice, 'evil is determined as that which of necessity *ought not to be*' (PR: 139R). As such, and despite being rooted in the individual's subjective conscience, morality still maintains objective standards of right and wrong. Rather than choose the evil of its particular natural drives and desires, morality requires the will to use its freedom to affirm the universal good.

Because evil entails the affirmation of the individual's pure subjective desire in opposition to the universal good, it shares a similar structure to crime. While evil affirms the wills subjectivity in opposition to the universal good, crime affirms the wills subjectivity in opposition to the universal objective agreement of the contract. However, evil's violation of universal right is more serious than crime's violation because: 1) the freedom of morality is a more developed form of freedom than that of abstract right and so the form of freedom that evil violates is a higher form of freedom than that violated by crime; 2) evil violates the other's *moral* subjectivity not just his abstract right as a person; and 3) evil is grounded in the individual's natural drives and desires, which means that its acts are not only more vicious and malicious, but also entail a more primordial violation of right than those constitutive of crime. In other words, while all evil involves criminal activity, not all criminal activity is evil.

However, while Hegel makes it clear that evil arises when the individual *chooses* to privilege his own subjective desires and drives in opposition to the welfare of others, because 'the *origin of evil* in general lies in the mystery [...] of freedom' (PR: 139R), it is impossible to explain why the individual makes this choice. Evil remains one of the mysteries of human being (Dews, 2008: 9–10). However, it seems to me that there is an intimate connection between alienation and evil that may go some way to explaining why the individual chooses to commit evil acts.

As noted, evil arises because the individual insists that the realization of his true free self is achieved when he sets aside the universal interest and simply follows his natural drives and desires. In other words, evil arises when the individual understands himself to be a self-enclosed, unencumbered, natural being as opposed to the organic, socially embedded, rational being he truly is. This alienated self-understanding leads him to wilfully usurp both the rationality and freedom of others. However, by purposefully acting in contradiction to the universal freedom of others, evil violates the universal freedom upon which his genuine freedom depends. By acting capriciously to satisfy his natural desires, he fails to become genuinely free and so is alienated from what he truly is and should be.

But the individual's self-estrangement is not simply a cause of his evil acts; self-estrangement results from his evil acts. Evil and alienation form a self-re-enforcing cycle: affirming his natural desires and failing to understand that his freedom is dependent on whether he affirms and realizes the freedom of others lead the evil individual to affirm his natural desires over the universal good. The evil acts that result cause revulsion amongst others and lead them to turn against him. This leads to the social alienation that re-enforces his sense of self as a self-enclosed, unencumbered, natural being and so makes it more likely he will continue to wantonly affirm his natural desires over the universal good.

While further elaboration is beyond the scope of this book, this does tentatively reveal an intimate connection between evil and alienation. While Hegel is probably right to note that there is no way to determine at what point the individual's self and social estrangement will lead him to act in an evil manner, we must recognize that an individual's self and/or social alienation plays a fundamental role in his decision to commit evil acts.

Overcoming the danger inherent to conscience (i.e. that it choose the horrors of evil over the righteous of universal good) requires that conscience's decisions be guided by an objective end. But, as demonstrated, this objective end cannot be the empty objective formalism of abstract right. It needs to be an end that is objective insofar as it directs, without constraining, the individual's activities. As such, neither the freedom of abstract right nor the freedom of morality *taken on its own* is sufficient. To overcome the vacuity of both abstract right and morality Hegel insists that it is necessary to combine the objectivity of abstract right with the subjective universality of morality.

This combination can only be satisfactorily achieved when the objective end of individual action is the realization of *universal freedom* and when this objective end does not emanate from the individual's subjective conscience, but emanates from and is re-enforced by his social world. By existing within certain objective institutional structures and social norms that affirm and re-enforce the primacy of universal freedom, each individual will spontaneously and unreflectively act in a manner that affirms the freedom of all (PR: 141). While the individual will still have to choose to act in a way that affirms the freedom of the other, he will instantaneously know what right entails and so will not have to fall back on his subjective conscience to know how to act. Hegel calls this socio-cultural formation 'ethical life.'

8
Realizing Freedom: Hegel and Ethical Life

The previous analyses of abstract right and morality showed that, while they disclose important truths about the conditions necessary to secure individual freedom, each is partial and necessarily requires additional structures. The possibility of crime inherent to contract can only be corrected through an impartial, moral individual that can discern what just punishment would right the criminals wrong. As such, abstract right necessarily requires and so logically morphs into the universal orientation of morality. Similarly, the possibility that the moral individual may choose the horrors of evil necessarily requires that the content of the good be taken out of an individual's subjective hands and placed in a socio-cultural formation that has the affirmation of the other's freedom as its end. Hegel calls this social formation 'ethical life.'

Ethical life is constituted by specific institutional state structures that lock together to embed individuals within social networks. Its interlocking structures ensure that when an individual expresses himself, his actions simultaneously contribute to the welfare and freedom of others. Far from being an obstacle to their freedom, a particular form of 'society and the state are [therefore] the very conditions in which freedom is realised' (PH: 41).

However, we have to be clear that Hegel does not maintain that true freedom requires that the individual identify with *any* state or community. For this reason, Shlomo Avineri is wrong to simply maintain that 'ethical life is defined by Hegel as the identification of the individual with the totality of his social life' (2003: 87). Such an understanding underpins Karl Popper's (2003: 24) infamous charge that Hegel's social philosophy sanctions not only political quietism, but also totalitarian government. As noted in the previous chapter, this is not the case. Hegel does not maintain that individual freedom requires that the individual subordinate his actions to those of *any* state. He maintains that true individual freedom requires the individual to exist within and work to further the ends of a *particular* state.

More specifically, 'the individual attains his right only by becoming the citizen of a good state' (PR: 196), which means a universally free and rational state. According to Hegel, the state is rational when it is grounded in rational analysis and conforms to the conception of freedom found in ethical life, which, we must remember, he has justified by showing the contradictions inherent to other forms of freedom.

In broad outline, this requires that: 1) the individual see the state as an extension of his own subjectivity; 2) the objective structures of the state bind individuals together to form a collective universally free whole that allows each to freely express themselves as far as possible, but not so far as their individual actions undermine the universal freedom of the state; and 3) when the state acts to limit the individual's activities to secure the freedom of others it does so only to the extent that limiting the individual's subjective freedom contributes to or safeguards the universal freedom of all. If any of the conditions of the rational state are not met, the state is not rational, and because the realization of individual freedom requires membership of a rational state, the individual remains alienated from his essential freedom.

How to overcome our alienation from our world is, therefore, central to Hegel's social philosophy. Answering this question leads him to outline the objective structures and subjective comportment necessary to allow individuals to overcome their alienation from the social world and, as a consequence, be truly free. But it is not the case that 'alienation arises when the goals, norms or ends which define the common practice or institutions begin to seem irrelevant or even monstrous, or when the norms are redefined so that the practices appear a travesty to them' (Taylor, 1998: 90).

The problem with this suggestion is that it insists that the individual is alienated whenever he does not see himself in the objective structures of the state. But, according to Hegel, alienation is not simply dependent on the individual's subjective interpretation of his relation to the state; after all, the individual may feel intimately related to a state that is unfree. Alternatively, the individual may not understand what freedom actually entails and so may feel alienated from a state that actually contains the rational objective structures necessary for the realization of universal freedom.

Hegel does not sanction reconciliation with any state, nor does he maintain that subjective belief alone is sufficient for the individual to overcome his alienation from the actual world. As Frederick Neuhouser notes, 'beyond this subjective "certainty" on the part of social members that their social world constitutes a home, that world must in "truth" *be* a home, which means [...] that it must enable its members to realise their true essence' (2000: 114). True freedom can only be found within certain objective structure because it is only objective structures that co-ordinate each individuals activity in a way that secures the universal freedom upon which individual freedom depends.

Thus, for Hegel, the individual is alienated from his social world when: 1) the objective structures of the rational state *do not* exist and the individual reflectively understands this; 2) the objective structures of the rational state *do not* exist but the individual thinks they do; and/ or 3) the objective structures of the rational state *do* exist, but the individual does not recognize this or does not understand that relating to them in a specific manner is necessary to realize his own freedom.

Importantly, the co-ordination that occurs between the individual and his community is not a thought-out reflective process engineered or instantiated by a totalitarian regime. Hegel's rational state is so organized that the objective structures spontaneously interlink to form a coherent, flexible, and organic social whole. As Mark Tunick notes, Hegel 'details how through the institutions of private property and contract individuals objectify their wills and are recognized by others in a common will; how through marriage an individual comes to be an ethical being; how in civil society, by working in corporations, we work for still a greater universal objective; and how all of these stages prepare us to be citizens in the state' (2001: 81). It is because each individual's activity is mediated through a range of social functions, each of which is supported by a community-orientated culture, that each spontaneously and voluntarily acts in a way that secures other's freedom.

Ethical life is, therefore, a unified (although not necessarily harmonious) social whole in which each individual identifies with his community and actively, if not always reflectively, works to realize the freedom of all citizens. But this does not mean that there is no difference or diversity in ethical life. Individuality is a key aspect of ethical life in that it safeguards the creativity, innovation, and subjective expression that are necessary to ensure that society continues to reinvigorate itself and does not stagnate.

However, Hegel recognizes that individual self-expression cannot be valued over all else because having every individual do as they please when they please would lead to conflict and social disharmony. The resultant atomism would lead to social breakdown, alienation, and unfreedom. Thus, for Hegel, individual self-expression is not the same as individual freedom. To become free, the individual needs to ensure that his self-expression is embedded within, and contributes towards, the establishment of particular social bonds and norms. Only by being a member of, and actively contributing towards, a particular social body will the individual overcome his self and social alienation and be truly free.

While the individualistic bent of civil society provides ethical life with difference and diversity, this individualism needs to be tempered so that it accords with the freedom of others. Again, however, this is not achieved through force or external imposition; it is achieved through education and the instantiation of a culture that brings the individual to spontaneously and voluntarily temper his activity so that it accords with the universal interest. While ethical life contains room for individual self-expression, each individual understands what true freedom entails and spontaneously and voluntarily acts in accordance with this end. As such, there will not be any *fundamental* conflict over the meaning of freedom that would disrupt the overall harmony of the community (Hardimon, 1992: 179).

Ethical life performs a balancing act: it must allow the individual to freely express himself as far as possible, but not to the extent that his subjective freedom undermines the freedom of others. Co-ordinating the activity of all citizens not only requires the creation of specific objective structures, but also that the individual fulfil certain duties within these structures.

But again Hegel warns us that we should not think that these duties limit the individual's freedom. It is only from the standpoint of abstract freedom that the individual's duty appears as a limitation on his freedom. Because the will is defined by activity, its abstract freedom is not the full realization of its free will; fully realizing its ontological potential requires concrete action. But, as noted, achieving anything concrete requires that the infinite will limit itself to a finite concrete activity. Fulfilling his duty allows the individual to fully realize the freedom implicit to his will because it makes his infinite abstract freedom concrete and actual in a way that contributes to the development of the universal freedom necessary for the realization of his own freedom. This is why Hegel notes that 'in duty, the individual liberates himself so as to attain substantial freedom' (PR: 149). But, for Hegel, this is insufficient; the individual will only be free when *he* realises and understands that his duty delineates his 'substantial being' (PR: 148).

It would appear, therefore, that, on this point, Hegel and Sartre agree: practical freedom requires that the individual fulfil certain duties. For Sartre, the practical freedom the individual wins by being a member of an organized group requires that he fulfil a certain function; whereas, for Hegel, securing his practical freedom requires that the individual contribute to a particular social formation in a particular way.

However, while both thinkers agree on this point, they do differ on one very important point: the relationship between the individual's ontological structure and his practical freedom. As I have argued throughout, Sartre maintains a distinction between the ontological freedom of the individual's consciousness, which is a condition of its being, and his practical freedom which needs to be concretely realized. Hegel, however, collapses the distinction between the individual's ontological and practical freedom. For Hegel, the individual's ontological structure is dependent on the degree to which he is practically free. Thus, while both thinkers agree that being *practically* free requires that each individual act in a particular way in a particular social formation, they differ in terms of what this means for the individual's ontological structure. Put simply, contra Sartre, Hegel maintains that the individual's ontological structure is intimately related to his social duty.

But in terms of their analyses of the activities necessary to secure the individual's practical freedom, Hegel's analysis goes beyond Sartre's by describing the particular duties and roles that each individual must fulfil. Whereas Sartre simply maintains that enhancing the individual's practical freedom to the greatest degree requires that he identify with and fulfil a particular function in an organized group, Hegel describes in much greater detail the particular social roles and duties the individual must fulfil if he is to overcome his alienation from the actual world.

Furthermore, whereas Sartre appears to maintain that the individual simply has to choose to undergo the conversion that will allow him to adopt the universal orientation, Hegel recognizes that the process through which the individual comes to see that his world is an extension of himself is more complicated. It requires that he be embedded in structures that gradually bring him to the universal perspective, that he interact with others in a particular way, exist in a particular culture, and have undergone a particular education. Only when each of these universal relations is correctly developed will the rational state exist and the individual develop the subjective ethical outlook that will allow him to identify with the rational state in the way necessary to allow him to be truly free.

According to Hegel, the structure of ethical life takes the form of concentric rings where the most immediate form of universality, as found in the family, is superseded by the more developed form of universality of civil society, which in turn is superseded by the final form of rational universality found in the rational state. But the creation of these objective structures is not enough; achieving organic unity with his world also requires the individual to correctly express himself in each sphere. In other words, the free individual is a member of a particular form of family, expresses himself in a particular form of civil society, and exists in a rational state.

But the movement between the various forms of universality is not simply a one-way linear development to a higher form of universality. Each is required to organically unify the individual with his world. However, because the universality of the state is the highest form of universality, it takes precedence over the universality of the family and civil society. In other words, because the family and civil society exist within the state, it is the job of the state to co-ordinate the activities of civil society and the various families to ensure the coherency, rationality, and freedom of the whole.

The ontological and ethical importance of family

For Hegel, becoming 'a *member*' (PR: 158) of a family is the most immediate way in which the individual becomes conscious of being part of something greater than himself. In other words, family is important because it brings the individual out of his pure self-interestedness and points him towards his social being. But not all families are ethical; to be ethical, a family must fulfil three conditions.

Marriage is the first condition of the family. While individuals can exist without getting married, it is only if they seek and gain the recognition of their community that their union becomes *ethical* (PR: 161–162). According to Hegel, marriage creates a standing ethical union between individuals where each shares common values and norms and cares for someone else. Through these shared values and norms, marriage allows the individuals to create a union that transcends their own individuality. But marriage does not simply allow the two individuals involved to create and participate in a union that transcends their individuality; marriage plays a role in integrating the individuals into their community.

By recognizing that only marriage as institutionalized through the laws of the community can make their union ethical, individuals come to recognize that their freedom depends on gaining recognition from others. With this recognition, they see that living in a community, as opposed to setting themselves in opposition to it, is necessary for their own freedom. In other words, through marriage, individuals come to respect and see the virtue of belonging to a community.

But while the community confers ethical status on the lovers by virtue of recognizing them as a married couple, so the community's capacity to confer this status is dependent on the lovers' seeking the community's recognition of their union. The act of marriage is, therefore, an example of mutual recognition between: a) the lovers; and b) the lovers and their community. While the community recognizes the couple's union as an ethical one, the couple recognize the community as being capable of conferring this status. Through this dialectical interaction the individuals come to see the necessity of their community while the community recognizes the necessity and ethical validity of its individuals.

But Hegel is clear that the true form of marriage requires a *'union* of the natural sexes' (PR: 161). In other words, the ethical relation of marriage can only occur between a man and a woman; same-sex marriages are not ethical according to Hegel. Hegel thinks this, not only because the notion of same-sex marriage was not around in his time, but also because, for him, the two sexes perform different, but complementary, ethical roles in the family.

Marriage arises when a man and a woman freely consent to give themselves to one another and thereby establish the common union of the family. This union allows the two independent persons to unify in the higher ethical life of the family. But the family is not simply a union of two individuals; marriage brings two individuals together in such a way that they create an entity that takes on the life of *'a single person'* (PR: 162). Because members of the family are to have specific functions, the family requires that each limits his/her activity. 'In this respect, their union involves a self-limitation, but since they attain their substantial self-consciousness within it, it is in fact their liberation' (PR: 162).

As noted, the two sexes perform separate, but ultimately complementary, familial roles. Hegel's argument emanates from his logic of the concept, insofar as the truth of each concept is composed of a combination of particularity and universality. If the truth of the concept were simply its universal aspect, it would remain empty and formal. It is only when the universal aspect of the concept is made concrete through the actions of particular individuals that it becomes fully realized. For example, the universality of the concept 'good' is, on its own, empty and formal. It is only when individuals imbue it with concrete content by actually enacting it in reality that the formal, emptiness of the universal becomes concrete and true. As such, the true, ethical moment of the family depends upon the combination of particularity and universality.

According to Hegel, the sexes are naturally able to fulfil the different, but complementary, roles necessary to ensure that the family is ethical. In other words, the combination of the sexes, one of whom represents particularity, the other universality, creates an ethical, spiritual 'entity' that transcends both. With this, Hegel goes beyond claiming that the sexes are naturally different to the far more controversial claim that these natural differences are rational and delineate how an individual must act (Franco, 1999: 244–245).

The male fulfils the universal aspect of the family by being the fig-ure-head for the family in its dealings with the wider community. His self-knowledge, membership of a family, and interaction with his com-munity allow him to transcend the particularity of the family and align the family's ends with those of the wider community. In contrast, the female finds her 'substantial vocation in the family' (PR: 166). Her free-dom is found in tending to the particularity of the family; she does not engage in affairs that encompass the wider community. Because of this, Hegel maintains that while women are to be educated, it is not neces-sary to educate them in artistic pursuits, philosophy, or science (PR: 166A). These are only necessary for those who are to act in the com-munity and since women are not to fulfil this role, there is no need for them to be educated in these disciplines.

However, Hegel goes further and insists that women are not to become leaders of the community because 'when women are in charge of gov-ernment, the state is in danger, for their actions are based not on the demands of universality but on contingent inclination and opinion' (PR: 166A). Hegel's understanding of the family is, therefore, very bour-geois: the male is the head of the family, the female subordinate to him and in charge of maintaining the household.

But Hegel does not think that limiting a woman's place to the house-hold necessarily limits her freedom. Because the essence of what it is to be a woman is aligned to her role as guardian of the family, limiting herself to this role does not limit her freedom; it actually realizes her implicit ontological potential as a woman.

Furthermore, because she is the backbone of the family, and because the male is only able to act in the wider community by virtue of his family, his actions are dependent on the female's guardianship of the family. Thus, while it initially appears that Hegel is simply excluding women from ethical life, he does maintain that women have a crucial, albeit supportive, role to play in ensuring the creation and continuation of a rational community.

Despite these suggestions, and, indeed, their consistency with his logical categories, Hegel's division of the sexes is, no doubt, not one that we would share today; indeed, it shows a major failing in his attempts to secure universal freedom. There are, at least, two reasons for this: in the first instance, Hegel claims, in his analysis of the onto-logical structure of consciousness, that consciousness is composed of an implicit, non-determining ontological potential that needs to be made actual by the actions of consciousness. The key point here is that an individual's ontological potential is *individual* and is not deter-mined, although may be shaped, by his/her natural sex. However, in his discussion of the capabilities of women, Hegel maintains that, irre-spective of their individual capabilities, *all* women, by virtue of being women, are so constituted that they are simply incapable of success-fully interacting with the wider society. It appears, therefore, that it is natural being (i.e. sex), not individual capability that defines an individual's being.

Secondly, while Hegel maintains that an individual can only be truly free if and when he is a member of a family, participates in civil soci-ety, and adopts the universal orientation that brings him to purpose-fully affirm the freedom of all citizens, his insistence that women are to be confined to the family prevents them from participating in civil society and adopting the universal orientation that would allow them to see their world as an extension of themselves. As one commentator notes, because she is 'trapped within the family, woman is denied social awareness through labour and human interaction. Similarly, she can never experience the highest order of freedom for she is denied a space within the public realm' (Landes, 1981: 23). Failure to allow women to participate in the public realm prevents them from shaping it in their image and ensures it always appears as something opposed to them. They cannot, therefore, shape the world in the way that allows them to overcome its other-ness and so fail to fulfil the fundamental condition of Hegel's conception of freedom.

But it could be objected that, for Hegel, the organic unity between a man and a woman constitutive of marriage allows a woman to achieve true freedom by virtue of the mediation of her husband's activities in the world. In other words, women find fulfilment in the social status and activities of their husbands.

However, insisting that a woman's freedom is realized through her husband's social activities violates Hegel's insistence that genuine freedom requires that each be able to work on and shape his/her world in accordance with the requirements of ethical life. If the woman is dependent on her husband's activities to shape the wider community in the image of ethical life, she will not engage in the process of self-objectification that brings her to recognize that the social world is an extension of herself. The self-knowledge that results from the process of self-objectification can only truly affect the individual if he/she actually objectifies him/herself and subsequently identifies with the object created. The individual cannot truly overcome his/her alienation from the social world unless he/she works on it directly. But, by confining women to the pure particularity of the family, Hegel prevents women from doing precisely this. The consequence can only be that women will continue to see their social world as something opposed to them and so will fail to meet the conditions Hegel insists are necessary for them to be truly free. But, importantly, because universal freedom is a necessary condition of individual freedom, the failure to secure the freedom of women also undermines the freedom of men.

An alternative to this would be, for Hegel, to claim that 'freedom' means fundamentally different things for the sexes: on the one hand, men require a fuller, social conception of freedom; while, on the other hand, women require a more limited, private, family-oriented conception of freedom. The problem with this argument is that it contradicts Hegel's painstaking analysis of the logical development of the concept to a fixed, unitary absolute meaning.

However, rather than simply writ off Hegel's analysis of women, perhaps there is a way we can modify it somewhat to make it more consistent with his analysis of the conditions necessary to secure universal freedom. Rather than delineate familial roles by sex, Hegel could describe the conditions necessary for the family to be ethical (for example, that it have a particular and universal orientation), but leave it up to the individual couple to determine how these conditions would be fulfilled within their particular relationship. This would not immediately exclude women from public life and would allow Hegel to: a) remain consistent with his claim that it is an individual's will, and not nature, that realizes the ontological potential to be free implicit to his ontological structure; and b) be consistent with his analysis of the unitary meaning of freedom. This would offer women the possibility of shaping her society in her image which would allow her to overcome the other-ness of her community in the way that Hegel maintains is necessary to truly realize individual freedom. Guardianship of the family could then fall to either member of the family, or indeed, it could be the job of both.

This alternative accepts Hegel's point that the ethical moment of the family is found in the combination of particular familial concern and concern for the wider community, but questions whether the particular is the exclusive domain of the female and the universal the exclusive domain of the male. In its place, it suggests that each individual in the marriage, regardless of sex, can and should be concerned with both their particular family and their wider society.

However, maintaining that both parties to the marriage are constituted by a concern for their particular family and the wider community can mean one of two things: 1) that both parties are composed of the same degree of concern for their particular family and the wider community; or 2) that while the two parties are composed of a universal and particular concern, each has a different mix of particularity and universality.

Edward Halper has discussed and dismissed both options. He maintains that if the will of each person in the marriage is composed of the same mixture of particularity and universality then 'the two could not be bound by the diversity of their wills and would, in consequence, lack the unity essential to marriage' (2001: 852). According to Hegel's logic, however, a successful, ethical marriage is constituted by a combination of two different, but complementary, wills. As such, a marriage between two individuals in which each is composed of the same mixture of particularity and universality would necessarily fail to be ethical and, perhaps, wouldn't have the difference necessary to keep it interesting for each party.

Secondly, Halper examines the other alternative; that is, that the two parties are constituted by different combinations of universality and particularity and apply these flexible combinations in different ways at different times to different tasks. However, he maintains that it then becomes necessary to determine how the couple will divide the tasks constitutive of family life. The conclusion Halper arrives at is that either one person exhibits a natural talent for certain familial duties and so naturally gravitates towards them or, if this is not the case, and so as to avoid conflict, the couple need to come to some arrangement. According to Halper, however, the problem with this is that 'such an arrangement would amount to a contract, and [for Hegel] marriage is not a contract' (2001: 853).

But it is questionable whether dividing tasks in this manner would constitute a formal contract. It is quite conceivable that, in-line with

Hegel's valuation of culture and social norms, the two parties to the marriage would reach an *implicit, informal* agreement as to who was to do which jobs when. Surely this implicit, informal agreement is at the very heart of an ethical, loving relationship. Rather than have to spell out every move, obligation, and duty, the ethical unity of marriage emanates from and is constituted by implicit, informal, tacit understandings and norms between the two individuals. It is, therefore, quite possible that each partner could: 1) combine a universal concern for the community with a particular concern for the family in different ways; and 2) fulfil different, but complementary tasks without a formal agreement being created. In this case, both partners would be able to fulfil the conditions (i.e. membership of a family, a relationship of mutual recognition, and participation in public life) necessary for them to be free and to do so in a way that also secures the organic unity of the family.

Familial property and the ethical role of children

The second aspect of the family is property. Because the family is a single entity, it takes on the characteristics of a person and so gains the same abstract rights to property as a person. Because the male is the head of the household, he interacts with the wider community and 'is primarily responsible for external acquisition and for caring for the family's needs, as well as for the control and administration of the family's resources' (PR: 171). This creates common familial property which every member of the family has a right to, even if its distribution is controlled by its male head.

However, possessing property is not the end or full realization of a marriage. This brings us to the third aspect of the family: children. A child allows each individual to see the love each has for the other expressed in the objective form of another human being. There is, however, some confusion regarding the ethical moment in the family's relationship to its children. On the one hand, the *Philosophy of Right* appears to implicitly indicate that it is only if the couple naturally produce a child that they will see their union in objective form (PR: 173). However, in the *Philosophy of Mind*, Hegel refines this somewhat by indicating that the ethical moment of the family is not found in the natural generation of children, but 'in the second or spiritual birth of the children – in educating them to independent personality' (PM: 521). In other words, the ethical moment is found in *raising* children, not in *naturally generating* them. We will see that, while the first interpretation creates problems in

Hegel's account, insofar as it prevents same-sex couples from fulfilling the conditions necessary to be truly free, the later interpretation may be more satisfactory.

Children are important to a couple because they validate and re-enforce the ethical commitment each has made to the other. It is the family's role to bring up, educate, and look after its children. This education and upbringing must seek 'to raise the universal [orientation] into the children's consciousness and will' (PR: 174). In other words, it is the family's duty to educate its children to be good citizens of the community by teaching them to adhere to and purposefully seek to further the universal freedom of the community. This requires discipline so as to break the child's natural will. Only when this is broken can the child be raised 'out of the natural immediacy in which [he] originally exist[s] to self-sufficiency and freedom of personality' (PR: 175).

This again reiterates the point made in Chapter 5 concerning the difference between Hegel's and Sartre's conceptions of consciousness. For Sartre, it would appear that the consciousness of an adult and the consciousness of a child are constituted by the same ontological structures. The difference appears to be in the degree to which each is capable of reflectively understanding its ontological nothingness with the child being less capable of reflectively understanding what it truly is ontologically. For Hegel, however, not only does the child have a lower capability of reasoning than the adult, but the ontological structure of a child is different to that of an adult.

Importantly, while Sartre maintains that the consciousness of adults and children 'possess' the same ontological structures, Hegel maintains that the ontological structure of a child's consciousness alters and develops into that of an adult. This requires that: a) the rational aspect of the will becomes dominant over the natural drives and desires; and b) the child comes to realize that he has abstract rights as a person.

This allows the child to become an independent person in his own eyes and in the eyes of others, which allows him to own property and found his own family. By asserting his individuality in this way, the child's family recedes in importance and he himself establishes his own family. Through this movement, the chain of the generations is played out: the family develops, realizes itself in children, and then sees its immediate importance recede as the child asserts his own individuality. He, in turn, tries to overcome his own particularity through getting married and having children who, in turn, repeat the process.

Through this process, the original family dissolves into a multiplicity of families each of which is opposed to other families as an individual is to other individuals. The interaction between families and the means through which each family gains the resources needed to meet its needs is mediated through civil society and the state.

However, before moving onto discuss civil society, and while Hegel's treatment of the family goes far beyond that offered by Sartre, I would like to return to a potential problem in Hegel's account of the family. As noted, Hegel insists that not only do the sexes have different ontological structures, but realizing the freedom implicit to both requires that each sex fulfil different familial obligations. As such, the male realizes his freedom by being married and interacting with his wider community, while the female realizes it by taking care of the family. With this, Hegel either excludes women from public life and so undermines his claim to be describing a universally free society or insists that freedom means different things for man and woman, which undermines the unitary conception of 'freedom' his logic defends. This led me to suggest that this issue could be rectified if it is accepted that, contra Hegel, an individual's sex does not necessarily delineate or determine the activities necessary to realize his/her freedom. This would prevent women from being excluded from public life simply because they are female and so would give them the possibility of shaping the community in the way that Hegel insists is necessary for individuals to be truly free. This does not mean that each female would necessarily shape their community in the necessary manner. It simply means that whether she does or not is up to her own will (in conjunction with her social circumstance), it is not up to nature. This appears to be more attuned with Hegel's insistence that freedom is not predetermined by nature (i.e. sex) or history; it is realized by human will.

However, while this alteration in Hegel's argument would allow both sexes to fulfil the criteria that Hegel maintains is necessary for all to be free, his insistence that: 1) an ethical marriage only occurs between a man and a woman; and 2) children are fundamental to the ethical validity of the family appears to prevent same-sex couples from fulfilling the conditions of universal freedom upon which his rational state depends.

Admittedly, this is probably not an issue that arose in Hegel's time and he certainly does not address it, but this does not mean it is not an important issue that does not impact on his attempt to describe a universally free society. Indeed, if Hegel is to remain relevant to contemporary social theory/political philosophy, I think we have to see whether his thought is adaptable to new circumstances, occurrences, and social formations.

In relation to the first point, I have already argued that, while Hegel is right to insist that an ethical family needs to be so structured that it combines concern for itself with concern for its wider community, we must de-couple this from his insistence that natural sex determines individual familial activities. Rather than maintain that the male is necessarily concerned with the wider community and the female necessarily with the particular family, Hegel's theory of freedom requires that we reconceptualize the relationship between the universal and particular aspects of the ethical family to not only recognize that natural sex does not determine which aspect each partner will undertake, but that, in fact, the ethical family requires that both members be concerned with their particular family and wider community.

De-coupling familial activities from natural sex in this way not only frees women from the home and so allows them to shape their society in the way that Hegel's conception of genuine freedom requires, but also means that family forms other than the heterosexual, male-dominant family Hegel values can be described as ethical.

If it is accepted that same-sex couples can marry and if both partners combine concern for their particular relationship with concern for their wider community, their union would: 1) fulfil the first condition of an ethical marriage, insofar as they would form a stable relationship constituted by concern for the particular family and universal society; 2) allow Hegel to incorporate a more diverse range of individuals into the rational state; 3) overcome the division between heterosexual and same-sex individuals that may threaten the overall harmony and freedom of ethical life; and 4) bring Hegel's rational state closer to realizing the universal freedom it aims to achieve.

However, while this shows that Hegel's framework can be reconceptualized to recognize that same-sex couples can fulfil the first condition of an ethical marriage, we are still left with the issue of how they can fulfil its second condition: children.

Identifying if and how Hegel's framework can accommodate this issue requires that we remember that Hegel does not always appear to be absolutely clear or consistent in his statements on where exactly the ethical moment of the child lies. While one apparent option necessarily excludes same-sex couples from creating an ethical family, the other does not.

If the ethical moment of the child/family relationship is found in naturally generating children, then, given that same-sex couples cannot naturally produce children, they are necessarily naturally excluded from fulfilling the conditions of an ethical marriage upon which true individual freedom is based. This excludes them from society and undermines the universal freedom of ethical life.

However, we arrive at a very different conclusion if we: 1) accept that same same-sex couples can get married; 2) recognize that they can structure the relationship in such a way that it combines concern for the family with concern for the wider community; and 3) take seriously the *Philosophy of Mind's* insistence that the ethical moment of the family is found in raising children. Indeed, if we extend this further to accept that raising adopted, as opposed to naturally generated, children is sufficient to realize the ethical bond of the family then this issue is one step closer to resolution. The final hurdle is to accept and affirm that same-sex couples can actually adopt children. With this, Hegel would be able to allow same-sex couples to fulfil the conditions of the ethical family (marriage and raising children) which realizes, or at the very least does not undermine, the conditions of universal freedom upon which his rational state depends.

However, while Hegel's general framework allows for this conclusion, he would have to: a) drop his insistence that only heterosexual relationships are ethical; b) rethink where exactly the universal and particular orientations of the family are located; and c) insist that same-sex couples be able to adopt children. In other words, he would have to fundamentally alter his notion of the ethical family to one that even the most liberal of contemporary societies do not find uncontroversial (Nicolacopoulos & Vassilacopoulos, 1999: 166–169, 184). While there is nothing to prevent social attitudes from moving in this direction, the extent of the reformulation required does, I think, show that significant questions remain regarding Hegel's description of the ethical family and, by extension, his attempt to describe a universally free society.

But despite this, I do not think that we should simply discard his discussion of the family. After all, Hegel does bring our attention to the importance of family, in terms of the well-being of the individual and the community, in a way that other social theorists have been unable or unwilling to do. Indeed, Sartre, to my knowledge, does not even discuss familial, or family/society, relations. By discussing it, Hegel at least brings it to our attention. Importantly, however, he recognizes that the family must feed itself. This requires that it engage in civil society.

Civil society and individual need

Hegel maintains that civil society is the sphere of ethical life that mediates the relationship between the family and the state. It is the arena within which disparate individuals attempt to satisfy their own material needs by interacting with others in a way that conforms to the rules of market exchange. Through buying and selling goods and services, each individual is able to satisfy his own material needs while also contributing to the life of his community.

In order to buy or sell the goods to satisfy his material needs, however, the individual must work (PR: 196). Through work, individuals are able to produce goods to sell to others or sell their labour to others in exchange for money to buy goods produced by others. As Hegel explains, 'I acquire my means of satisfaction from others and must accordingly accept their opinions. But at the same time, I am compelled to produce means whereby others can be satisfied. Thus, the one plays into the hands of the other and is connected with it' (PR: 192A). By requiring individuals to act as both a producer and a consumer (Greer, 1999), civil society is so structured that when an individual's self-interest leads him to act in the world, his self-interested actions also satisfy 'the welfare of others' (PR: 182A). In this way, civil society creates a system of mutual interdependence wherein the actions of one individual impact on and condition the activities of another (PR: 187).

But while Hegel recognizes that individuals interact with one another in civil society to satisfy their material needs, commentators usually fail to recognize that he understands that not all needs are the same. While Sartre simply identifies that humans have material needs, Hegel differentiates between *absolute* needs and *relative* needs.

Absolute needs describe those material needs that are absolutely necessary for the biological existence and survival of the individual. For this reason, they are ahistoric and universally applicable. Hegel includes 'food, drink, and clothing' (PR: 189A) under absolute needs. Because his existence depends on the satisfaction of his absolute needs, the individual must satisfy these before he can freely choose how he will express himself. Importantly, those individuals that fail to satisfy their absolute needs are said to be absolutely poor.

But Hegel recognizes that the individual does not simply have fixed, universal, absolute, material needs. Because the human being is an imaginative, social, 'spiritual being' (PR: 190A), his material needs can multiply inexhaustibly. So it may come to be that the individual 'needs' a mobile phone, laptop computer, etc. These needs are not *initially* material *needs*; they are *initially* material *desires*. In time, however, active participation in the life of the community can require that the individual owns and is able to use these material things (PR: 190A; 191A).

Because these needs emanate from the social life of the community, they are contingent on the existence and social life of that particular community. For this reason, they are *relative* needs; what a particular individual in one community needs to actively participate in the life of his community is not necessarily the same as what another individual living in another community requires. It must be remembered, however, that relative needs are grounded in the satisfaction of absolute needs. It is only because the individual has first satisfied his absolute need for food and water that he can then set about desiring other goods, which in time, may become relative needs.

There are, at least, two aspects to Hegel's analysis here. First, that active participation in the life of certain communities requires ownership of certain goods simply to function and participate in that society. Secondly, because he insists on an intimate and constitutive relationship between individual identity and social recognition, Hegel maintains that the individual may come to 'need' certain goods simply because others have them too. In other words, desires turn into needs because being recognized by others as a valid, free member of the society requires that the individual possess certain goods.

This is an interesting and important socio-ontological insight; not only are humans able to alter and change their desires/needs, but the logic of the process that determines the requirements for active participation in the social life of the community is so structured that it tends towards complexity. For example, whereas ownership of a mobile phone was once unheard of, then subsequently became a reality for a select few, it has subsequently become so all-pervasive that active participation in the life of certain communities requires the individual to possess a mobile phone.

But the distinction between absolute and relative needs also plays a crucial role in Hegel's discussion of poverty. Just as the individual's failure to satisfy his absolute needs ensures he is absolutely poor, so failure to satisfy his relative needs ensures he is relatively poor. Thus we find that Hegel's analysis of relative and absolute needs implicitly differentiates between individuals that are: 1) both absolutely and relatively poor by virtue of not being able to satisfy either their absolute needs or the relative needs that will allow them to actively participate in the life of the community; 2) relatively poor insofar as they do not possess the means that will allow them to actively participate in the life of the community, but who are *not* absolutely poor; they have satisfied their absolute need for food and water; and 3) not absolutely or relatively poor; they have satisfied their absolute needs and their relative needs, thereby allowing them to actively participate in the life of the community. This does not mean that each individual possesses the same wealth or the same goods; it simply means that each has been able to satisfy his absolute needs while also acquiring the minimum goods that will satisfy his relative needs and allow him to actively participate in the life of the community. Thus, if actively participating in the life of the community requires the individual to possess a laptop computer, those that do have met this relative need. It does not mean that each individual can only possess *one* laptop computer; it means that possessing one laptop computer is necessary to have overcome the relative need of that particular society. Those that do meet this standard can no longer be said to be relatively poor in respect to this need.

But it may be asked: at what point should the individual divert his resources away from satisfying his absolute needs to satisfying his relative needs? While this movement must occur at some point, insofar as being fully integrated into the community requires that the individual satisfy both his absolute and relative needs, and while Hegel never explicitly mentions this, the logic of his argument warns against two possibilities: first, that the individual should not simply focus on 'keeping up with the Jones' by, for example, working to possess all manner of 'mod-cons' to the detriment of adequate nutrition.

Secondly, the individual should not simply focus on satisfying his absolute needs. This would stunt his social existence because he would not have the means that would enable him to actively participate in the life of his community. Satisfaction of both his absolute and relative needs is required to allow the individual to actively participate in the life of his community.

There is, therefore, a balance to be struck between satisfaction of the individual's absolute needs and satisfaction of the relative needs necessary to allow him to actively participate in the life of his community. While the relationship between the two will depend on the context and community, Hegel's basic point is that the individual must aim for a well-rounded satisfaction of all his needs: he should not ignore his absolute needs (food and water) simply to buy the latest mobile phone/laptop computer if he already has one that allows him to actively participate in the life of his community and especially if such action would mean he is unable to satisfy his absolute needs.

While contingencies such as individual skill, education, place of birth, and especially the wealth the individual is born into play a large role in whether the individual is able to actually satisfy his material needs (PR: 233), it is work that allows the individual himself to satisfy his own particular needs. By preparing goods to sell to others, or selling his own labour in exchange for money to purchase the goods he needs, the individual is able to attain the means to satisfy his needs (PR: 196A).

To maximize the return from his efforts, thereby allowing him to better satisfy his needs, work becomes subject to a *'division of labour'* (PR: 198). This division allows each individual to specialize his activity and so become more efficient and productive. However, in this specialization, 'work becomes increasingly *mechanical,* so that the human being is eventually able to step aside and let a *machine* take his place' (PR: 198). There is clearly a form of constraint on the individual's freedom here, insofar as the division of labour prevents the individual from freely expressing himself. However, surely this only applies to certain forms of work (Knowles, 1983: 59). After all, work constitutive of the division of labour that allows the individual to subjectively express himself in the task is very different to work that is purely repetitive and requires no subjective expression.

In truth, while this is an aspect of Hegel's thought that does need to be developed, perhaps Hegel's description of the specialization and alienation that accompanies the division and mechanization of the labour process should be read as a warning not a general description of all forms of work. While a division of labour is necessary to ensure the smooth efficient functioning of civil society, the division of labour must not go so far that work becomes so mechanical that the individual is prevented from expressing himself in the role he undertakes. This will allow the individual to express himself subjectively in his role, preserve the efficiency constitutive of the division of labour, maintain the freedom that accompanies civil society, and allow the individual to satisfy his material needs.

While work becomes subject to a division of labour, and because certain jobs share similar characteristics, Hegel holds that the individuals of these tasks come to form *'universal masses'* (PR: 201); or, as he calls them, 'estates.' Estates are umbrella organizations under which the disparate individuals of civil society coalesce depending on their particular vocation. Thus, agricultural workers will coalesce under the agricultural estate; public workers will coalesce under the universal estate; and workers in civil society will coalesce under the estate of trade and industry by becoming a member of a trade association; or, as Hegel calls them, 'corporation[s]' (PR: 249).

I will return to the role of the corporation, but at this point it is necessary to note that the estates play a crucial role in Hegel's civil society and rational state. Which estate the individual belongs to will depend on contingent factors such as his family, location, subjective disposition, and individual skill (PR: 206). It is the job of the estate to: 1) oversee the work of its members; 2) educate its members in terms of the work required and the wider world, thereby bringing each individual out of his attitude of pure self-interest (PR: 201A); and 3) cultivate a sense of '*honour*' (PR: 207) in each of its members. This sense of honour brings each to uphold the values and norms of his estate, which, as we will see, is directed towards realizing the ethical end of the rational state: the universal freedom of all its citizens. In this way, the individuals of estates voluntarily adopt norms and values that bind each to the other. Through this common bond, individuals of the same estate come to support one another while also becoming aware that each exists as a member of a wider community. For this reason, Hegel writes that 'a human being with no estate is merely a private person and does not possess actual universality' (PR: 207A).

But the fragmentation of the workforce into estates and the pride each worker takes in his membership of an estate does not mean that the estates are akin to a closed guild each acting to further its own ends at the expense of other aspects of society. Hegel explicitly rejects this (PR: 255A). Individuals of estates support their own members while also voluntarily comporting themselves in accordance with the universal freedom of all members of the state. It is for this reason that Richard Teichgraeber's (1977: 61) insistence that the various estates undermine the unity of the state because they compete with one another for influence and power fails to understand the complementary role each aspect of Hegel's rational state plays in the realization of its end: the universal freedom of all its citizens.

Hegel recognizes that the estates can act competitively towards one another and the state, each seeking to secure its own ends at the expense of others, but he holds that such action is ultimately self-defeating because it will undermine the state that the activities of civil society depend upon. For Hegel, the estates must not *simply* act of pure self-interest. Each estate must comport itself towards other estates and the state in a way that realizes the universal freedom that is the goal of Hegel's rational state. The important point is that, contra Teichgraeber, the estates are not to have alternate ends to the state; the estates must *voluntarily* comportment themselves in such a way that their activity works to realize the end of Hegel's rational state: the universal freedom of all its citizens (PR: 255A).

Hegel's civil society is, therefore, a system of mediated interactions. While each individual focuses on his own ends, his individual actions bring him into contact with others who are also trying to satisfy their material needs. Implicitly employing Adam Smith's invisible hand argument, Hegel maintains that the individual's self-interested pursuit of his own needs simultaneously provides the means for others to satisfy their needs. For example, the individual can buy someone else's products to satisfy his need. This enriches the other, thereby allowing him to satisfy his needs, while simultaneously allowing the individual to satisfy his own needs. Alternatively, the individual can employ someone to produce goods to sell on the market, thereby enriching the other through his wage and himself through the profit gained from selling the goods produced by the other's labour. Civil society is so structured that when an individual's self-interest leads him to act in the world, his self-interested actions also satisfy 'the welfare of others' (PR: 182A). As Hegel explains, civil society creates 'a system of all-round interdependence' (PR: 183) in which the satisfaction of the individual's needs 'are interwoven with, and grounded on, the subsistence, welfare, and rights of all, and have actuality and security only in this context' (PR: 183).

But while civil society binds each individual together in a relation of mutual entwinement where 'in my furthering my own end, I further the universal, and this in turn furthers my end' (PR: 184A), because the individual of civil society focuses solely on his own self-interest it appears to each that the wider community is opposed to his actions. For this reason, most people regard the payment of taxes as an imposition on their freedom; in actuality, however, taxes pay for the upkeep and functioning of the state that allows the individual to freely express himself in civil society (PR: 184A). However it may *appear* to the individuals involved in civil society, the rules, norms, and laws that allow them to freely express themselves in civil society are, in actuality, dependent on the very 'thing' they view as opposed to their freedom: the state.

Civil society and the problem of poverty

As noted, civil society is the arena within which individuals buy and sell the goods and services that allow them to satisfy their absolute and relative needs. Importantly, however, an 'unrestricted' (PR: 243) civil society only offers the individual the '*possibility*' (PR: 230) of satisfying his material needs. Whether he is able to satisfy his material needs depends on 'the individual's own arbitrary will and particular nature' (PR: 230), as well as existing objective structures, the comportment of others, and contingent circumstances. Because the satisfaction of his material needs is subject to these contingencies, the individual may not actually be able to satisfy them. With this, poverty arises.

Poverty is an important existential issue because the individual is left with both his absolute and relative material needs while at the same time being unable to satisfy them. If this happens, his very existence is threatened.

But Hegel also maintains that the individualistic ethic of an unrestricted civil society will tend to weaken, if not destroy, the social bonds necessary to secure true individual freedom (PR: 245). The resultant atomism can lead to the breakdown of social bonds and, in general, an anomic society. By tearing the community's social bonds and support networks apart, civil society and the atomistic ethic that underpins it not only prevent the individual from satisfying his material needs, but also prevent him from satisfying his spiritual or social needs (PR: 241).

In other words, poverty alienates the individual both from his own spiritual being and from his society. The social fragmentation and disharmony that can result from poverty is a real threat to the universal freedom Hegel holds to be a condition of genuine individual freedom. For this reason, 'the important question of how poverty can be remedied is one which agitates and torments modern societies' (PR: 244A).

To secure the universal freedom that his description of the rational state aims to, Hegel must account for how he is to integrate the poor into the rational state despite an aspect of it, the smooth working of civil society, appearing to inevitably exclude the poor from actively participating in the life of the community. Because poverty necessarily results from the activities of civil society, Hegel must either find some way to integrate the poor into society while also maintaining civil society or abandon his insistence that civil society is an integral aspect of the rational state.

Because he insists that civil society is the arena within which the individuality, difference, and diversity necessary to prevent social stagnation is located, Hegel maintains it is a key aspect of the rational state and so must be maintained. With this, he turns to the former option.

It is safe to say, however, that the dominant historical interpretation is highly critical of Hegel's attempt to overcome poverty while maintaining a form of civil society. For these commentators, Hegel's failure to solve the problem of poverty fatally undermines his attempt to describe a rational, universally free state. For example, while Shlomo Avineri recognizes that Hegel's analysis of poverty is subtle and multidimensional, he holds that 'the extraordinary thing about Hegel's discussion of these social problems in the *Philosophy of Right* is that in an analysis which attempts to depict how modern society in its differentiated structure is able to overcome its problems through mediation, the only problem which remains open and unresolved according to Hegel's own admission is the problem of poverty' (2003: 148). Similarly, David Kolb argues that 'Hegel confessed he saw no solution to growing inequities in the distribution of wealth and the creation of a rabble (*Pöbel*) not caught up in the attempt to mediate all social oppositions' (1986: 33). Frederick Neuhouser writes that 'despite protracted attempts to do so, Hegel (to his credit) never actually finds a solution to this pre-eminently modern social ill that he can wholeheartedly endorse' (2000: 172). Richard Teichgraeber's insistence that Hegel fails to negate poverty or integrate the poor into society leads him to hold 'that something is seriously wrong with the "architectonic of reason" which Hegel claims he has constructed' (1977: 63), and Allen Wood (1995: 152, 260) maintains that Hegel's rational state is not able to secure the universal freedom it aims to because the smooth working of a crucial aspect of it, civil society, necessarily leads some of its citizens to the un-freedom of poverty.

In contrast to this viewpoint, however, are numerous commentators that have argued that not only does Hegel offer solutions to the problem of poverty, but that these have a good chance of succeeding. For example, Stephen Houlgate provides a detailed discussion of Hegel's analysis of poverty and identifies many of the policy proposals he offers to integrate the poor into the life of the state. However, Houlgate maintains that the corporations play the crucial role because membership of one embeds individuals within support networks that allow them to satisfy their material and spiritual needs (2005: 204–206).

While recognizing that Hegel holds that managing poverty requires that production be regulated, with the corporations playing a role in this management through the self-regulation of production, Joel Anderson (2001: 195) maintains that Hegel's logic implicitly discloses that simply focusing on managing poverty through the regulation of production will fail to adequately manage the problem. The intimate relationship between production and consumption means that managing poverty requires an alteration in both production and consumption patterns.

In a similar vein to Houlgate and Anderson, Paul Franco also offers a defence of Hegel's analysis of poverty. While Franco is somewhat critical of the effectiveness of the proposals he understands that Hegel offers, he ultimately defends Hegel's position by introducing policy proposals, such as 'private charity, taxation of the wealthy, job-creation and train-ing' (1999: 275), that he argues complement Hegel's own proposals. While it is contentious whether Hegel does in fact dismiss the policy proposals that Franco insists he does, the general point of Franco's dis-cussion is to show that, contrary to some commentators, not only does Hegel propose solutions to the problem of poverty, but he recognizes that 'the effective management of the problem of modern poverty requires a complex blend of these strategies' (1999: 275).

While agreeing with Houlgate, Anderson, and Franco that Hegel does offer a range of solutions to the problem of poverty, including market regulation, wealth distribution, voluntary alterations in production and consumer practices, and membership of a corporation, which do not undermine his attempt to describe a rational, universally free state, I do not aim to reiterate their defence here. What I aim to do is contribute to the defence of Hegel instantiated by these commentators by making explicit what is sometimes alluded to but never made fully explicit in their respective analyses; that is, that the success of the policies that Hegel proposes to manage the problem of poverty is dependent on the cultivation of a specific community-orientated social culture and indi-vidual mentality. To this end, I will argue that: 1) Hegel's analysis of poverty is not purely economic, but recognizes that there is a cultural/psychological aspect to poverty; 2) the success of the policy proposals that Hegel proposes to manage poverty is dependent on the cultivation of a specific culture/ethic; and because of this 3) the development of a specific culture/ethic is crucial to the management of poverty.

Cultures of poverty: honour and the rabble

While commentators often fail to recognize this point, Hegel's analysis of the dangers inherent to civil society does not contain a critique of *all* forms of civil society. It offers a two-pronged critique of a particular, 'unrestricted' (PR: 243) form of civil society. On the one hand, there is an *objective* critique that recognizes that an unrestricted civil society can prevent the individual from satisfying his objective absolute and relative material needs; on the other hand, there is a *subjective* critique that recognizes that the atomist ethic of civil society wrenches the individual away from the organic support networks that could provide him with spiritual and social support. The conclusion drawn is that managing poverty is not simply an objective matter of satisfying the individual's material needs; an individual's subjective spiritual needs must also be met.

It is for this reason that charity alone, whether at the hands of private donors, wealthy private institutions, foundations, and/or monasteries, will not solve the problem (PR: 242R). First, private charity is subject to the arbitrary whim of the charity-giver. This ensures that the individual may not be covered by the individual's charity and/or could, at any moment, fall foul of the donor's mood. For Hegel, the contingency of poverty cannot be managed through the contingent means of charity.

Secondly, and more importantly, simply giving the poor the means to satisfy their absolute and relative material needs only satisfies their objective material needs; it does not satisfy their subjective spiritual needs. Simply receiving money from the rich to alleviate their material needs is 'contrary to the [ethical] principle of civil society and the feeling of self-sufficiency and honour among its individual members' (PR: 245). In other words, charity does not cultivate the individual's sense of honour; it threatens to affirm the individual's sense of social rights while undermining his sense of social responsibility.

If the poor individual's spiritual, or social, needs are not met, he can turn into a member of the rabble. Hegel's discussion of the rabble in terms of the causes of its formation plays a crucial role in, what Shlomo Avineri calls, Hegel's analysis of the 'culture of poverty' (2003: 150). This term describes the norms, values, beliefs, and general subjective attitudes that tend to be exhibited by the poor. While Avineri rightly notes an important aspect of Hegel's analysis, it is important to note that there is not simply one unitary culture of poverty. The poor can choose how they live their poverty by choosing to adopt one of two general cultural formations, which correspond to two general mentalities, each of which has degrees and differentiations within it. For this reason, it is more appropriate to state that Hegel implicitly undertakes an analysis of the *cultures* of poverty.

Hegel notes that if the individual is unable to satisfy the material needs that will allow him to actively participate in the life of his community, he may alter his subjective disposition and comportment towards his community. If the individual is excluded from actively participating in the life of his community, he can come to see his community as an obstacle to the realization of his material needs rather than viewing it as the means through which his material needs are satisfied. If this occurs, he may turn away from his community which may lead him to lose the 'feeling of right, integrity [*Rechtlickkeit*], and honour which comes from supporting oneself by one's own activity and work' (PR: 244).

Honour is a key term in Hegel's analysis of poverty and in his analysis of the means through which the social problems associated with poverty can be overcome because without a sense of honour, the individual will tend to focus on his own self-interest and so will not make the ethical move that leads him to identify with, and seek to further, the universal freedom of his wider community.

But Hegel's explicit comments on the subject can quite easily be taken to mean that developing a sense of honour is only a possibility for those working (PR: 244). Hegel is most explicit on this in his criticisms of charity (PR: 245). As noted, Hegel argues that if the individual does not work and is simply taken care of by others, he can quite easily forget or ignore that he is and should be responsible for his own existence. Only work develops the individual's sense of self-responsibility and allows him to care for himself while contributing to the wider community.

However, it may be objected that full employment would lead to the overproduction that causes poverty (PR: 245). From this, it appears that linking work to an individual's sense of honour undermines Hegel's attempt to manage poverty.

But while this conclusion does appear to arise from Hegel's explicit comments, we can reconstruct his argument to make it coherent with other aspects of his social philosophy and, in particular, his proposals to manage poverty. Doing so requires that we engage with the relationship between: 1) honour and work; and 2) honour and the notion of 'supporting oneself by one's own activity' (PR: 244).

In the first instance, I want to suggest that developing a sense of honour is not as dependent on work as Hegel's explicit comments appear to make out. While the self-sufficiency that comes from work is the most *immediate* way in which the individual can develop a sense of honour, whether the individual develops a sense of honour is not *primarily* dependent on whether he works. Primordially, honour relates to a sense of self-understanding and identity that the individual chooses to adopt. The individual of honour takes responsibility for his existence, seeks to take care of himself, and recognizes that he is part of a wider community. While the individual should try to work to take care of himself, if for one reason or another he is not able to, he can still comport himself with honour even though he receives material and emotional support from others.

Secondly, I want to suggest that the notion that developing a sense of honour requires that the individual support himself by his own activity does not mean that the individual's sense of honour is dependent on him becoming fully self-sufficient. Hegel's insistence that the individual of honour supports himself by his own activities should be taken to mean that the individual acts with honour whenever he recognizes that he is *responsible* for his own existence. By taking responsibility for his existence, the individual will recognize and accept that, while the satisfaction of his material needs is dependent on interaction with others, ultimately, it is his responsibility to ensure that he obtains the resources that will allow him to satisfy his material needs.

This does not mean that the individual cannot obtain emotional and material support from others. It means that when the individual of honour receives support from others, he will recognize that, ultimately, it is his responsibility to provide for himself. While he is justified in accepting other's help, the individual of honour does not simply sit back and let others look after him. While accepting other's help, he will try to make his dependency on others as temporary as possible by purposefully amending his situation to ensure he can secure the resources that will allow him to satisfy his own material needs.

This allows us to distinguish between the *poor honourable individual* that chooses to take responsibility for his existence despite receiving material help from others and the *poor dishonourable individual* that receives material help from others but does not take responsibility for his existence. When the former receives material help from others, his sense of honour means he feels an obligation to act in a way that: 1) acknowledges his dependence on others; and 2) seeks to make his dependence on others as temporary as possible. In contrast, the latter simply takes the help on offer and runs. He does not attempt to take responsibility for his existence, but holds that it is the job of others to provide the material resources to satisfy his material needs.

By losing his sense of community and the honour that accompanies it, the poor dishonourable individual does not feel bound by the norms, values, and beliefs of his community. Importantly, however, while his estrangement from his community leads him to turn away from its social norms, values, and beliefs, he continues to maintain that he is entitled to claim rights from his society. The individual who rejects his social responsibilities towards his community while still maintaining that he has the right to expect his community to take care of him becomes part of the rabble (PR: 244A).

It is important to note, however, that the poor individual does not have to be absolutely poor to become a member of the rabble; he only has to be relatively poor to risk falling into the rabble mentality because, as explained, relative poverty prevents him from possessing the goods that will allow him to actively participate in the life of his community. Because his relative poverty excludes him from the life of his community, the individual may choose to reject his responsibilities to society while still claiming his society owes him certain rights.[3]

Furthermore, the relatively poor individual's descent into the mindset of the rabble is a subjective decision. While the impact of his immediate community plays a role in this decision, it is only if the individual chooses to accept the mindset of the rabble that he will adopt it. Thus, the individuals of the rabble mentality are not completely blameless for their predicament. While the satisfaction of the material aspect of their relative poverty is beyond their control insofar as it is, to a large degree, subject to contingencies, how the individual approaches his poverty is not subject to such contingency: it is the individual that chooses how he will live his poverty. For this reason, he is responsible for the frivolity and laziness that accompanies his decision to adopt the rabble mentality (PR: 244A).

Such is the threat of the rabble mentality to the universal freedom of the community that Hegel implicitly holds that the question of how to prevent and/or overcome the *rabble mentality* is the central problem of modern discussions of poverty. Overcoming the rabble mentality is so difficult because it relates to the spiritual, or social, aspect of individual existence. While the objective aspect of poverty can be quite easily overcome through redistributions of wealth, or charity, the subjective aspect is far more difficult to overcome. It requires that the individual develop a sense of individual and social honour. If this double sense of honour is cultivated, the individual will recognize that he has social rights and that these are dependent on whether he fulfils certain social responsibilities. He will not, therefore, join the rabble in believing he has social rights but no social responsibilities.

Breaking the rabble mentality

While Hegel's comments on this issue are fragmentary, he does hint at a way to break the rabble mentality that is applicable: 1) to those individuals that have already adopted this mentality and so are blocking progress towards the formation of a universally free society; and/or 2) should individuals choose to adopt this mentality despite the objective structures and social norms necessary to secure the rational, universally free society being in place.

The latter is possible because: a) the state 'exists in the world, and hence in the sphere of arbitrariness, contingency, and error, [...]' (PR: 258A) and so it is possible that, even if the structures necessary to realize the universally free society are currently in place, their dependence on the actions and understanding of its citizens means they are subject to future alteration; and b) Hegel's indication that the rich can also choose to adopt the rabble mentality indicates that the adoption of the rabble mentality is not primarily based on whether the individual's material needs are satisfied; it is due to the way in which the individual comports himself in relation to his wider society (PR: 244A). As such, it is quite possible that even if society has in place the means to satisfy each individual's material and spiritual needs, some individuals may choose to adopt the mentality of the rabble. For these reasons, Hegel has to describe how he would break the rabble mentality in those that currently exist in accordance with it so as to allow for the creation of a universally free society and outline how he would break the rabble mentality if it is chosen by individuals who actually live in a society that has the means to satisfy each individual's material and spiritual needs.

Hegel recommends the same, hard-headed solution to both problems: 'the most direct means of dealing with [...] with the renunciation of shame and honour, [...] laziness and extravagance which give rise to a rabble [mentality] is to leave the poor to their fate and direct them to beg from the public' (PR: 245R).

It is important to note, however, that Hegel does not hold that the poor *in general* should simply be left to their own devices. As explained, he proposes a combination of solutions to alleviate and manage the problem of poverty. However, his overall point is that the alleviation of poverty cannot simply be something that society does *to* the individual. The alleviation and management of poverty requires both the intervention and support of the wider community *and* for the individual to choose to comport himself with honour; that is, he must take responsibility for his situation and seek to alleviate his poverty in a way that conforms to the ethical end of Hegel's rational state: the universal freedom of all its citizens.

Thus, if society is so structured that it is not capable of securing its citizens material and spiritual needs, it must be reformed so that it does. But if the various stakeholders (i.e. the Government, corporations, and consumers) are doing all they can to secure the means to satisfy the individual's material needs and he still chooses to adopt the rabble mentality that leads him to purposefully and continuously turn away from his community then Hegel holds it is entirely justifiable to simply leave him to fend for himself. Rather than continue to support an individual who flouts social norms, breaks laws, is rude, lazy, unhelpful, and lacking in honour, the community can simply decide to revoke his social rights and leave him to fend for himself.

Leaving the poor individual to fend for himself would, hopefully, remind him of the necessity and pleasure to be found in a recognized social existence. Even if the individual became self-sufficient through begging, not only would he not be participating in the social structures, such as membership of a corporation, that Hegel maintains are necessary for him to secure his true freedom, but, if he is rational, he would sooner or later come to the realization that his existence depends on others. This would, hopefully, but would not necessarily, lead him to alter his mentality and comportment towards others in a way that accepts and affirms the positive role that others play in the fulfilment of his freedom. Of course, if the individual is not rational, he would have to deal with the consequences of his actions. His existence would be an unhappy, unfulfilling struggle for survival that would prevent him from attaining the material and spiritual/social conditions that would allow him to be truly free.

Hegel's proposal is implicitly underpinned by the following argument: while the individual has a right to be taken care of by his community, in exchange for this right he has a responsibility to, at the very least, not undermine the universal freedom of the community. If the individual does not seek to contribute to the universal freedom of his community, by for example continuously breaking its laws, the other members of the community are perfectly within their right to withdraw their support for the individual and leave him to fend from himself.

Importantly, however, and in-line with Hegel's insistence on the concrete nature of ethics, at what point each community decides to withdraw support from the individual who violates its rules and norms would be a matter for each particular community. This does not mean the community cannot subsequently reinstate their support for the individual, but this would be contingent on the individual first demonstrating, through his actions, that he supported and was willing to actively participate in the realization of other's freedom.

Poverty and the community-orientated culture/ethic

While Hegel's analysis of the rabble mentality discloses one general culture of poverty, a culture he clearly holds to be debased, his discussion, and statement that 'poverty in itself does not reduce people to a rabble' (PR: 244A), implicitly discloses another culture of poverty that he is far more supportive of. Indeed, I will argue that Hegel's rational state requires that each individual adopt the mentality that corresponds to this particular culture.

For Hegel, the realization of the universal freedom of his rational state is not subject to a transcendent imperative with its own metaphysical teleology; it is dependent on the actions and mentality of the individuals that compose it (PR: 265A). Thus, while the individual of Hegel's rational state is to be free as far as possible to choose his own existence, he must also comport himself with a specific general ethical orientation; one that is compatible with the freedom of others. Rather than simply seek to further his own ends, Hegel holds that securing the freedom of every citizen requires that each cultivates the ethical disposition that brings him to recognize and work towards the freedom of all (PR: 260). If the individual has cultivated this universally orientated, or put differently, this community-orientated mentality, he will recognize that his freedom is dependent on the existence of a rational, universally free state and, importantly, will actively act in a manner that realizes this. While it is primarily the responsibility of the family to educate the individual towards the universal disposition, Hegel holds that the state and corporation also have roles to play in this respect (PR: 240).

Engendering a community-orientated mentality in each individual leads each to spontaneously and unreflectively act in a way that instantiates new community-orientated social values and norms. In turn, these community-orientated social values and norms cultivate and re-enforce the individual's community-orientated mentality. The dialectical interplay between social norms and individual thought ensures that social culture and education play a crucial role in the management of poverty and the attainment of universal freedom. Without a community-orientated culture and the education that instantiates and supports such a culture, Hegel implicitly holds that it is not possible for society to be universally free.

Thus, while the individual's social situation and interaction play a role in whether he adopts the rabble mentality, the individual must also choose whether to accept and act in accordance with this community-orientated mentality. Those that do not will, as noted, descend into the debased life of the rabble. For those that do, however, Hegel appears to hold that they will act with honour. They will recognize and uphold their responsibilities to the community by affirming its rules, norms, general values, and beliefs. They will continue to act in a way that affirms the universal freedom of the community and will actively seek to participate in the life of the community. Importantly, even if the individual is both relatively and absolutely poor, the adoption of the community-orientated mentality will ensure that he continues to have respect for himself and others and so will not descend into the debased mentality of the rabble. Put simply, the poor individual that chooses to adopt the community-orientated mentality will recognize and accept that he is entitled to claim social rights to the extent that he recognizes and actively affirms his social responsibilities. If he receives material help from others, he will continue to comport himself with honour and dignity and, indeed, will actively try to do everything he can to alter his situation so that he can gradually wean himself off the material help he receives from others. Of course, other factors may prevent this, but the important point is that the individual that has adopted the community-orientated mentality will not simply sit back and live off the largesse of others.

Thus, Hegel's analysis implicitly discloses that the individual can choose to live his poverty in accordance with either the culture of the debased rabble mentality or the culture of the noble community-orientated mentality. While the satisfaction of the individual's objective material needs and subjective spiritual needs may be subject to contingency, the individual must also choose how he will live his poverty. Some will choose to turn away from society and forego their responsibilities to society. They will become lazy, rude, and lacking in honour; they will, in short, become part of the rabble. Others will recognize the necessity of living in society and will seek to uphold its laws, contribute to the life of the community, recognize that they have social responsibilities, and, in general, comport themselves with honour. Of course, their material poverty may actually prevent them from achieving this, but, importantly, their sense of honour will lead them to act in a way that respects and values the life of their community.

The distinction Hegel makes between absolute and relative needs, which, as I noted earlier, leads to a distinction between absolute and relative poverty, and the distinction introduced to differentiate the two general cultures of poverty leads Hegel to implicitly recognize four general types of poor individual: 1) the absolutely poor individual of the rabble mentality; 2) the absolutely poor individual of the community-orientated mentality; 3) the relatively poor individual of the rabble mentality; and 4) the relatively poor individual of the community-orientated mentality.

This distinction is important for understanding the role poverty plays in Hegel's rational state and the solutions he proposes to allow individuals to cope with the alienating consequences of poverty. In particular, it allows us to discuss the sort of poverty Hegel is trying to overcome and that which he is not. This is because Hegel's rational state is not one in which everyone has equal resources or wealth. 'Hegel believes some inequalities are inevitable and defensible' (Williams, 1997: 240) because poverty (or, put differently, inequalities in wealth): 1) inevitably result from the competition inherent to a market economy, which it will be remembered is the economic formation that Hegel maintains best secures and affirms the individual's social freedom; and 2) is the price to be paid to secure diversity, difference, and individual self-expression, which is necessary to prevent a society in which 'all cows are black' (PS: 9).

Importantly, however, in Hegel's rational state each individual will have satisfied his absolute material needs; satisfied his relative material needs and so be able to actively contribute to the life of the community; live in accordance with the community-orientated mentality; and live in, and actively contribute towards, support networks that care for and affirm the other's freedom.

Culture and the public authority

To demonstrate the important, but often ignored, role that a community-orientated culture plays in Hegel's proposals to manage poverty, it may be helpful to briefly demonstrate how three of Hegel's proposals to manage poverty are dependent on, and in turn instantiate, a community-orientated culture.

One of the crucial ways in which Hegel proposes to manage the problem of poverty is by establishing a 'public authority' (PR: 235) to regulate the market, ensure contracts are upheld, and maintain the rule of law. But the public authority also has another crucial role in the management of poverty. The dialectical relationship between the individual and the community means that, while the individual has a duty to live in accordance with and affirm the rules and norms of his community, he also has 'a right to demand that, within this context, [his] particular welfare should also be promoted' (PR: 229A). It is the job of the public authority to provide a minimum level of social provision. This social provision includes 'street lighting, bridge-building, the pricing of daily necessities, and public health' (PR: 236A), which will greatly increase, although will not guarantee, that each will secure the means that will enable him to satisfy his absolute material needs.[4]

But Hegel recognizes that the welfare provision of the state cannot simply emanate from a distant faceless bureaucracy. If it did, the individual may accept the state's material offerings without recognizing his responsibilities towards society; he would be in danger of descending into the mentality of the rabble. To prevent this, the public authority's welfare scheme must be accompanied by two further developments.

In-line with his insistence that the subjective spiritual aspect of poverty is just as important as the satisfaction of the individual's objective material needs, Hegel recognizes that there must be support networks in place to care for and provide the subjective spiritual support each individual needs (PR: 242). In the first instance, the family provides such support. However, Hegel also maintains that these familial bonds must be complemented by social structures and support networks that individuals can fall back on as and when they need to. There are two ways civil society achieves this: 1) through the individual being a member of a corporation; and 2) through the activities of the public authority.

In the case of the public authority, managing the problem of poverty requires that it not only satisfy each individual's objective material needs through regulation of the market and, if need be, welfare provision, but that it also satisfy each individual's subjective spiritual needs.

However, Will Dudley objects that 'since people do not identify themselves with the public authority' (1997: 53), it is not possible for the public authority to fulfil this role. Instead, he maintains that only the corporations can bring individuals to temper their particular self-interest to accord with the universal interest of all.

In contrast, however, I want to suggest that individuals can come to identify with the public authority, but that this requires the cultivation of a specific community-orientated culture and that individuals and the public authority adopt a specific mentality that leads each to act in a specific way towards the other. This requires two things: first, that the public authority puts in place objective policies and structures that allow individuals to interact with the public authority in ways that bring individuals to see that the public authority is an extension, not a constraint, on their freedom. The public authority must not only actively work to secure the freedom of all citizens; it must do so in an open and transparent manner. This will also require that individuals recognize that the public authority is doing this and, crucially, that it is doing this because this action is necessary to secure the universal freedom upon which their individual freedom depends. This is why education and the activities of the corporation are so crucial; they educate individuals in the requirements of universal freedom and instantiate a community-orientated mentality 'in' them.

However, bringing individuals to recognize that the public authority is an extension, not a constraint, on their freedom also requires that civil servants take an active and caring approach to individual circumstances. While it is up to each individual civil servant to choose to act in a support manner towards the individual concerned, their choice can be influenced by an education that affirms the community-orientated mentality, membership of an estate that realizes and affirms the community-orientated mentality, and the development of a particular community-orientated organizational culture in the public authority that encourages its employees to act in accordance with and, indeed, affirm a community-orientated mentality in-themselves and others. This will lead civil servants to act professionally in their dealings with citizens and actively take into account an individual's circumstances when devising solutions to his problems. Importantly, and while Hegel never mentions this, this will require that each civil servant be given sufficient formal power and authority to devise and implement policy solutions specific to each particular citizen's circumstance. By meeting face to face with a supportive civil servant, rather than simply receiving money from 'the government,' an individual on welfare will be more likely to recognize his debt to society. As such, he will be less likely to simply take the money and run as the individual of the rabble does. For this reason, the attitude, comportment, and capabilities of civil servants, in conjunction with the proper education and membership of a corporation, plays a fundamentally important role in the prevention and/or overcoming of the rabble mentality.

Secondly, Hegel's welfare state also requires the development of a community-orientated culture. Rather than simply take an interest in his own particular existence, Hegel argues that each individual must develop the mentality that takes an interest in the wider community and actively seeks to contribute to its life and activities (PR: 187). This contribution could take the form of charity or voluntary work, but more generally it takes the form of a specific subjective orientation: the individual must remain open to his society and actively comport himself in a way that works to realize the universal freedom of all its citizens.

We have seen that the public authority's role in managing the problems of poverty is, in part, dependent on civil servants cultivating and comporting themselves in accordance with the community-orientated ethic. But it also requires that civil servants purposefully aim to cultivate a community-orientated ethic in each individual they interact with. Of course, this cultivation is also dependent on individuals receiving a certain community-orientated education and having this education re-enforced by informal support networks and membership of a corporation, but the important point is that the civil servants of the public authority have a role to play in this process. Cultivating this ethic will, hopefully, ensure that the individual that receives objective material support from the public authority will recognize that he has a responsibility to his community to provide for himself at the earliest opportunity; he will not, therefore, simply maintain that the community should provide for his needs indefinitely.

Culture, poverty, and the role of the corporation

Another crucial means through which Hegel aims to manage the problems of poverty is through membership of what he calls the corporation. As Stephen Houlgate (2005: 204–206) has undertaken an extensive analysis of the contents and form of the corporation and the role it plays in Hegel's attempts to manage the problems of property, I will not engage with these aspects of his thought. What I will do, however, is emphasize what is implicit to Houlgate's analysis; that is, that the activities of the corporation will only succeed in managing poverty if its members live in accordance with a community-orientated culture/ethic.

It is important to recognize, however, that while we tend to associate corporations with multi-national companies, this is not what Hegel means by corporation. As Houlgate explains, for Hegel, 'corporations are voluntary associations of manufacturers, craftsmen or traders who have come together with the explicit intention of furthering the rights and welfare of those who work in a particular sector of the economy, and of ensuring that the labour of one person in that sector does not destroy the labour of another' (2005: 204).

By anchoring the individuals of the same general work, each of whom exists in accordance with the self-interested disposition inherent to civil society, into a common group formation, membership of a corporation not only brings the individual to identify with a group formation that transcends his own individual standpoint, but, by cultivating a specific universally orientated mentality, also helps him to overcome the purely self-interested ethical disposition inherent to civil society. 'In this way, [the individual recognizes] that he belongs to a whole which is itself a member of society in general, and that he has an interest in, and endeavours to promote, the less selfish end of this whole' (PR: 253).

But the corporation does not simply bestow an abstract sense of personhood on the individual; it actively cares for its members. Educating its members both in terms of the skills required to be a member of the corporation and in terms of their responsibilities towards the wider community, caring for their subjective well-being through the mutual support and recognition it provides its members, and caring for their objective material needs through the provision of goods and services allows the corporation to become 'a *second* family for its members' (PR: 252). Importantly, because the corporation cultivates a sense of community and, because each member can find honour in his membership of a corporation, he recognizes his duties and responsibilities to other members and his wider community. The sense of honour the individual receives as a result of belonging to a corporation ensures that if and when the individual receives objective material support from his corporation this: 1) does not violate his sense of honour in himself and his community; and 2) compels him to honour his duty to care for himself and his community (PR: 253R). Thus, the individual of the corporation does not simply reject his social responsibilities while claiming his social rights as the rabble do; nor does the objective material support of the corporation violate the individual's sense of self-worth in the way that private charity does. Membership of a corporation secures the individual's objective material and subjective spiritual needs.

But corporations also fulfil another crucial role in the management of poverty: the self-regulation of production. Rather than value an ethic of ever expanding production, the corporations must come to understand the necessity of *voluntarily* limiting their production so that it accords with that which is capable of being comfortably consumed. For example, rather than seek to maximize its profits by producing as much as possible, the corporation must teach its members to accept a steady rate of return and attain this steady return through action that conforms to and affirms the ethical end of Hegel's rational state: the universal freedom of all its citizens.

From this, we can see that the fostering of a community-orientated culture plays a crucial role in the transformation of the activity and mentality of corporations. The corporations must come to recognize that they are not opposed to each other, or to the state; they have to realize that 'the end of the corporation, which is limited and finite, has its truth in the *end which is universal* in and for itself and in the absolute actuality of this end' (PR: 256). In other words, the corporation does not exist in opposition to the state; it is, in actuality, dependent on the life and vitality of the state for its content. When corporations come to recognize their dependency on the state, Hegel maintains they will temper their self-interest to accord with the ethical ends of the state; they will, in other words, act in a way that realizes the freedom of all citizens. It is for this reason that corporations represent the 'ethical moment of civil society' (Williams, 1997: 256).

Importantly, however, while Hegel maintains that the spiritual nature of social entities, such as corporations, means they cannot be reduced to the sum of their individual parts, he also recognizes that the structure and content of social entities is dependent on the activities and understanding of the individuals that compose them. As such, whether corporations undertake the activities necessary to realize the freedom of all citizens will depend on the activities and understanding of its members.

However, in the same way that an individual's self-understanding and social mentality shapes and is shaped by the objective structures and cultural norms and values of his society, so an individual's decision regarding whether to act in accordance with the community-orientated mentality is not made in strict independence from the activities of the corporation; membership of a corporation plays a fundamental role in instantiating and supporting the formation of the community-ori-entated mentality 'in' individuals in the first place. The relationship between the individual and corporation is dialectical: the corporation provides material and social support to its members and educates them in the need to adopt a community-orientated mentality while corporations only gain life and meaning through the activities of individuals. To ensure a rational, universally free society, individuals must not only choose to become members of corporations; they must also choose to act in ways that support and affirm the ends of the corporation. In turn, the ends of the corporation must be aligned with and actively affirm the objective structures and social norms that realize a rational, universally free society. For this reason, simple membership of a corporation is not enough. If the community-orientated culture necessary to secure a universally free society is to be realized: a) individuals must be members of a corporation; b) corporations must act in accordance with the ends of the universally free society by regulating production and affirming a culture that affirms the ends of the universally free society; c) individuals must recognize the need to adopt a community-orientated mentality; and d) individuals must actually choose to adopt and affirm this mentality.

Culture, poverty, and consumerism

But while Hegel holds that managing the problems of poverty requires that civil society be regulated and that the corporation voluntarily shape its production in accordance with the needs of the wider society, Joel Anderson (2001: 195) argues that Hegel's logic reveals that this alone is insufficient. The intimate relationship between production and consumption means that if production is to be regulated so must consumption. Thus, managing poverty requires an alteration in production patterns and an alteration in consumer attitudes and consumption patterns.

For Anderson, the best way to alter consumption patterns to accord with that produced while still preserving the individual's capacity to choose how to express himself is for the individual consumer himself to choose to voluntarily alter what he consumes so that it mitigates the poverty of others and affirms their freedom. Individual consumers must develop the social awareness that brings them to either spend their money in ways that contribute to the alleviation of poverty or to not spend at all if their consumption would likely lead to a significant imbalance between production and consumption. Developing this social awareness is dependent on education and the individual choosing to adopt a community-orientated mentality.

But, for Anderson, this does not entail individuals simply purchasing ethically superior products. It requires more than this insofar as consumers must: 1) understand the impact their consumption patterns have on the wider community; and 2) alter their purchasing habits to accord with current production patterns. Rather than simply consuming 'ethical' rather than 'unethical' products, Anderson argues that consumers must alter their consumption patterns to accord with what is required to maintain a relatively stable equilibrium with current production capabilities and/or help others who may be struggling:

> For example, if I am aware that a favourite restaurant is having trouble attracting business, I may frequent it more often to help keep it afloat. If a craze for this Christmas season's 'hot' toy is leading to wide retail and production fluctuations, I may choose a different gift for a child. Or I may purchase goods that are produced by labourers earning a living wage, so as to resist the downward pressures on wages that come from uncertainty and fierce competition. In small ways, these choices help to support rational and stable growth in consumer demand (2001: 196).

This re-enforces the point that for poverty to be successfully managed and for the poor to be integrated into the life of Hegel's rational, universally free state requires that each citizen adopt and affirm a community-orientated mentality. It is only by adopting this mentality that individual consumers will come to recognize the impact that their consumption patterns can and do have on the wider community. Only then will they explicitly act in a way that contributes to the realization of universal freedom.

Thus, while Sartre does not engage with the issue of poverty nor provide concrete policy proposals beyond a vague if committed pact of solidarity with the poor in the name of a general revolution, Hegel once again goes beyond him by offering a sustained and detailed analysis of the issue and proposing complex, detailed, radical, and far-reaching policy proposals to manage poverty and alleviate the alienating social problems that tend to accompany it. Government, in the form of the public authority, has a key role to play by providing objective structures and policies to ensure each individual is able to satisfy his absolute and relative material needs; trade associations, in the form of corporations, have a crucial role to play both materially and spiritually; consumers must alter their consumption patterns to accord with current production patterns and the situation of others; and each individual must choose to live in a way that explicitly affirms their self-honour and their membership of a rational community.

However, the success of these policy proposals is dependent on a radical alteration in the culture of civil society and society at large away from a culture that affirms pure individual self-interest to one that affirms a culture of community in which each individual explicitly recognizes, cares for, and affirms the other's freedom. Whether Hegel's proposals to manage the problem of poverty are workable or simply a logical dream will probably remain an important if contentious issue. But, as he recognizes, the issue of poverty and its alienating consequences is a problem that results from human actions. Its resolution will, therefore, depend on our understanding and actions.

We have to remember, however, that while civil society plays a crucial, if often misunderstood, role in Hegel's analysis of ethical life, both civil society and the family exist within and gain meaning from the third and most universal form of ethical life: the state. Without the state to bind the individuals of civil society together, the conflictual nature of civil society would lead to atomism and social breakdown. Thus, because the unrestricted activities of civil society would lead to a situation of conflict, poverty, extremes in wealth distribution, and general social disharmony, the state is necessary to temper the worst excesses of civil society and ensure and preserve the freedom of all citizens. But it is important to note that while, from a purely logical standpoint, the state is necessary to contain the fragmentation and difference constitutive of civil society, in actuality, the state *precedes* civil society (PR: 182A). It is only because of the overarching structures of the state that the difference of civil society is possible.

Freedom and the state

Because it is the universal substance that provides meaning and coherence to both the family and civil society, Hegel maintains that the state is the highest form of universality; it is the embodiment of ethical spirit (PR: 257). With this, Hegel is trying to say that, because it provides laws, customs, and culture that shape and give meaning to individual lives, the state is at the very heart of social life. For this reason, it is intimately connected to what is ethical. But again, not all states are ethical; securing a universally free society requires a specific state.

Importantly, the state is not simply a static thing that exists in opposition to its citizens. As a living entity, the state has a will of its own manifested in a particular spirit or culture that gives meaning to and so shapes its content. The state's immediate content emanates from custom with this emanating from the 'self-consciousness of the individual' (PR: 257). But, crucially, the state also provides the individual with meaning; 'it is only through being a member of the state that the individual [*Individuum*] himself has objectivity, truth, and ethical life' (PR: 258R). But this does not mean that the individual is subservient to the community. As Hegel notes, 'particular interests should certainly not be set aside, let alone suppressed; on the contrary, they should be harmonised with the universal, so that both they themselves and the universal are preserved' (PR: 261R).

Rather than being a defender of totalitarianism, Hegel goes to great lengths to explain that the state and the individual are dialectically entwined in that each gains meaning and content through the other. While objective structures are necessary to ensure the smooth functioning of the community and, through legally enforceable rules that define acceptable individual behaviour, the freedom of all citizens, these objective structures must only impinge on the individual's subjective freedom to the degree necessary to secure the freedom of all citizens. Furthermore, its citizens must understand the necessity of the state and be willing to identify with it. This will only happen if each individual realizes that his essential freedom requires that he 'lead a universal life' (PR: 258R). If the individual does not develop this subjective ethical disposition, he will continue to see himself as an inviolable entity opposed to his community. This may lead to the conflict and social disharmony constitutive of abstract right and/or morality.

Therefore, while membership of a family and civil society provide the individual with knowledge of what is acceptable behaviour, because neither the family nor civil society is focused on the well-being of the whole community, their individualistic, particular orientation must be tempered by conscious membership of the wider community. Hegel calls this universal orientation 'patriotism' (PR: 268). Far from being a narrow, nationalistic chauvinism, patriotism simply delineates the adoption of a subjective attitude in which the individual orientates himself towards and cares about his wider community. Because the content of the state is dependent on its citizen's activity and understanding, it is only if its citizens will universal freedom that it will be realized. As Hegel notes, 'since the state is not a mechanism but the rational life of self-conscious freedom and the system of the ethical world, the *disposition* [of its citizens], and so also the[ir] consciousness of this disposition in *principles*, is an essential moment in the actual state' (PR: 270R).

From this, we see that Hegel does not insist that individual freedom requires that he simply identify with *any* state; the individual must only identify with the state insofar as it secures the universal freedom of the community. This requires compromise and the development of laws and customs that bring each to recognize that his freedom is dependent on the freedom of others. It also means that there is a critical aspect to Hegel's description; if the state does not secure the freedom of all citizens, its structures must be altered. But altered how?

This point is often ignored in the secondary literature, but is crucially important when trying to understand what Hegel is trying to achieve in his description of a rational state and when defending him against the charge that he is an apologist for totalitarian government. Understanding Hegel's thinking on this issue, however, requires that I return to his ontology of spirit.

As discussed in Chapter 5, Hegel maintains that spirit is the universal ontological substance of existence that is manifested, to various degrees and forms, 'in' different entities. In turn, spirit's content emanates from the activities and understanding of the entities it constitutes. The important point for the present discussion is that existence is *always* a form of spirit; or, put differently, that each particular culture and/or epoch is simply constituted by a different form of spirit constituted by varying degrees of freedom and rationality. The aim of Hegel's social philosophy is to outline the objective structures and subjective disposition that lead ethical life to be fully rational and hence fully free. According to Hegel, his rational state is the only social formation that secures the freedom of all citizens.

But, we must also remember that Hegel maintains that the development of spirit is wholly historical. It is not simply an event that bursts fully formed 'into' the world; spirit requires a specific developmental journey to fully realize itself with this developmental journey requiring that it learn from its previous failings in a particular way.

The combination of his insistence that: 1) the realization of freedom requires an organic development in the objective structures and culture of that society; and 2) the actual world is (to varying degrees) rational, leads him to warn that we should not aim to (or indeed think we can) start from scratch, devise a perfectly rational abstract system, and then impose this onto concrete reality. We should look for those moments of rationality in the current system and amend the other aspects of that system to complement the objective structures and social norms that already exist that do realize the freedom of all citizens. In other words, if individuals are not able to satisfy their material and social needs in a particular social formation, Hegel insists on piecemeal reform of that current system rather than revolution.

But Hegel warns that 'the state is not a work of art, it exists in the world, and hence in the sphere of arbitrariness, contingency, and error, and bad behaviour may disfigure it in many respects. But the ugliest man, the criminal, the invalid, or the cripple is still a living human being; the affirmative aspect – life – survives [*besteht*] in spite of such deficiencies, and it is with this affirmative aspect that we are here concerned' (PR: 258A). Life in Hegel's rational state is not perfect, nor should we expect it to be.

Because it is dependent on individual activity, it can be subject to arbitrary action, misunderstandings, and wrong. However, Hegel thinks that not only are the structures he describes flexible enough to incorporate these contingencies into its existence, but when individuals understand what universal freedom entails and comport themselves accordingly, they will voluntarily act in a way that does not create fundamental conflict. While conflict, diversity, and difference are crucial aspects of Hegel's rational state, this difference will not *fatally* undermine the rationality and freedom of the whole.

The constitution of Hegel's rational state

For Hegel, the rational state is a constitutional state (PR: 273) grounded in the preservation of an individual's right to property, freedom of speech, and freedom of religion. Its internal structure takes the form of a democratic, constitutional monarchy constituted by a division of powers between the legislature, executive, and judiciary (PR: 273). But while the rational state must conform to this division, the specifics of this division will be determined by the spirit, or culture, of each particular community. It is for this reason that a constitution cannot be imposed on another culture; it must develop organically from within the history of that particular community (PR: 274A).

The monarch stands at the head of the state and combines the universality of the state with the particularity of an individual person. This combination allows the monarch to be the concrete embodiment of the state. Because the monarch is the focal point for the state, he embodies the state's sovereignty and is the 'decisive moment of the whole' (PR: 279R).

But the role of the monarch is somewhat problematic (Westphal, 1999: 262). On the one hand, Hegel insists that the monarch must use his skill and judgement to fulfil the duties of the office and to provide oversight to other aspects of the state. In the first instance, the monarch does this by deciding who will be his close confidents. However, as Sartre will note (EH: 39–41), this predetermines the type of advice the monarch receives, which, in turn, means the decision is actually the monarchs. As such, it would appear that the monarch's role is not simply formal and empty, but requires a specific character, deft judgement, and a high degree of intelligence (PR: 283).

On the other hand, however, Hegel contradicts this by insisting that the monarch is not to actively participate in the creation and determination of law. 'In a fully organised state, it is only a question of the highest instance of formal decision, and all that is required in a monarch is someone to say ' "yes" and to dot the "I"; for the supreme office should be such that the particular character of its occupant is of no significance' (PR: 280A). Because the monarch's role is purely formal, it is not dependent on his skills or character; the monarch simply has to use his sovereign status to sign a bill into objective law. It is difficult to see how Hegel is able to satisfactorily reconcile his claim that the particularity of the monarch in terms of his judgement and vitality is important to the role while simultaneously claiming that the monarch is merely a formal figure-head that unites the disparate groups into a coherent, unified whole.

Furthermore, it is difficult to see how Hegel can consistently maintain that the monarch should inherit his position, while also claiming that the offices of the state 'can neither be sold nor inherited' (PR: 277A). While Hegel insists that state offices be earned on merit, the monarch becomes sovereign by virtue of the contingencies of history. Now it may be that Hegel means to say that the monarch's role is purely formal and, because of this formality, is the only office that can be inherited, but he needs to explain this exception especially in light of his comments regarding the relationship between the monarch's judgment and function. Because Hegel does not explain this, the role of the monarch appears to be somewhat confused.

But the monarch's decisions need to be made actual; this is the job of the executive. The executive is the mediating link between the monarch and the individuals of the state; it not only carries out the monarch's decisions, but ensures they are adhered to. As such, the police and the judiciary are, at one and the same time, independent from *and* intimately linked to the executive.

Importantly, however, the executive must undertake its activities in a way that does not alienate the individuals from the state. In other words, citizens must see the executive as an expression of their own will. To achieve this, and while the executive must contain specialists who understand the specific areas under its remit, it is also to contain a number of 'ordinary' elected citizens. This will maintain an organic link between the populace and the executive while also ensuring that the executive cares for, tends to, and works in a manner that secures the freedom of all citizens (PR: 288).

Efficiency and effectiveness dictate that the executive be split into various departments headed by individuals who are in direct contact with the monarch (PR: 289). This direct contact allows the monarch to have the information that allows him to determine how to act and which bills to sign, while also allowing the department heads to pass on information that can effect policy to that which is required 'on the ground.' While the government is split between different functions and forms, each is intimately and organically linked to others. The result is an interconnected structure of networks and departments that bring the disparate aspects of the community under a rational governance framework.

The overall aim of the various departments is to act in a way that co-ordinates individual activity in a way that realizes the universal freedom of the community. But while the activities of the various functions are determined in accordance with those necessary to realize the freedom of all citizens, because the manner in which its duties are fulfilled is left to the individual to decide, the individual office holder is able to freely express himself within his function. This allows him to find satisfaction within his official duties (PR: 294A).

But while the individual office holder must carry out the functions of his office in a way that affirms the universal freedom of the community, his action cannot simply be mechanical. Because he must bind individuals to the community, not only must the office holder offer subjective support to others, but he must undertake his duties in a polite, professional manner. 'This provides a spiritual counterweight to the mechanical exercises and the like which are inherent in learning the so-called sciences appropriate to these [administrative] spheres' (PR: 296) which will allow individuals to identify with the state. The executive must, therefore, not only fulfil objective tasks, it must also offer subjective counsel and support. Whether it is able to achieve this will shape whether the individual identifies with the state or views it as something opposed to him.

But Hegel recognizes that the executive's central importance and the fact that its activity is undertaken by people of the middle class may mean it becomes politicized. In other words, the middle class functionaries may subvert the ends of the executive to advance their own class ends not the universal freedom of the wider community. To prevent this, Hegel argues that the monarch must oversee the executive's actions from above. This again demonstrates that the monarch's role is not simply a passive and formal one; he must use his judgement to fulfil his tasks. Similarly the corporations must undertake this activity from below. The activities of the executive will, therefore, be scrutinized from above by the monarch and from below by the corporations (PR: 297).

The activities of the monarch and the executive are linked to those of the legislature. It is the legislature that passes the bills the monarch signs into law and which the executive makes actual and/or ensures are upheld. But there is not a definitive distinction between the different realms of the state; when it comes to creating laws, the monarch, legislature, and executive must all discuss their content.

Public opinion must also be consulted and considered. This will make individuals feel that their views matter and integrates the public into the workings of the state. If the state takes into consideration and reflects public opinion, individuals are far more likely to identify with it and feel at home living within it.

But this does not mean that the state must become a slave to public opinion; far from it. While Hegel notes that public opinion must be respected, he also writes that its general ignorance should be *'despised'* (PR: 318). The general ignorance of each individual means that if the content of public opinion violates the universal freedom of the community it must be ignored and the state must attempt to change it so it accords with the conditions of universal freedom. This, however, does not mean a totalitarian form of ideological manipulation; it means that reasoned arguments be put forward that show the limitations of the public's opinion on that issue. In other words, Hegel wants to instantiate a public discourse; he does not advocate that the executive simply impose its views onto the populace.

Concluding remarks

We can see from this, albeit brief description, that Hegel's rational state is a 'system of mediation' (PR: 302A). The individual exists in a family, which exists in civil society, which exists in the state. The individual is integrated into civil society through membership of the corporation, and through membership of his corporation, into the state. At the same time, the state's public authority oversees civil society to ensure its activities accord with and re-enforce the freedom of all members of the community. Similarly, the actions of the various state organs must interact with the corporations, the estates, and individuals in a specific way to incorporate their views into the laws of the state. When this mutually dependent network of objective structures is combined with Hegel's insistence that each aspect must actively create and comport itself in accordance with a culture that affirms the freedom of all citizens, we begin to get a better idea of the impressive architectonic of rationality Hegel has constructed.

In contrast, while the *Critique of Dialectical Reason* does provide a detailed description of the ways in which he understands that different group formations enhance or constrain the individual's practical freedom, Sartre never discusses the subjective comportment and objective social structures necessary to allow consciousness to be practically free in the world to anywhere near the same degree as Hegel does. Indeed, it is difficult to see how Sartre could outline the subjective comportment and objective structures necessary to allow consciousness to be practically free in the world given his rejection of a priori, transcendent, ethical imperatives and his insistence that consciousness's practical freedom is won by overcoming the resistance of the objective structures and social norms of the concrete world.

Hegel, however, shows that consciousness only fully overcomes its alienation if it fully understands its ontological structure and realizes the ontological potential implicit to its ontological structure. Importantly, Hegel goes to great lengths to outline the specific objective structures and subjective comportment necessary to realize this implicit potential. These include being married and having children, actively participating in a certain form of civil society, identifying with a certain form of the state, and purposefully working towards the realization of the other's freedom.

In terms of actions, therefore, Hegel's social philosophy demands a great deal from us. It not only demands that we act in a manner that we would no doubt find difficult, but also challenges us to question our deepest held assumptions about a range of social issues including the family, male/female relations, the ethical role of children, individual needs, poverty, freedom, the role of the state, the individual's relation to the state, and the relationship between the various aspects of the state. Importantly, however, Hegel himself recognizes that while 'we ought to will something great [...] we must also be able to implement it, or else our willing is futile' (PR: 124A). Paraphrasing Karl Marx,[5] the question becomes: has Hegel merely interpreted the world or is he capable of actually changing it? In other words, is Hegel's rational state capable of being actualized?

There are certainly those who do not think it is. For example, Allen Wood maintains that the vision is too great. According to Wood, 'the nation-state cannot serve the exalted function in human life which Hegel assigned it. Neither it nor any other modern institution provides the transition of individual into communal life in the way Hegel's theory demands' (1995: 259). For him, the complex structures of Hegel's rational state ensure it is nothing but an unrealizable utopian dream.

But this misses the point. Hegel does not argue that there is a modern state that conforms to this model. He recognizes that no existing single state is universally free because none combines all the objective structures necessary for the realization of the rational state with the specific subjective attitude on the part of its citizens that would secure universal freedom. His point is that when the concept 'freedom' is properly understood, we will realize that it is only when these objective structures and subjective attitude are made actual that universal freedom can and will be truly realized. With this, the question becomes not whether Hegel's state exists in the world, but whether it can actually be realized.

While Wood thinks it is a utopian dream that cannot be realized, I am much less pessimistic. After all, as far as I can see, there is nothing in Hegel's architectonic that is beyond the realm of human action. Admittedly, it will be extremely difficult to create all the objective structures, have them interact with each other in the necessary manner, and ensure that individuals adopt the necessary supportive attitude towards the wider community, but I do not think that extreme difficult alone is sufficient to preclude the possibility. Of course, as Hegel recognizes, whether it is actualized or not is due to our own historical actions.

But this leads me to another question: does Hegel's rational state actually realize the universal freedom it aims to? While sharing Hegel's optimism regarding the issue of whether the structures of his rational state could be made actual, I would suggest that, as it stands, Hegel's rational state does not realize the universal freedom it aims to achieve. In particular, because it excludes: 1) women from extra-familial activities under the pretext that freedom means something different for men and women; and 2) same-sex couples from fulfilling the conditions of a 'genuine' family which, it will be remembered, is necessary to ensure genuine individual freedom, Hegel's architechtonic not only employs a dual conception of 'freedom' and so contradicts his insistence that 'freedom' has a universal meaning, but, by failing to consistently identify where the ethical moment of the child lies, also fails to secure freedom in either its male or female versions for same-sex couples. Because these groups are unable to fulfil the conditions Hegel insists are necessary to be fully free, they remain excluded and alienated from ethical life. This not only impacts on their freedom, but due to universal freedom being a condition of individual freedom, also prevents other citizens from being free. When these are combined with the confused role of the monarch, we see that in a number of areas Hegel's architectonic either no longer speaks to us or aspects of it are simply in tension with other aspects of his thought.

But while it doesn't quite realize the universal freedom it sets out to achieve, I think we must recognize and appreciate that Hegel's attempt is a magnificent and unparalleled achievement. The insights it provides to the multiple issues it discusses and the general logical framework it uses to 'solve' these issues goes far beyond the work of Sartre and, indeed, any other thinker. Indeed, on a number of issues, such as crime, the importance of family and culture to individual and social identity, the issue of poverty, intersubjective relations, and the intimate ontological relationship between the individual and his community, Hegel is still highly relevant.

But while we have much to learn from Hegel, this does not mean that we should simply abandon Sartre. It means we must learn from each thinker with a view to looking afresh at the issues they so painstakingly analysed. Not only are the issues that Hegel and Sartre discussed still relevant today, but, as they remind us, their resolution depends on us first recognizing that they are ours to solve; whether we do so or not is up to us.

Notes

1. Similarly, Walter Kaufman (1966: 151) argues that Sartre owed a great deal to Hegel, Bruce Baugh notes that 'Sartre's attitude towards Hegel was deeply ambivalent: he was both attracted to Hegel's dialectic and deeply mistrustful of it' (2003: 94), Herbert Marcuse insists that *Being and Nothingness* is 'in large parts a restatement of Hegel's *Phenomenology of Mind*' (1948: 311), Tom Rockmore maintains that 'Sartre seems never to have been knowledgeable about Hegel, although Sartre was influenced by him' (1993: 171) and Pierre Verstraeten argues that 'an implicit undercurrent [of Sartre's thought] frequently borrows from, is inspired by, or simply re-invents Hegelian thinking' (1999: 354).
2. The translator of the English version of the *Critique of Dialectical Reason* has called this group formation the 'fused group.' However, I have chosen to use the term 'group-in-fusion' because it emphasizes the open ended, dynamic nature of this group formation in a way that the term the 'fused group' fails to convey.
3. Stephen Houlgate (2005: 202) points out that Hegel recognizes that the rich can also become part of the rabble if they reduce social interaction to purely economic considerations and so maintain that everything has its price and/ or show a callous disregard for the welfare of others. It would appear from this that the crucial factor that determines whether or not a rabble mentality forms is not due to economic circumstances, but is due to the subjective ethical disposition the individual adopts with regard to his wider society (PR: 244A).
4. Thus, Richard Teichgraeber's insistence that 'Hegel's idea of the state has virtually nothing to do with a welfare state system' (1977: 61) fundamentally fails to understand the positive role the public authority plays in Hegel's rational state. Because it is tasked with securing the material needs of its citizens through wealth redistribution and public works, Hegel's rational state is a welfare state.
5. 'The philosophers have only *interpreted* the world, in various ways; the point, however, is to *change* it' (Marx, 1992: 423).

Bibliography

Anderson, J. (2001), 'Hegel's Implicit View on How to Solve the Problem of Poverty: The Responsible Consumer and the Return of the Ethical to Civil Society,' in: Williams, R.R. (ed.), *Beyond Liberalism and Communitarianism: Studies in Hegel's* Philosophy of Right, State University of New York: Albany (pp. 185–206).

Anderson, T. (1993), *Sartre's Two Ethics: From Authenticity to Integral Humanity,* Open Court: Chicago.

Aronson, R. (1980), *Jean-Paul Sartre: Philosophy in the World,* Verso: London.

Avineri, S. (2003), *Hegel's Theory of the Modern State,* Cambridge University Press: Cambridge.

Baron, K. (2001), 'The Poetics of Morality: The Notion of Value in the Early Sartre,' *Sartre Studies International,* vol.7, n.1 (pp. 43–68).

Baugh, B. (2003), *French Hegel: From Surrealism to Postmodernism,* Routledge: London.

Baxter, B. (1982), *Alienation and Authenticity,* Tavistock: London.

Berthold-Bond, D. (1989), *Hegel's Grand Synthesis: A Study of Being, Thought, and History,* State University of New York Press: Albany.

Boileau, K. (2004), 'How Foucault Can Improve Sartre's Theory of Authentic Political Community,' *Sartre Studies International,* vol.10, n.2 (pp. 77–91).

Butler, J. (1987), *Subjects of Desire: Hegelian Reflections in Twentieth-Century France,* Columbia University Press: New York.

Catalano, J.S. (2007), 'The Meaning and Truth of History: A Note on Sartre's *Critique of Dialectical Reason,*' *Sartre Studies International,* vol.13, n.2 (pp. 47–64).

Catalano, J.S. (1986), *A Commentary on Jean-Paul Sartre's* Critique of Dialectical Reason: *Theory of Practical Ensembles,* vol.1, University of Chicago Press: London.

Caws, P. (1979), *Sartre,* Routledge & Kegan Press: London.

Cooper, D.E. (1999), *Existentialism: A Reconstruction,* Blackwell: Oxford.

Daigle, C. (2004), 'Sartre and Nietzsche,' *Sartre Studies International,* vol.10, n.2 (pp. 195–210).

Darnell, M.R. (2004), 'Being-looked-at: Ontological Grounding for an Ethics in *Being and Nothingness,*' *Sartre Studies International,* vol.10, n.1 (pp. 15–24).

Derrida, J. (2006), *Spectres of Marx: The State of the Debt, the Work of Mourning and the New International* (trans. Kamuf, P.), Routledge: London.

Detmer, D. (2008), *Sartre Explained: From Bad Faith to Authenticity,* Open Court Press: Chicago.

Detmer, D. (1988), *Freedom as Value: A Critique of the Ethical Theory of Jean-Paul Sartre,* Open Court: Chicago.

Dews, P. (2008), *The Idea of Evil,* Blackwell: Oxford.

Dudley, W. (1997), 'Freedom and the Need for Protection from Myself,' *The Owl of Minerva,* vol.29, n.1, Fall (pp. 39–67).

Due, R. (2005), 'Freedom, Nothingness, Consciousness: Some Remarks on the Structure of *Being and Nothingness,*' *Sartre Studies International,* vol.11, n.1&2 (pp. 31–42).

Due, R. (2000), 'Self-Knowledge and Moral Properties in Sartre's *Being and Nothingness*,' *Sartre Studies International*, vol.6, n.1 (pp. 61–94).

Dupré, L. (1972), 'Hegel's Concept of Alienation and Marx's Re-Interpretation of It,' *Hegel-Studien*, vol.7 (pp. 217–236).

Eshleman, M.C. (2008), 'The Misplaced Chapter on Bad Faith, or Reading *Being and Nothingness* in Reverse,' *Sartre Studies International*, vol.14, n.2 (pp. 1–22).

Farrell- Fox, N. (2003), *The New Sartre: Explorations in Postmodernism*, Continuum: London.

Ferrara, A. (1997) 'Authenticity as a Normative Category,' *Philosophy and Social Criticism*, vol.23, n.3 (pp. 77–92).

Flynn, T.R. (1984), *Sartre and Marxist Existentialism: The Test Case for Collective Responsibility*, University of Chicago Press: London.

Franco, P. (1999), *Hegel's Philosophy of Freedom*, Yale University Press: London.

Fry, C.M. (1988), *Sartre and Hegel: The Variations of an Enigma in* L'Etre et le Néant, Bouvier Verlag: Bonn.

Gadamer, H.G. (1976), *Hegel's Dialectic: Five Hermeneutical Studies* (trans. Smith, C.P.), Yale University Press: London.

Glenn Jr, J.D. (1984), 'Marcel and Sartre: The Philosophy of Communion and the Philosophy of Alienation,' in: Schilpp, P.A., & Hahn, L.E. (eds), *The Philosophy of Gabriel Marcel*, Open Court: Illinois (pp. 525–550).

Greene, M. (1966), 'Alienation within a Problematic of Substance and Subject,' *Social Research*, vol.33 (pp. 355–374).

Greer, M.R. (1999), 'Individuality and the Economic Order in Hegel's *Philosophy of Right*,' *European Journal of the History of Economic Thought*, vol.6, n.4 (pp. 552–580).

Halper, E.C. (2001), 'Hegel's Family Values,' *The Review of Metaphysics*, vol.54, n.4, June (pp. 815–858).

Hardimon, M.O. (1994), *Hegel's Social Philosophy: The Project of Reconciliation*, Cambridge University Press: Cambridge.

Hardimon, M.D. (1992), 'The Project of Reconciliation: Hegel's Social Philosophy,' *Philosophy and Public Affairs*, vol.21, n.2, Spring (pp. 165–195).

Hartmann, K. (1966), *Sartre's Ontology: A Study of* Being and Nothingness *in the Light of Hegel's Logic*, Northwestern University Press: Evanston.

Heidegger, M. (2003), *Being and Time* (trans. MacQuarrie, J., & Robinson, E.), Blackwell: Oxford.

Heidegger, M. (1988), *Hegel's* Phenomenology of Spirit, Indiana University Press: Indianapolis.

Heter, T.S. (2008), *Sartre's Ethics of Engagement: Authenticity and Civic Virtue*, Continuum: London.

Heter, T.S. (2006), 'Authenticity and Others: Sartre's Ethics of Recognition,' *Sartre Studies International*, vol.12, n.2 (pp. 17–43).

Honneth, A. (2005), *The Struggle for Recognition: The Moral Grammar of Conflicts*, Polity Press: London.

Houlgate, S. (2005), *An Introduction to Hegel: Freedom, Truth, and History*, Blackwell: Oxford.

Houlgate, S. (1991), 'Power, Egoism and the "Open" Self in Nietzsche and Hegel,' *Journal of the British Society for Phenomenology*, vol.22, n.3, October (pp. 120–138).

Hyppolite, J. (1997), *Logic and Existence* (trans. Lawlor, L., & Sen, A.), State University of New York Press: Albany.

Hyppolite, J. (1974), *Genesis and Structure of Hegel's* Phenomenology of Spirit (trans. Cherniak, S., & Heckman, J.), Northwestern University Press: Evanston.

Kain, P.J. (2005), *Hegel and the Other: A Study of the* Phenomenology of Spirit, State University of New York Press: Albany.

Kaufman, W. (1966), *Hegel: Re-Interpretation, Texts, and Commentary,* Weidenfeld & Nicholson: London.

Kirsner, D. (2003), *The Schizoid World of Jean-Paul Sartre and R.D. Laing,* Karnac: London.

Kirsner, D. (1985), 'Sartre and the Collective Neurosis of Our Time,' *Yale French Studies,* n.68 (pp. 206–225).

Knowles, D. (1983), 'Hegel on Property and Personality,' *The Philosophical Quarterly,* vol.33, n.130, January (pp. 45–62).

Kolb, D. (1986), *The Critique of Pure Modernity: Hegel, Heidegger, and After,* Chicago University Press: Chicago.

Landes, J.B. (1981), 'Hegel's Conception of the Family,' *Polity,* vol.14, n.1., Autumn (pp. 5–28).

Levy, B.H. (2003), *Sartre: The Philosopher of the Twentieth Century* (trans. Brown, A.), Polity Press: Oxford.

Levy, N. (2002), *Sartre,* Oneworld: Oxford.

Ludwig, W.D. (1989), 'Hegel's Conception of Absolute Knowing,' *The Owl of Minerva,* vol.21, n.1 (pp. 5–19).

Luft, E.V.D. (1989), 'An Early Interpretation of Hegel's *Phenomenology of Spirit,*' *Hegel-Studien,* vol.24 (pp. 183–194).

Lukács, G. (1975), *The Young Hegel: Studies in the Relation between Dialectics and Economics* (trans. Livingstone, R.), MIT Press: Massachusetts.

Maker, W. (1994), *Philosophy without Foundations: Re-thinking Hegel,* State University of New York Press: Albany.

Manser, A. (1966), *Sartre: A Philosophic Study,* Athlone Press: London.

Marcuse, H. (1996), *Reason and Revolution: Hegel and the Rise of Social Theory,* Humanities Press: New Jersey.

Marcuse, H. (1948), 'Existentialism: Remarks on Jean-Paul Sartre's *L'Etre et le Néant,*' *Philosophical and Phenomenological Research,* vol.8, n.3, March (pp. 309–336).

Martinot, S. (2005), 'The Sartrean Account of the Look as a Theory of Dialogue,' *Sartre Studies International,* vol.11, n.1&2 (pp. 43–61).

Marx, K. (1992), *Early Writings* (trans. Livingstone, R., & Benton, G.), Penguin: London (pp. 279–400).

McBride, W.L. (1991), *Sartre's Political Theory,* Indiana University Press: Indianapolis.

Meyers, M. (2008), 'Liminality and the Problem of Being-in-the-World: Reflections on Sartre and Merleau-Ponty,' *Sartre Studies International,* vol.14., n.1 (pp. 78–105).

McCulloch, G. (1994), *Using Sartre: An Analytical Introduction to Early Sartrean Themes,* Routledge: London.

Mirvish, A. (2002), 'Sartre on Friendship: Promoting Difference while Preserving Commitment,' *Journal of the British Society for Phenomenology,* vol.33, n.3, October (pp. 260–272).

Moellendorf, D. (1992), 'A Reconstruction of Hegel's Account of Freedom of the Will,' *The Owl of Minerva,* vol.24, n.1 (pp. 5–18).

Natanson, M. (1980), 'The Sleep of Bad Faith,' *New Literary History,* vol.12, n.1, Autumn (pp. 97–106).

Nicolacopoulos, T., & Vassilacopoulos, G. (1999), *Hegel and the Logical Structure of Love: An Essay on Sexualities, Family, and the Law,* Ashgate: Aldershot.

Neuhouser, F. (2000), *Foundations of Hegel's Social Theory: Actualising Freedom,* Harvard University Press: London.

Pinkard, T. (1996), *Hegel's Phenomenology: The Sociality of Reason,* Cambridge University Press: Cambridge.

Pippin, R. (2008), *Hegel's Practical Philosophy: Rational Agency as Ethical Life,* Cambridge University Press: Cambridge.

Pippin, R. (1989), *Hegel's Idealism: The Satisfaction of Self-Consciousness,* Cambridge University Press: Cambridge.

Poellner, P. (2004), 'Self-Deception, Consciousness and Value: The Nietzschean Contribution,' *Journal of Consciousness Studies,* vol.11, n.10–11 (pp. 44–65).

Poellner, P. (2003), 'Non-conceptual Content, Experience and the Self,' *Journal of Consciousness Studies,* vol.10, n.2 (pp. 32–57).

Popper, K. (2003), *The Open Society and its Enemies: Hegel and Marx,* vol.2, Routledge: London.

Rae, G. (2010), 'Alienation, Authenticity, and the Self,' *History of the Human Sciences,* vol.23, n.4 (pp. 21–36).

Rockmore, T. (1993), *Before and After Hegel: A Historical Introduction to Hegel's Thought,* University of California Press: London.

Rose, D. (2003), 'Sartre and the Problem of Universal Human Nature Revisited,' *Sartre Studies International,* vol.9, n.1 (pp. 1–20).

Rosen, S. (1974), *G.W.F. Hegel: An Introduction to the Science of Wisdom,* Yale University Press: London.

Rosenthal, A.L. (1971), 'A Hegelian Key to Hegel's Method,' *Journal of the History of Philosophy,* vol.9 (pp. 205–212).

Roth, M.S. (1988), *Knowing and History: Appropriations of Hegel in Twentieth-Century France,* Cornell University Press: London.

Santoni, R.E. (2008), 'Is Bad Faith Necessarily Social?' *Sartre Studies International,* vol.14, n.2 (pp. 23–39).

Santoni, R.E. (1995), *Bad Faith, Good Faith, and Authenticity in Sartre's Early Philosophy,* Temple University Press: Philadelphia.

Schacht, R. (1970), *Alienation,* Anchor Books: New York.

Sprigge, T. (1984), *Theories of Existence,* Penguin: London.

Stern, A. (1968), *Sartre: His Philosophy and Existential Psychoanalysis,* Vision: London.

Taylor, C. (2003), *The Ethics of Authenticity,* Harvard University Press: London.

Taylor, C. (1998), *Hegel and Modern Society,* University of Cambridge Press: Cambridge.

Taylor, C. (1975), *Hegel,* Cambridge University Press: Cambridge.

Teichgraeber, R. (1977), 'Hegel on Property and Poverty,' *Journal of the History of Ideas,* vol.38, n.1 (pp. 47–64).

Tunick, M. (2001), 'Hegel on Political Identify & the Ties that Bind,' in: Williams, R.R. (ed.), *Beyond Liberalism and Communitarianism: Studies in Hegel's Philosophy of Right,* State University of New York Press: Albany (pp. 67–90).

238 Bibliography

Ver

Verstraeten, P. (1999), 'Hegel and Sartre,' in: Howells, C. (ed.), *The Cambridge Companion to Sartre*, Cambridge University Press: Cambridge (pp. 353–372).

Wang, S. (2006), 'Human Incompletion, Happiness, and the Desire for God in Sartre's *Being and Nothingness*,' *Sartre Studies International*, vol.12, n.1 (pp. 1–17).

Ware, R.B. (1999), *Hegel: The Logic of Self-Consciousness and the Legacy of Subjective Freedom*, Edinburgh University Press: Edinburgh.

Warnock, M. (1970), *Existentialism*, Oxford University Press: Oxford.

Webber, J. (2009), *The Existentialism of Jean-Paul Sartre*, Routledge: London.

Webber, J. (2002), 'Motivated Aversion: Non-Thetic Awareness in Bad Faith,' *Sartre Studies International*, vol.8, n.1 (pp. 45–57).

Williams, R.R. (1997), *Hegel's Ethics of Recognition*, University of California Press: London.

Williams, R.R. (1992a), *Recognition: Fichte and Hegel on the Other*, State University of New York Press: Albany.

Williams, R.R. (1992b), 'Sartre's Strange Appropriation of Hegel,' *The Owl of Minerva*, vol.23, n.2 (pp. 3–14).

Williamson, I., & Cullingford, C. (1997), 'The Uses and Abuses of "Alienation" in the Social Sciences and Education,' *British Journal of Educational Studies*, vol.45, n.3, September (pp. 263–275).

Westphal, K. (1999), 'The Basic Context and Structure of Hegel's *Philosophy of Right*,' in: Beiser, F.C. (ed.), *The Cambridge Companion to Hegel*, Cambridge University Press: Cambridge (pp. 234–269).

Wood, A. (1995), *Hegel's Ethical Thought*, Cambridge University Press: Cambridge.

Yovel, Y. (1979), 'Existentialism and Historical Dialectic,' *Philosophy and Phenomenological Research*, vol.39, n.4, June (pp. 480–497).

Zahavi, D. (2008), *Subjectivity and Selfhood: Investigating the First-Person Perspective*, MIT Press: Massachusetts.

Zahavi, D. (1999), *Self-Awareness and Alterity: A Phenomenological Investigation*, Northwestern University Press: Evanston.

Zheng, Y. (2002), 'Sartre on Authenticity,' *Sartre Studies International*, vol.8, n.2. (pp. 127–140).

Zheng, Y. (2001), 'On Pure Reflection in Sartre's *Being and Nothingness*,' *Sartre Studies International*, vol.7, n.1 (pp. 19–42).

Index